Presidents, Congress, and the Public Schools

Presidents, Congress, and the Public Schools

The Politics of Education Reform

Jack Jennings

HARVARD EDUCATION PRESS
CAMBRIDGE, MASSACHUSETTS

Library of Congress Control Number 2014959082

Paperback ISBN 978-1-61250-796-5
Library Edition ISBN 978-1-61250-797-2

Published by Harvard Education Press,
an imprint of the Harvard Education Publishing Group

Harvard Education Press
8 Story Street
Cambridge, MA 02138

Cover Design: Ciano Design
Cover Image: Chris Minerva/Getty Images
The typefaces used in this book are Minion Pro and Scala Sans

This book is dedicated to the many fine people I have encountered during my career, especially to three special persons whose humanity, dedication to helping others, hard work, intelligence, and sense of humor have enlivened and enlightened my life during our time together on Capitol Hill and at the Center on Education Policy:

Toni Painter
Diane Stark Rentner
Nancy Kober

Contents

Foreword

FOR INSPIRATION ABOUT the historical and contemporary struggles of American education, a good place to look is on the back of a one-dollar bill. Although no longer the official motto of the United States, the original dictum, *e pluribus unum*, is still relevant enough to be on our Great Seal, and in just three easily translatable Latin words summarizes two and a half centuries of the American experiment in divided democracy. The tension between the many and the one, between the pluribus and the unum, has no simple or obvious resolution, and certainly not when it comes to education. As Jack Jennings so eloquently explains in this book, simplistic arguments that federal involvement in education has been either its savior or its curse are rhetorically extravagant, ahistorical, and empirically dubious. The story is more complicated, and more interesting.

One might think, for example, that a "system" of 14,000 independent school districts operating in fifty states, all with their own authority for what gets taught, to whom, and how, is a recipe for disaster. How to reconcile this "chaos," as a former Harvard president called it, with its remarkable accomplishments is a puzzle that has attracted considerable attention by scholars, policy makers, and journalists. On the one hand, we have (at least until recently) led the world in opening education to the masses, an investment in human capital that deserves much of the credit for the unparalleled gains in economic productivity and quality of life through much of the twentieth century. And a large part of this success is due to the agility and innovative capacity of school districts and their communities, unencumbered by the logy machinery of centralized government. On the other hand, persistent and vexing inequalities in resources and educational attainment—by region, race, and socioeconomic status—gnaw at our national fabric and give rise, thankfully, to periodic calls for national action. We have understood, perhaps somewhat grudgingly, that some problems can't be solved without the visible hand of government.

The academic word for our political arrangement is "federalism," loosely defined as the rules governing the diffusion of decision making between the federal government and the states. This concept is by no means easy to implement, and the federal role in education, perhaps more than in other sectors, has always been contested and constrained. To appreciate the difficulty of reconciling our pluribus with our unum, one need only recall that it took us 214 years to even try to write a set of national education goals!

As we approach the fiftieth anniversary of the Elementary and Secondary Education Act of 1965 (ESEA)—arguably the most significant federal legislative accomplishment in the history of education—and as the nation continues to debate the promise and peril of national standards, it is the ideal moment for a reasoned consideration of the future. What can or should the federal role be? With Jack Jennings to guide us through this process of national reflection, we are in good hands. As staff director and then general counsel for more than twenty-five years to the most influential House committee on education policy, and as founder of a nationally renowned nonpartisan center providing research on key educational policies, Jack is in the unique position to describe the influential role the federal government has played in education policies for the last fifty years, the development of the current standards movement as a natural outgrowth of these efforts, and the lessons from this history about how to go forward.

In the pages that follow, Jack expands the lectures he delivered at The George Washington University in spring 2014. He reviews the history and unravels some of the mystery of federal involvement since the passage of ESEA and offers a fresh set of ideas about where and how the federal government could now focus its efforts. The questions are complex: no doubt there is validity to the criticisms expressed about the woes of local and state control of schools, the politics of school boards, and the damaging consequences of inconsistent state standards. But whether a system of national standards to guide teaching, learning, and resource allocation is a necessary or sufficient remedy is not obvious; and again, many people worry that the word "national" is code for federal, an affront to our history and a misguided response to the problems of fragmentation.

Jack's treatment of these and related issues is gripping and is bound to shake many preconceived beliefs. Even the most faithful worshipers of free markets who dislike government intervention and distrust centralized authority concede that in education we are better off today than fifty years ago, and that the federal role—the combined (and often colliding) efforts of the Supreme Court, Congress, and the White House—deserves a good part of the credit. The passage of ESEA, just about a decade after the landmark Supreme Court case outlawing racial segregation in schools, was an instance of political adaptation to increasingly obvious and unacceptable inequities. How it was framed and how it evolved as the pains of implementation began to be felt is a story with many lessons. Anyone who thinks that large-scale educational change via federal legislation can "get it right" from the beginning should take a deep breath and study the facts summarized in this volume, along with the interpretations of its wise and experienced author.

Readers may marvel, for example, at how a system designed for fragmented governance nonetheless spawned an array of complex federal policies and, more amazingly, how often public programs were reengineered. Agility in government, especially in our system with its fetish for checks and balances and diffused authority, is more challenging than in the private sector, where different rules of innovation and accountability apply. And the tensions are palpable: some critics decry the slow pace of government bureaucracy and its potential to suffocate creative problem solving, while others play the "evidence card" to stall enactment of policies that haven't been fully researched. Finding the sweet spot between inaction and irresponsible action is part of the art of governing. On balance, I would argue that the federal role in education should be complimented for its dexterity, made possible in large part by the tenacity of our public servants, including Jack, in their pursuit of laws, policies, and programs aimed at enhancing the public good. One hopes they will have the resources and the will to continue.

But here, too, the road ahead is bumpy, and travelers are well advised to pack this book for the trip. Jennings is one of the best guides imaginable for a journey to the future of federal education policy. As a courageous defender of the virtues of bipartisan discourse (a seemingly lost art on Capitol Hill), and an incredibly lucid writer, he provides here a rich blend of personal reflection and research-informed analysis leading to provocative recommendations. He uses his knowledge of the history of education reform, his personal involvement for nearly the last half century, and current research to provide a clear roadmap to the future. You will see how some of his original beliefs about the role of the federal government have evolved, and how he candidly explains the need for national standards. He also takes on the notion that education is not a federal issue, and shows that it truly is a fundamental right compatible with our core culture, Constitution, and politics. He knows politicians well, and wants them—regardless of what side of the aisle they represent—to be held to their rhetoric that education is a civil right.

Surely readers will disagree with aspects of Jack's book, but I know that stimulating a vigorous debate is one of his highest priorities. The future of American education may be uncertain, but with people like Jack continuing to think and write and argue about it, the quality of debate and the possibility for progress are guaranteed.

—Michael Feuer
Dean and Professor of Education
The George Washington University
President, The National Academy of Education

Introduction

PEOPLE HANDLE THEIR fiftieth birthdays differently. Some do their best to ignore it. Some revel in it. But nearly everyone realizes that it is a landmark in their life.

The fiftieth anniversary of the signing of the Elementary and Secondary Education Act of 1965 (ESEA) is such an occasion. As the main source of federal aid to states and local school districts for half a century, this ambitious and encyclopedic law has reshaped American education and influenced the schooling of millions of American children over a fifty-year period. While the federal government had been peripherally involved in public education prior to 1965, ESEA marked the beginning of broad federal involvement in the daily operation of schools. This change has had a profound effect.

Made up originally of five major sections, ESEA has provided many billions of dollars over the last half century to improve American education. Nearly every public school in the country, and many private schools as well, received new books and audiovisual aids to improve library services. Innovative programs were funded in scores of school districts. Educational research was expanded. State governments were nudged to take a stronger role in improving their schools. Public school districts and private schools were induced to forge unprecedented new relationships to provide extra assistance for students from low-income families who attended private and religious schools. The centerpiece of the law forcefully directed

1

the attention of teachers and administrators toward better serving economically and educationally disadvantaged children.

After its creation in 1965, ESEA soon settled into a schedule of reviews and renewals by Congress every four or five years. That routine led to the expansion of federal aid over the years to meet new needs, either through the creation of additional programs or through the expansion or redirection of current aid programs.

ESEA thereby opened the door to educational interventions for all types of students. Children of migratory farm workers were educated while their parents worked in the fields. Students who were placed in facilities for neglected children received additional classes. Children who did not speak English learned the language. Gifted and talented children received special attention and assistance.

ESEA also served as the exemplar for the creation of other federal laws benefitting children. Most notably, the Individuals with Disabilities Education Act (IDEA) took children with mental and physical disabilities out of their homes or state institutions for "handicapped children" and placed them in regular classrooms at neighborhood schools. That law further revolutionized the treatment of children with disabilities by guaranteeing them the services they needed to be educated.

During its regular reviews of ESEA, Congress also established education policies that went beyond specifying the characteristics of funded programs. For instance, intense debates occurred about the merits of busing school children as a means to integrate schools. As a consequence, laws were enacted over the years that progressively restricted that practice and in effect overturned a U.S. Supreme Court ruling. Those busing battles also helped to refashion the Democratic and Republican parties into what they are today.

Below are a few examples of the many concrete effects of policies that came about due to ESEA and other education laws that followed its example:

- Most students are now tested yearly in response to federal prescriptions enacted in the No Child Left Behind Act (NCLB), the reauthorization of ESEA signed in 2002.

- Young children with disabilities are provided with preschool programs through funding from IDEA.
- Pupils who struggle to keep up academically receive extra instruction and other supports, which is paid for by federal funds under ESEA's Title I (the main federal program).
- Immigrant children are learning English in federally funded classes.

Over the years, ESEA's legislative prescriptions and the related funding assistance it provides for public education have helped millions of students learn better and ultimately lead more productive lives. These efforts have had their shortcomings, but most observers agree that overall, the country is better off as a result.

Even Chester E. Finn Jr., a former high-ranking official in the first President Bush's administration and an often-cited skeptic of federal aid (some of whose criticisms are quoted later), after reviewing major developments in federal involvement in education, concluded:

> None of it worked quite as well as ardent advocates had hoped. All brought unintended consequences, pushback, and sizable financial burdens. But American education is a very different enterprise—and, for the most part, a better enterprise—as a result of these game-changing initiatives from Washington.[1]

Just as reaching the age of fifty encourages people to think back on their lives, this milestone anniversary of ESEA's enactment also presents an opportunity for reflection. What accomplishments flowed from that event? What problems did the law create as it evolved? What have we learned from a half century's experiences with federal intervention in education? How might these lessons refine our understanding of the federal role in education and point us toward ways to do things differently?

To assist in the process of reflection, this book first explores the reasons why these federal programs and policies came about and how they developed over the last fifty years. This will take us from the 1960s and 1970s, when federal financial assistance was welcomed by educators as a way to expand services for children with special needs, to the present day, when federal mandates for extensive, high-stakes student testing are seen by many teachers as converting schooling into joyless, rote learning, especially for disadvantaged children.

The book then examines the major Department of Education programs affecting elementary and secondary education. These constitute more than 80 percent of that agency's budget for public elementary and secondary education, and are the federal programs that educators know best. Particular emphasis is given to ESEA's Title I program, the largest federal aid program and a model for other equity programs. The IDEA, the second biggest program, and the English Language Acquisition Act, also receive considerable attention. The Charter School Grants program as well as several major civil rights directives from federal courts and from federal regulations are also discussed. I will assess the relative effectiveness of these approaches and consider some of the other strategies the federal government has used to effect change in education.

Thus, although it does not include every federal program or policy, this book presents a comprehensive review of federal involvement in public schooling. The aim is to show the extent of the federal role in education and illustrate the various tools at the federal government's disposal. These examples challenge the widespread belief that the federal government has only a limited role to play in education, and show how federal education policy has been closely intertwined with a wide range of social issues. (A chronology of major events in education policy is provided in the appendix.)

Finally, I will propose a new approach to federal education policy, one that expands and transforms the federal role. The congressional creators of federal aid in the 1960s believed that the obstacle to better schooling was a lack of money: once sufficient funding was provided to equalize expenditures among school districts, it was assumed that educators would know what to do to improve education. In contrast, the architects of the standards/tests/accountability reforms of the 1990s and 2000s believed that student academic achievement could be improved by setting high academic standards, using tests to measure attainment of those standards, and holding teachers and schools accountable for poor results. Providing more money to assist with this job was not necessary in the minds of many proponents of this second reform.

Neither of those two extremes has proved to be correct in its assumptions. The past fifty years' experiences have shown that education is too complex to have easy answers. The truth lies in taking the best from each reform movement. Thus, I propose a significant expansion of federal aid to schools that is not restricted to particular categories of students but that is contingent on states' willingness to address the most fundamental issues that impede educational progress.

In addition, I believe this expanded general aid program, which could be called the United for Students Act (USA), must be complemented by legal efforts to ensure that children have the constitutional right to a good education. This strategy is consonant with the widely touted claim that education is the civil rights issue of our time. If so, it deserves the full protection and sanction of constitutional law.

A SEAT AT THE TABLE

My views on the federal role in education were heavily influenced by my two careers: as the principal education expert for twenty-seven years in the U.S. House of Representatives, and as founder and CEO of the Center on Education Policy (CEP) for the next seventeen years.

In my first career in Congress, I got to know the original congressional authors of ESEA, including Representatives Carl Perkins (D-KY), Edith Green (D-OR), John Brademas (D-IN), Patsy Mink (D-HI), and Roman Pucinski (D-IL), along with Senators Ted Kennedy (D-MA) and Jacob Javits (R-NY). Talking to them and listening to them gave me a good idea of how ESEA came about and what the expectations were at the time of its creation.

During my time working for Congress I was the legal counsel and staff director responsible for ESEA, its subsequent amendments, and similar statutes. In that capacity, I dealt directly over the years with three different chairmen of the Committee on Education and Labor of the U.S. House of Representatives, set up hearings and chose witnesses to testify, drafted legislation to renew and revise programs, and helped the committee's chairmen to shepherd the legislation through the subcommittee, the committee, and the House. Once the Senate passed a companion bill, I was the chief negotiator for the House in staff meetings preceding Senate-House conference committees to agree on the terms of the final legislation. During the actual conference committees, I assisted the chairmen, and once agreement was reached I worked with them to obtain House approval of the legislation that would become the law. In all these activities, I was the chief representative of the House committee in working with the presidential administrations, dealing with lobbyists of the organizations representing all the groups affected, and explaining the details of the legislation to the news media.

I was an "insider," to use Washington, DC, lingo.

When I left Congress at the end of 1994, I refused job offers from law firms, universities, and organizations. Instead, I set up the Center on Education Policy to provide independent, objective analysis of federal laws and policies, which I believed was sorely lacking amid a sea of reports and publications that used selected facts to justify established positions. CEP also analyzed key state-level policies and produced publications on the conditions of American public education. I limited the Center's funding to grants from charitable foundations, and refused government funding and support from education organizations because I wanted CEP to be independent and not influenced by the views of government funders or private interests. At that time, it was easier to be independent with foundation funding than it was with other sources of support.

Among the many products of CEP was a series of reports on the implementation of NCLB, which became mandatory reading for those in the news media, the Congress, the Department of Education, the White House, and associations representing education and business at the state and national levels. Those reports, which were released periodically over the course of nearly a decade, provided timely, comprehensive, readable, and factual information on NCLB, unmatched by any other group. In 2006, *Education Week*, the leading trade newspaper in this area, conducted a poll of national leaders in education and reported that CEP was one of the ten most influential education organizations in the country. CEP was by far the smallest of the ten in staffing and had the least amount of funding; others included the U.S. Congress, the U.S. Department of Education, the Bill and Melinda Gates Foundation, and established, larger groups.[2]

During those two long careers, I was privileged to have a seat at the table as federal aid to education evolved from its modern beginnings until today. That unique long-term perspective undergirds the views presented in this book. Based on those experiences, I lay out the fifty-year history of federal aid, as well as incidents that I observed or participated in first-hand that illustrate the human side of policy making.

During this lengthy involvement with the federal role in the schools, I saw the good that came from this assistance and direction, such as the inclusion of children with disabilities in regular classrooms and the provision of extra services to disadvantaged children who needed them to succeed. But I also saw the limitations of federal programs and some of the difficulties they created for educators and administrators, such as imposing too many regulations on administrators while providing too little federal funding to fulfill the promise of the federal laws.

FEDERAL AID REIMAGINED

After reflecting on the record of federal aid, I have come to the conclusion that a different role is needed for the future. We have been too indirect in our approach, and now a more specific way to school improvement based on research is needed.

The current aid programs and the mandates for extensive testing are rooted in the times in which they were created. They are premised on the belief that *indirect* educational assistance and *external* insistence on extensive testing are the primary ways by which the federal government should encourage local educators to improve the schools. Both approaches have brought about some good, such as making better use of student achievement data to identify and address gaps in learning. But providing a little extra help for disadvantaged students, while laudable, is not nearly enough in a school system that permits spending far more money on advantaged students than it does on those who are disadvantaged. That fatal flaw is combined with another—imposing extensive testing on resentful teachers. We must leave history behind us and find a more *direct* way to improve the quality of American education. This goal is urgent because the world is changing rapidly.

The United States faces two large challenges in elementary and secondary education. All of our students need to learn more, and every student should receive the same high-quality education regardless of family income or the property wealth of his or her school district.

Contrary to common belief, American students are not doing worse than they did in the past; rather, despite challenging demographic changes, students are holding their own in academic achievement or even doing better as measured by national test scores. Some other indicators also show progress: the graduation rate from high school is at a historic high, college-going rates have increased significantly since 1980, and the proportion of students aged seventeen to twenty-four who are high school dropouts has fallen by more than half since 1970.[3]

Granting these positive trends, what is different from the past—and what presents an urgent challenge to the United States—is that other countries' students are taking education very seriously and are doing better than ours on several important measures of educational progress. From the 1940s through the 1990s, the United States led the world on many indicators of educational achievement, but that record has been eroding as the educational levels of other nations have risen. In 1995, the United States ranked second after New Zealand in higher education graduation rates among nineteen OECD countries with comparable data, but by 2010 it ranked thirteenth among twenty-five such countries. This relative decline in rankings occurred not because the United States was doing worse, but because other countries were doing better.[4] (OECD is the Organization for Economic and Cultural Development, an association of the world's economically advanced countries that tracks economic and educational trends in its member countries.)

Another indicator of the relative performance of American students comes from the international test called the Program for International Student Assistance (PISA). In results released in 2013, even our top high school students did not perform as well in mathematics as top students in many other economically advanced countries.[5] PISA mainly assesses students' achievement in reading, mathematics, and science, and is designed to measure students' ability to solve problems and apply their knowledge to real-life problems.[6]

In a meeting several years ago, President Obama asked the president of South Korea about his biggest challenge in education. President Lee answered that parents in South Korea were "too demanding." Even the poorest parents insisted on a world-class education for their children, and his nation had to spend millions of dollars each year to teach English to students in first grade, because parents won't wait until second grade.[7]

A worldwide job market exists today in which American students will have to compete for jobs with Korean students, among many others, once they leave school. We ignore at our peril the economic and technological changes that have led to higher educational demands. As Marshall S. Smith, a former professor and high-ranking official in the Carter and Clinton administrations, has noted,

> The challenges of a global economy, a complex and changing international environment, and the technology and communication revolutions have dramatically increased our collective national need to ensure our future prosperity. As a nation, we are ever more dependent on the quality of our human capital to carry us into a productive and safe future. Our schools are better than many think, but we must ask them to change and become smarter.[8]

A final factor that should compel us to improve the schools is the extent of poverty in the United States and the implications that has for the life opportunities of children born poor. As the U.S. Secretary of Education's Equity and Excellence Commission stated in its 2013 report, America does not compare favorably on this measure with other OECD nations:

> Our poverty rate for school-age children—currently more than 22 percent—is twice the OECD average and nearly four times that of leading

countries such as Finland. We are also an outlier in how we concentrate those children, isolating them in certain schools—often resource-starved schools—which only magnifies poverty's impact and makes high achievement that much harder.[9]

To solve those two big problems—broad improvement of the schools and a better education for disadvantaged students—the United States should follow through on its ideals and truly provide a good education for every student.

In light of these challenges, I propose that we replace the current federal programs and directives with a new policy in which the federal government, working with the states, aims directly to improve classroom teaching and learning. The objectives of this new approach should be to improve students' readiness for school, raise the quality of the teaching force, encourage mastery of more challenging curricula, and provide sufficient funding for schools to do the job. The current policy of inserting a little extra help for students into an inequitable system of schooling has not brought about the quality of education we need. The other current federal strategy—demanding extensive testing of students—has not resulted in a broad increase in student achievement. These reforms rooted in past times must be abandoned as ineffective. Instead we should adopt a more direct and equitable way to bring about real improvement.

In addition, we must put in place legal and constitutional guarantees of students' rights to a good education. Presidents George W. Bush and Barack Obama have called education the civil rights issue of our time. It is, but presidential rhetoric won't win that battle. What is needed is a guarantee that is as strong as the Civil Rights Act of 1964, which helped to win the struggle for rights in the 1960s.

This book represents a major evolution in my own views. In the nearly three decades I worked for Congress, I helped to create the targeted funding programs and also the standards/testing/accountability framework. In various public forums, I argued for these approaches and defended them against criticism. But my views are different now because progress has not been sufficient and because the world is changing at such a fast pace that I feel we cannot procrastinate. If we want to bring about improvement, we must let go of resistance to change and sweep aside old excuses to adopting new and better ways.

Writing this book has cast me in a different role, since I have usually been a behind-the-scenes actor. When I worked for Congress, the elected representatives were the ones who received attention from the news media while, out of public view, I worked at writing the legislation and getting it through the Congress. In doing that, I listened to all sides, respected different points of view, and compromised to secure agreement to move the legislation. In my second career with CEP, I wanted the facts to speak for themselves. Nearly every report was authored by the experts who did the research, and I put my name on very few publications. In other words, I am not inclined to seek public attention for its own sake; rather, I have a reputation for understatement.

I mention these personal factors because I believe so strongly that the country must change its approach to school improvement, and do so rapidly and thoroughly. This book looks at history with an objective eye, analyzes research to identify the most serious problems impeding improvement, and then sets out a series of measures that must be taken to move us forward.

I believe that this reorientation of national efforts to improve the public schools will make America a world leader again in the area of education. But I also recognize that others may have different ideas. My hope is that in joining this debate we take the time to consider our past experiences with federal aid and also what research shows us about the impact of federal intervention. That is what I do in this book.

In the spring of 2014, I was privileged to be a guest lecturer at The George Washington University at the invitation of Michael Feuer, dean of the Graduate School of Education and Human Development. With the support of the Spencer Foundation and its president Michael McPherson, I was able to spend time researching, writing, and lecturing about federal aid to education. This book grows out of that lecture series. I am thankful to anyone who takes the time to read it, but I would be more appreciative if readers then did something about implementing the solutions to bring about improvement. Having knowledge without taking action is not good enough. American schools can be the best in the world, and American students can be both knowledgeable and creative. But, we must get moving—and right now!

After all, people celebrating their fiftieth birthday decide to either continue down the same path or else move their lives in a new direction. Federal policy can't keep doing what it has been doing. It is time to look to a new future and follow a new path.

Part I

EQUITY AND THE ORIGINS OF ESEA

THE UNITED STATES is a polyglot country and always has been. There is no single dominant nationality as in France or Germany, nor a predominant religion as in Italy. And most Americans, with the notable exception of African Americans descended from slaves, had ancestors who came from a wide variety of countries of their own free will to start a new life, or are immigrants themselves.

In such a diverse country, there are few common institutions in which most people participate. Public education is highly important for that reason alone—it is one of the few common experiences that most Americans share. Today, more than 90 percent of the nation's children attend public schools, and so the overwhelming majority of tomorrow's leaders, workers, and other citizens will have been educated in public schools.

The importance of public education to the well-being of the country and to the social cohesion of the nation has been noted for decades by national politicians, but it has proved to be difficult to move beyond rhetoric to federal action in support of public education. There are political reasons, as well as constitutional reasons, why this is so.

Part I of this book will describe the political struggles that accompanied the creation of the modern federal role in public elementary and secondary education. Bringing greater equity to schooling was the initial focus of this federal involvement, but in the views of many that effort did not produce the desired increases in educational achievement. Ultimately, this led to a different approach based on academic standards, tests, and accountability.

This part presents the story of how the federal government adopted the pursuit of equity as the focus of its education policy. It examines the political forces that shaped the implementation and evolution of that policy and assesses the initial impact of Title I aid on student learning.

1

The Road to ESEA

THE U.S. CONSTITUTION establishes a complex structure of government for the country, and each state's constitution echoes this complexity. America is a federal system, not a centralized system of government. This means there are three levels of government—federal, state, and local—each with its own powers. And at each of those levels there are three branches—executive, legislative, and judicial—each with its own responsibilities. This complex structure was created to diffuse power, not to concentrate it, because the writers of the Constitution wanted to avoid placing all authority in the hands of the central government as had occurred in many European countries where kings and queens had absolute power over their "subjects." The down side of this diffusion of power in the United States is that it is difficult to take action, especially swift action when a crisis appears.

In some cases in the American system, the local, state, and federal governments each have clear responsibilities—for example, national defense and foreign affairs are responsibilities vested in the federal government, while the issuing of building permits is ordinarily a local function. Some responsibilities, however, are not so clearly vested, and some have shifted over time from one level to another or are shared by two or even among three levels. Education is an area in which all three levels of government have been involved, and recently new responsibilities have evolved for each level.

Naturally, tensions have arisen among the three levels of government as new societal challenges have presented themselves. This has certainly been the case as the nation sought to improve public education, and as federal support for that effort grew.

A quick review of how education is governed in the United States is helpful as a background for understanding these tensions. Local school districts and state governments primarily operate the public schools. Local school boards decide important issues such as teacher pay and classroom curriculum, and states regulate key areas such as the qualifications needed to become a teacher and the standards for the broad knowledge and skills students are expected to learn. In keeping with these responsibilities, about 90 percent of the funds for the schools come from state and local governments.

Over the course of American history, the federal government has also been involved in schooling. This federal involvement in education for more than two centuries may surprise some who believe that the Tenth Amendment forbids federal support of the schools. The Tenth Amendment, enacted in 1791, reserves to the states and to the people respectively powers not delegated by the Constitution to the federal government nor prohibited by it to the states.

Both before and after the adoption of the Tenth Amendment, however, Congress required territories that became states to establish public schools with the proceeds from federally granted land. In the middle of the Civil War, President Lincoln signed laws creating state colleges and universities. After the Civil War, the Republican-dominated Congresses established schools for the freed slaves in the southern states. In the twentieth century, Congress created national vocational education and school lunch programs, and provided financial assistance for World War II servicemen and women to go to college or postsecondary job training.

Thus, for most of American history, the federal government has had some involvement in education. Courts have sanctioned this role, when it has been challenged, by referring to other parts of the Constitution, especially the clause authorizing spending of federal funds to provide for the "general welfare of the United States." The Tenth Amendment may be invoked in debate about federal actions affecting the schools, but federal involvement in education has a sound basis both in our history and in legal interpretations of the Constitution.

Although longstanding, this national assistance in elementary and secondary education was not significant enough to support the ordinary operation of most schools. In the 1960s, that changed. The federal government became involved in the day-to-day education that takes place in the nation's classrooms. It was not an easy transition. To understand the impact of this change, one must first have a sense of how public schools operated before the decade of the 1960s.

PUBLIC SCHOOLING PRIOR TO THE 1960s

Geographically, the United States is a vast country. When the nation was new, in the 1700s and 1800s, the population was small and thinly spread out, especially in the areas of expansion beyond the original thirteen colonies. Since the federal government encouraged the establishment and operation of public schools as territories became states, schooling expanded as the population moved ever westward.

Two unique facets of schooling developed in the United States due to its large geographic size and the limited ability of state and federal governments to take on substantial responsibilities. First, locally elected school boards controlled education in their schools; and second, those boards were responsible for raising funds for the support of their schools.

To gain a perspective on the local nature of public education, consider these facts. In 1939–1940, there were 117,108 school districts in the country, with some states having a large number and other states fewer. By 1965–1966, these districts had been reduced to 26,983; and in 2009–2010, 13,620 remained. These districts were consolidated as the population in rural areas declined, as reformers advocated for larger districts to make it possible to offer more courses of study, and as roads and other means of transportation improved. The large number of districts, as late as 1940, shows the traditional local nature of American education, which generally persists today as exemplified by the still significant number of remaining districts.[1] Other countries have different histories and lack the degree of local control that exists in American schooling.

As in many other economically advanced countries, the average person in the United States became better educated over time. In 1940, America achieved a landmark when a majority of its seventeen-year-olds graduated from high school.[2]

At that time, local control of elementary and secondary education was still strong, as demonstrated by the sources of funding for public education. In 1940, local taxes paid for about 68 percent of the costs, the states supplied nearly 30 percent of the funding, and the federal government provided the few remaining percentage points.[3]

Children with disabilities stayed home or were sent to state institutions or separate local schools. Frequently, children who did not speak English had to learn the language without extra assistance. Girls and boys attended separate schools in some school districts. Until the 1960s, and despite the *Brown v. Board of Education* decision of 1954, racially segregated schools were the norm in the southern states and in many northern school districts as well.

Although state constitutions had provisions about state authority over public education, traditionally state governments did not aggressively exercise this power. Usually, the governors and the state legislatures limited themselves to revising the state's school financing system—which, as noted above, normally supplied less funding for education than local school boards did.

The federal government's role was even more limited. Funds for school lunches, vocational education, and some teacher training in mathematics and science came from the federal level, but these were ancillary supports for the schools. As the 1960s approached, the political environment evolved so that the governance and financial support of public education developed differently than during the previous decades of American history.

Popular pressure to change the limited federal role began after World War II. From the late 1940s through the 1950s, school enrollments increased dramatically due to the baby boom after servicemen and women returned home from the war and started families. Parents demanded more and better schools for their children, and wanted action from whichever level of government would provide it. National politicians responded to these demands.

In 1946, the U.S. Senate considered a bill to provide federal aid to education. During the debate on that legislation, Senator Robert Taft (R-OH), the sponsor of the proposal, stated his belief:

> Education is primarily a state function—but in the area of education, as in the fields of health, relief, and medical care, the federal government has a secondary obligation to see that there is a basic floor under those essential services for all adults and children in the United States.[4]

That proposal was not accepted, but this issue was considered further in 1948. During that debate, Taft referred back to his position on an *even earlier* congressional piece of legislation and explained how his position had changed:

> Four years ago I opposed the then pending Bill on this subject [federal assistance to education]; but in the course of the debate it became so apparent that many children in the United States were left without education, and then it became apparent, upon further study, that that was not the fault, necessarily, of the States where they lived, but rather, of the financial abilities of the States, that I could see no way to meet the condition which now exists regarding illiteracy in the United States and lack of education in the United States without some Federal assistance, particularly for those states which today are considered below the average of wealth in the United States.[5]

In 1948, President Harry Truman announced his support for federal general aid for public elementary and secondary schools, but he did not submit legislation to the Congress. Instead, he endorsed the bill drafted by Senator Taft.[6] That same year, Truman, who had been Franklin Roosevelt's vice president and succeeded him on his death, was elected president in his own right.

Taft's proposal was approved by the Senate but died in the House of Representatives. At that time, the House was the graveyard for education legislation.

Years later, in 1967, when I began working for the House Education and Labor Committee, the members of Congress on that committee liked to tell me that both John F. Kennedy (D-MA) and Richard Nixon (R-CA) had been members of the committee and that they together provided the votes in the 1940s to kill federal aid, but for quite different reasons. Congressman Kennedy opposed it because it did not include aid for Catholic schools, and Congressman Nixon opposed it because of federal intrusion in the schools. Those reasons illustrate the major roadblocks that for decades faced federal aid.

In the 1940s and early 1950s, Taft's support for federal aid was especially significant since he was considered a leader of the Republican Party's conservative wing. In 1952, Taft ran for the presidency but was defeated for the Republican nomination by General Dwight D. Eisenhower. Eisenhower then won the general election, defeating Democrat Adlai Stevenson and bringing into power a Republican-dominated Congress.

It is interesting to speculate on what might have happened if Taft had won that Republican nomination in 1952 and then the presidency, and had brought a Republican Congress with him into office. Would the country have had general aid to education in the early 1950s when the Republicans controlled the presidency and the Congress? Could Taft have found a way around the traditional obstacles to federal aid? If he had, there would have been a substantial federal role in education a decade before it actually came about.

For their part, several Democratic members of Congress during this period proposed major legislative bills to pay for teachers' salaries and school construction. But when the Democrats won control of the Congress in 1954, they were not able to overcome the impediments to enacting major federal aid to education, especially since President Eisenhower did not take a leadership role.

Instead, the Democrats took advantage of the anxiety that arose when the Soviet Union launched a spacecraft ahead of the United States. Both countries had been vying to be the first to have a man-made satellite orbit the Earth, and therefore show scientific and technological superiority over the other. This was the era of the Cold War when the Soviet Union sought to demonstrate the superiority of communism, while the United States and its Western European allies were asserting the values of democracy.

As Sputnik began circling the globe, the United States was taken aback by the scientific prowess of the Soviet Union. Congress reacted by passing a narrow bill focused on improving the teaching of science and mathematics, which President Eisenhower signed. Although the National Defense Education Act of 1958 (NDEA) was limited in funding and scope and in no way represented a major piece of legislation for general aid or teachers' salaries, it helped to open the door a few years later to a larger involvement by the federal government in education.

By the later 1950s, none of the major funding proposals for general aid, support for teachers' salaries, or school construction had become law because of three controversies. First, southern members of Congress were opposed to federal aid because they feared they would have to end racial segregation in schools in order to receive this funding. Despite the *Brown* ruling of 1954, southern schools were still largely segregated. Second, supporters of private schools wanted these schools included in any federal aid legislation. The Catholic bishops were especially adamant on this point and used their influence over members of Congress to block any bills excluding private schools. On the other side of the issue were the public school organizations. The National Education Association (NEA) was as adamantly opposed to aid to private schools as the bishops were in favor of it, and it used its influence to stymie aid to private and religious schools. The third obstacle was a fear that federal support for education would lead to federal control of curriculum, teacher hiring, and other issues that had traditionally been considered matters for local discretion. Generally, political conservatives were more bothered by this issue of federal control than were liberals. That is why Taft's support of federal aid as a conservative was so important.

It is possible that had Robert Taft become president, he could have found a way around the federal control issue, as well as the other two obstacles; but since that did not happen, it remained for a later president to find the solution. The road to success led away from general aid, teacher salaries, and school construction to a different type of assistance. In other words, the federal government was able to support the schools but only in a restricted manner focused on specific goals.

SETTLING ON OVERCOMING THE EFFECTS OF POVERTY

President Eisenhower symbolized the national politics of the 1950s. As the successful military commander of the coalition of nations fighting the Nazis during World War II, he had conveyed to the armed forces an air of quiet, competent leadership. As the country's president during most of the decade of the 1950s, his demeanor assured the people that the nation was in safe hands. His political philosophy was to leave most decisions to the states and local governments. That attitude fitted the times after the huge national mobilizations of people and resources that had been necessary to win World War II.

As the 1950s reached an end, so did agreement that Eisenhower's political attitude was appropriate to address the nation's problems. The issue of poverty grew in importance, fed by a book on poverty and hunger by Michael Harrington.[7] African Americans were becoming increasingly dissatisfied with the glacial pace of school desegregation in the South five years after the *Brown* decision. Parents, in general, did not see enough improvement in the schools their children attended.

In the presidential campaign of 1959, John Kennedy played on this growing discontent and called for more vigorous national action to address education, civil rights, and hunger. Richard Nixon, his opponent, adopted a more cautious stance. Kennedy won, and once elected, his administration drafted legislation to address those issues, including major legislation to provide aid to education.

Although Congressman Kennedy had opposed federal aid if it did not benefit private schools, President Kennedy as the first Catholic in that office proposed aid without including private schools. In politics, there is a saying: You stand where you sit. In Congress, Kennedy represented a heavily Catholic district. As president, he represented a broader constituency; however, another factor was also involved. During the presidential campaign, he had to counter accusations that as a Catholic he would only represent the positions of that religion. This education legislation gave him an opportunity to demonstrate his independence.

Regardless of his political motivations, Kennedy's bills dealing with education and other areas faced unmovable obstacles. The House of Representatives was a special problem, particularly the Rules Committee that controlled the flow of legislation to the full House. Southern Democrats controlled that committee and did not share Kennedy's enthusiasm for federal action since it endangered their racially segregated way of life.

President Kennedy's assassination in 1963 shocked the nation, and shattered the political status quo. Lyndon Johnson, the new president, adopted Kennedy's agenda as his own, and brought to the task the political skills he had honed as the masterful majority leader of the Senate before he became Kennedy's vice president.

The following year Johnson won the presidency in his own right. After being sworn in he continued to aggressively pursue Kennedy's education agenda—but with more success than the previous president had had. In 1965 Johnson found the road map leading to enactment of federal education legislation. His approach was to base federal aid on the number of children from low-income families who lived in a school district. This strategy served two purposes. First, it fit well with the temper of the times. Achieving greater equity and focusing on the effects of poverty and hunger were national issues, and fundamental to the agenda of the Kennedy-Johnson administration. And second, it also made room for a compromise on the religious and private school issue. The Johnson administration proposed providing federal support for education services to poor children who attended private schools, while vesting control over the administration of the services with public school districts. This solution did not fully please combatants on either side of the issue, but the bishops and the NEA saw that Johnson was determined to get a bill, and so they reluctantly accepted the compromise.

The obstacle that southerners presented in wanting to retain their racially segregated school systems was overcome by Johnson's success in passing—a year before ESEA—the Civil Rights Act of 1964, which gave the federal government tools to speed the dismantlement of such schools. This meant that pressure from the federal government to integrate those schools would increase, even if federal aid did not pass.

Finally, the fear of federal control of the schools was put aside because the Democrats had won the elections of 1964 so overwhelmingly, partially as a reaction to Kennedy's assassination. That party dominated the House and Senate, and Democrats from regions outside the South generally did not share the concern of conservatives about federal control of the schools. In other words, there were so many liberal members of Congress—including many who were newly elected in 1964 with President Johnson's landslide victory—that this objection was pushed aside. To make sure it was not an obstacle, a provision was included in the legislative bill that no federal official could exercise control over the curriculum or instruction of any school.

The legislative bill creating ESEA was written by the Johnson administration, not by Congress, and a draft was presented to Congress for action. The bill went through the Congress in record time with only a few changes—a technical revision in the private school provision and a major amendment changing the way that funds would be distributed under the Title I program for disadvantaged children. (The major parts of the law are referred to as "titles.") President Johnson and the congressional supporters of the bill felt that fast action was the only way to avoid getting bogged down in the traditional controversies, especially the religious/private school issue.

The funding amendment that was made to the administration's draft legislation ensured that the northern states, and especially the largest cities in those states, would receive somewhat more Title I funding. The adoption of that amendment showed how much members of Congress were concerned that their schools would receive what they thought was their fair share of the new money. The bill Johnson had submitted to Congress called for distributing Title I funds to states and school districts based on their numbers of children from families with incomes of $2,000 a year or less, as shown by the decennial census. The southern states would have received a large share of the funds using this method because according to the census they had the largest concentrations of poor families. Members of Congress from the large cities of the country's northeastern, mid-Atlantic and midwestern regions objected because they cited the higher cost of living in those areas than in the southern states. They argued that families could have incomes of $3,000 in the northern cities and still be poor. Their point of view was important, since the House Education and Labor Committee, which had jurisdiction over the legislation, included a large number of northern urban Democrats among its members.

Congressman Roman Pucinski (D-IL), who was my home congressman and who brought me to Washington in 1967 to head the staff of his subcommittee on elementary and secondary education, offered an amendment that added to the number of poor families from the census data those receiving welfare payments over $2,000 a year. That amendment was accepted by the House committee and increased the count of poor children by about 10 percent—enough to cause a boost in funding for the northern states.[8] The northern states made higher welfare payments than the southern states, and so they were the gainers once those families were included.

President Johnson reluctantly accepted that amendment because he needed the support of those urban Democratic members of the committee to fight for the bill in the House. Johnson refused to accept any other major amendments, however. In the Senate, which is proud of its independence and of any senator's right to offer amendments of any type to any bill, Senator Wayne Morse (D-OR), the sponsor of the legislation in that chamber, fought off all amendments in order to keep the bill moving. Thus, the Senate adopted the House-passed bill without change.

During the course of the Senate debate, Senator Morse used a great deal of the debate time explaining how the new federal funds would flow to school districts because that was a question frequently raised by senators. His explanation goes to the issue of Title I's purpose:

> The objective of the bill is to raise the level, state by state, of what we call
> the deprived school district, the slum school district, the poverty pocket

school district in that State, nearer to the level of the better school districts in that State, to narrow the gap between the low-level schools and the high-level schools. If a deprived child is already going to a high-level school, he is already getting the educational opportunity that we want to give him.[9]

The Senate committee report on the legislation further explained this focus on funding:

School superintendents, educational leaders, and research scholars have provided evidence that there is no lack of techniques, equipment, and materials which can be used or developed to meet this problem, but that the school districts which need them the most are the least able to provide the necessary financial support. There was virtually unanimous agreement among those testifying that aid to the educationally deprived child represented the basic approach to widespread improvement in the country.[10]

In the House of Representatives, Congressman Carl Perkins (D-KY), the prime sponsor of the legislation and later my boss for twelve years, echoed those sentiments in his comments during the debate on the bill:

In many rural areas and in small school districts the impact of title I [sic] will provide as much as a 30-percent increase in local school budgets during fiscal year 1966. In such communities the lack of local financial resources have kept these school districts from keeping pace with new teaching techniques, new equipment, and adequate curriculum offerings. In most of these school districts the average per pupil expenditures are well below the State average per pupil expenditure for the State in which the district is located.[11]

Obviously, the key congressional leaders wanted to provide extra financial resources to needy school districts to improve their education programs. Since Title I funds were distributed based on poverty, disadvantaged students would be helped in the process. These public officials and school leaders had little doubt that educators knew how to do this. It was just a matter of giving them the financial means to solve the problem.

To state these points more directly, the congressional sponsors believed that the problem was a lack of money, not an absence of expertise to better educate children. Title I was a funding mechanism, not a means of supporting a particular approach to teaching and learning. Later, Congress came to believe that the problem was not limited solely to funding, but also extended to how the funds were used and how to hold school districts that received money accountable for academic results.

In 1965, President Johnson considered ESEA the cornerstone of his Great Society program to improve social conditions in the country. Johnson wanted to end hunger and poverty in America, and to use the resources of the federal government to achieve that end. Medicare, Medicaid, Head Start, and many other programs remain today as stalwarts still helping to achieve that objective; but other programs created as part of that vision were less successful and have faded away.

Some of the highest hopes of the Great Society to bring about greater equity in the country were placed on the new education legislation. After finishing college, Johnson had been a teacher in a school district with a high concentration of poverty, and believed in the power of education to bring about change. Upon signing the Elementary and Secondary Education Act of 1965, he said, "As President of the United States, I believe deeply no law I have signed or will ever sign means more to the future of America."[12]

2

The Evolution of Title I, 1965–1978

WHEN ENACTED IN 1965, the Elementary and Secondary Education Act was composed of five parts. Title I, which received about 90 percent of all funding for this law, distributed these new financial resources to school districts based on the number of poor children in each district. The other four titles of the law provided funds for library books, innovative programs, research, and the expansion of state departments of education so they could operate these new aid programs in their states.

The first appropriation for ESEA was huge for the times, $1.1 billion. Even more significantly, the Johnson administration had written its legislation to swiftly grow to a larger appropriation of $8 billion by 1969 and then in later years to have "vastly greater disbursements than a mere $8 billion a year," according to Samuel Halperin, a key figure in the administration working to enact ESEA.[1] Unfortunately, the costs of the Vietnam War stymied that objective, but the way the law was written left no doubt that Johnson thought big.

The stated purpose of the new law was "to strengthen and improve educational quality and educational opportunities in the Nation's elementary and secondary schools." The particular objective of Title I was expressed in this way:

> In recognition of the special educational needs of children of low-income families and the impact that concentrations of low-income families have on the ability of local educational agencies to support adequate educational programs, the Congress hereby declares it to be the policy of the United States to provide financial assistance (as set forth in this title) to local educational agencies serving areas with concentrations of children from low-income families to expand and improve their educational programs by various means (including preschool programs) which contribute particularly to meeting the special educational needs of educationally deprived children.[2]

Soon after ESEA was enacted, a struggle ensued about the exact meaning of those words in Title I's purpose. Did they mean that the new money was to buttress the general finances of school districts that had concentrations of poor families, which impaired their ability to provide a good education, especially to poor children? Or did they mean that the funds were to be extra, earmarked by school districts for special, separate programs for "educationally deprived children"? The explanations provided by Congressman Perkins and Senator Morse, the prime sponsors of the bill, suggested that they leaned toward the first interpretation. However, some officials in the U. S. Office of Education (then part of the Department of Health, Education, and Welfare) expressed the latter opinion.

The legislation was ambiguous enough to support both points of view. A major reason for this uncertainty was that the whole undertaking was new, and so there was little experience upon which to draw. But also, the political dynamic was to patch together a bill that could get past the three major obstacles that had for decades stymied federal aid, as discussed in chapter 1. Ambiguity helped to get an agreement because different people could read into the language their own meanings. This technique of being ambiguous is not unusual in Congress, where many different and strongly held points of view need to be placated. As helpful as this may have been to getting the legislation through to enactment, it planted the seeds of disputes that grew once ESEA became law.

After the law was enacted and appropriations were provided, the funds started to flow to states and local school districts. Educators were pleased that they had new money to improve the schools. In the first years of ESEA, the Office of Education was challenged with distributing such large sums of money and simultaneously interpreting the legislation to set rules for the use of the funds. Local school districts had the funds in hand before the federal government figured out exactly how it should administer the new programs.

In 1967, President Johnson decided not to run for reelection, in large part due to popular opposition to the war in Vietnam. In 1968, Richard Nixon won the presidency and brought with him to Washington a number of new Republican members of Congress. Nixon and the Republicans triumphed due to the war but also due to declining popular support for Johnson's Great Society programs. So, the new president sought to repeal, simplify, and cut back on funding for those programs.

In education, Nixon sought to eliminate ESEA and send funds to the states as unrestricted block grants. But he also wanted to substantially cut the funding so these block grants would provide less for education than was being provided under ESEA.

Congressman Perkins was the primary opponent in Congress of Nixon's education proposals. Perkins, a Democrat, represented the mountainous eastern part of Kentucky, which was very poor and had little industry except for coal mining. Perkins was a true product of that area: an active farmer who spoke with a twang, dressed in ill-fitting and unfashionable suits even in Washington, had a sloping gait, and was altogether unpretentious.

Perkins's electorate was poorly educated, and his school districts had few financial resources. Like President Johnson, he became a school teacher after college, and later he attended law school. Today, Perkins would be considered a political populist and not necessarily a liberal. He voted for federal aid because that was the only way his area could prosper since it had few other financial resources or features attractive to industry. Although he identified as a southerner and associated with southern Democrats, he voted for the Civil Rights Act of 1964, one of only two southern Democrats to do so.

Since I later worked for Perkins for twelve years, I know that some more sophisticated members of Congress considered him a "country boy," a few called him "Pappy," and they underestimated his intelligence—a big mistake! He may not have had a degree from an exclusive college, but he knew people's natures. He also worked tirelessly for his district, going back to it every weekend when Congress was in session and staying there every time Congress was not in session.

Perkins was the member of Congress I admired the most, and the one from whom I learned the most, since we spent many hours together working on legislation or talking about politics and politicians. In the twenty-seven years I worked in Congress, I got to know thousands of office-holders. Of them all, Perkins was the most dedicated and hardest-working politician I met. His devotion to helping the poor and forgotten was remarkable. He was not a "show horse," which is what members of Congress call a colleague who is always quoted in the news media but never gets a bill passed. He was a "workhorse" who eschewed publicity and got laws on the statute books.

Nixon had a formidable opponent in Perkins, who used all the powers of his chairmanship of the House of Representatives' Committee on Education and Labor to fight the president's proposals. In this all-out rescue effort, Perkins worked closely with the national public education organizations. Tirelessly, he held hearings throughout the country and provided local school superintendents with the exact amounts of money they would lose if Nixon's legislation passed. Due to local opposition, Nixon's proposals died, and the new ESEA continued to be implemented. Local school administrators liked having the additional money with few strings attached, since at that point the funds were used somewhat like general aid rather than targeted assistance.

After the defeat of Nixon's proposals, the freedom that local administrators had with ESEA funds began to shrink as the Office of Education took a more assertive role. This action was precipitated in part by reports issued in the late 1960s by advocates for poor children who had uncovered instances where some school districts were misusing Title I funds—for example, to construct a swimming pool.[3]

In the 1970s, Office of Education administrators sought evidence from local school districts that disadvantaged students were receiving services paid for with Title I dollars. Federal programs became more strictly regulated by the U.S. government, and federal audits for compliance increased. During that time, Congress also attached more strings to the receipt of aid. Thus, federal aid became more tightly focused on meeting the needs of particular students with disadvantages. This was the shifting point from quasi-general aid to targeted aid for disadvantaged children, commonly known as "categorical aid."

John Hughes, the first director of the Title I bureau in the Office of Education, explained the point of view of the federal departmental officials as follows:

> Title I was greeted by the educational establishment as the first step toward general aid. Their persistence over the years in pushing for general aid led them to feel that finally the federal government was joining State and local authorities as a full-fledged partner in the financing of the schools. However, the specific provisions of Title I which identified its purpose of providing assistance to local agencies serving concentrations of children from low-income families was a different concept than general aid for all children. Indeed Title I was categorical aid for a specific purpose in the tradition of other education programs enacted by the Congress . . . The ultimate triumph of Title I was to firmly establish the principle of special assistance to the children of poverty as a categorical education program. The early efforts to establish sound principles of categorical aid paid off in the legislative reinforcement of these categorical concepts by the Congress during the 1970s.[4]

During this period, I was staff director and counsel for the subcommittee responsible for elementary and secondary education in the House of Representatives, and saw the evolution of Title I from general aid to categorical aid as John Hughes described. Floyd Stoner, who studied the early administration of the Title I program, aptly described this situation as one where Congress had one view of the nature of the program, and the federal program administrators had another. The administrators ultimately prevailed in making Title I a categorical program, and finally the Congress concurred to maintain the funding.

"Most Congressmen closely associated with the bill believed that they were passing general aid under another name," Stoner wrote. But some members of the executive branch wanted to use Title I as a way of bringing about reform. Therefore, the Office of Education drafted requirements to force changes in state and local administrative behavior despite opposition by influential members of Congress. Over time, many members were put in the awkward position of defending these restrictions in order to maintain the appropriations.[5]

By the early 1970s, the ambiguity of Title I's statement of purpose was resolved. Congressman Perkins, Senator Morse, and some other congressional sponsors had thought that Title I would be a means of equalizing the expenditures among local school districts, especially those with concentrations of poor children. Key administrators in the Office of Education believed that the program's purpose was to focus federal aid on disadvantaged children by providing them with extra assistance. The congressional sponsors were supported in their position by local school administrators, while the federal administrators were aligned with advocates for poor children. The latter group prevailed. Title I clearly became a "categorical" program for disadvantaged children.

In 1974, Congress undertook a periodic review of ESEA. Along with other education laws, ESEA was amended and renewed in a legislative package called the Education Amendments of 1974. (This type of generic title became common practice for omnibus sets of amendments.) These amendments added several provisions aimed at ensuring that Title I funds were providing extra services and that schools with Title I grants received an amount of state and local funding that was comparable to the amounts spent in schools with more advantaged students. This action was one indicator that Congress had begun to accept the idea of Title I as a tightly focused effort to help disadvantaged students.

POLITICAL SUPPORT GROWS, BUT DISPUTES CONTINUE

In the 1970s, the ESEA programs became a ubiquitous part of local schooling. Title I programs were spread throughout the country, as were other, smaller ESEA programs, such as assistance to improve school libraries.

In Congress, political support for these programs grew to the point that former congressional opponents changed their positions on this type of federal aid. In the House of Representatives, 80 percent of Democrats voted for the original ESEA, while only 27 percent of Republicans did so. In the reauthorization of 1974, 84 percent of Democrats voted in favor and were joined by 74 percent of Republicans. In the Senate, there was more bipartisan support from the beginning. In 1965, 93 percent of Senate Democrats voted "yes," as did 56 percent of Republicans. In 1974, again 93 percent of Democrats were in support, along with 72 percent of Republican senators.[6]

With this political acceptance of the expanded federal role in education, the congressional debates shifted to the characteristics of Title I and other programs and to the distribution of this new, substantial aid. The first major occasion for these debates was the 1974 review of ESEA.

As mentioned above, several amendments were adopted in 1974 that ratified Title I as a categorical program directed at providing extra services for disadvantaged children. But the first big battle that year was over the distribution of Title I funds among states and school districts. Congressman Al Quie (R-MN), who had become the leader of the minority Republicans on the education committee, offered an amendment to use student test scores to distribute funds instead of poverty data.

The debate over that measure was interesting for several reasons. Quie had argued, and voted, against the original ESEA. Several years later, he tried to eliminate some of its programs. But by 1974 he had accepted its existence and was trying to make it more effective based on his beliefs. That

was a significant step forward in stabilizing the new federal role in education. (By contrast, in 2010 most Republican members of Congress voted
against Obama's national health care reform, and in 2014 they were still
attempting to repeal the entire law.) Another interesting aspect of Quie's
amendment was that it was a precursor to the debates in the 2010s about
the use of student test scores for such purposes as evaluating the performance of teachers and determining their pay and retention.

Quie was a serious and studious lawmaker. Like Perkins, he was a
farmer and an admirer of horses. This gave him a common bond with the
chairman of the education committee, and made cooperation easier. Often,
during hearings, when witnesses who read aloud long statements word by
word saw Perkins and Quie lean back in their chairs behind the podium,
they thought the two legislators were discussing the witnesses' suggestions
when they were really discussing horses.

Quie kept in good physical shape and later in life rode on horseback the
entire continental divide from the southern U.S. boundary to the northern
end. He was just as agile in mind. Often I would see him reading committee reports and other materials to prepare for his congressional work.

Quie later ran successfully for governor of Minnesota. Perkins and I
had breakfast with him at the governor's mansion when our committee
held a hearing in the state. I asked him what he had learned about the difference in being a congressman and a governor. He answered that he had
learned two things. First, he knew much less about state government as a
congressman than he thought he did. Second, as governor there is no place
to hide. By that he meant, the news media followed a governor on a daily
basis, and he had to take public stands on all sorts of issues. As a congressman, he was much less visible in the news media, and constituents often
did not know how he voted or what his opinions were.

Quie was one of the members of Congress I most admired for his hon-
esty, intelligence, and hard work. He also chose good staff members, including Christopher T. Cross, who came from the Department of Health,
Education, and Welfare to be Quie's chief education aide during the 1970s.
Chris worked hard and challenged me to do my work better, which estab-

lished a respectful relationship between us that produced sound, bipartisan legislation.

This is not to say that, in my opinion, all of Quie's ideas made sense—for instance, his proposal to shift the distribution of the billions of dollars appropriated for Title I from using census and welfare data to using student test scores. His criticisms of the prescribed way of distributing funds were on target, but his alternative would have made things worse. As a rationale for his amendment, Quie criticized the use of decennial census data to determine local grants because this approach did not identify the children who needed academic assistance. A poor child was not necessarily a child failing in school. Furthermore, the census data, collected once every decade, became outdated within a few years due to population shifts. Quie made a good case, but Perkins and others opposed him, and his amendment was defeated because of concerns about distributing such large federal grants based on test scores, which could change dramatically and could be manipulated if receipt of funds was tied to those results.

After disposing of that alternative, congressional attention became fixed on the effects of the Pucinski amendment in the original Title I law, which annually added the number of children from families which received welfare payments over $2,000 to the counts of poor children from the decennial census. In 1965, the Pucinski amendment had increased by about 10 percent the number of poor children used to allocate funds, but by 1974, 60 percent of the children counted in the funding distribution formula were included due to that amendment.[7] The result was a huge shift of funds to the large northern cities, such as Chicago and New York, because the northern states had increased welfare payments substantially since 1965. The losers were the southern states and other rural areas of the country, where welfare payments continued to be low.

That shift of Title I funding imperiled support for the program, especially future appropriations, since southern members of Congress had a tendency to seek membership on the appropriations committees of both the House and the Senate. It would have been difficult to maintain Title I as a mostly urban education program that chiefly benefited northern states.

Kentucky was one of the losing states, and therefore Perkins fought to change the allocation formula by capping the effect of the welfare factor. Naturally, he was opposed by the urban congressional delegations, including many of his fellow committee Democrats. At that time, the education committee was weighted toward the northern states, and the Democratic side had many big city members.

At the time, I was Perkins's counsel. I did most of the staff work on the amendment to trim back on the welfare count and contributed to the political work to get that change accepted. This was ironic, since Congressman Pucinski had brought me to Washington and now I was trying to undo part of his handiwork. (Pucinski had left Congress in 1972 and so at least was not part of this fight.)

This battle showed me certain aspects about how Congress operates. The first one is obvious: staffers have to be loyal to the members for whom they work. Loyalty is valued above other attributes because a staffer does so much in the name of the elected member of Congress. I agreed with Perkins that the Pucinski amendment had gotten out of hand and was imperiling broad support for the program, but as Perkins's counsel I would have had to carry out his position even if I had disagreed with it.

Second, there are favors a committee chair can grant to help win the support of other congressional representatives. Perkins needed every vote he could get on his committee to counter the northern and big city members. Congressman Bill Lehman, a Democrat from the Miami, Florida, region, was in favor of Perkins's amendment, but Perkins wanted to make doubly sure of his support. So when Lehman asked for a trip to Israel to visit some schools, Perkins assented, even though he rarely approved foreign travel because scandals of this sort had plagued his predecessor as committee chairman. I was sent to accompany Lehman and another committee member—probably as a daily reminder of the vote facing them when they returned.

Third, members of Congress care a lot about how much federal money comes to their home districts. Although I was from Chicago, I had never met Dan Rostenkowski, the Chicago Democratic congressman who chaired the House Ways and Means Committee, the most powerful committee in the House and possibly in the Congress. When the debate started about the effects of the Pucinski amendment, I was summoned to meet with Chairman Rostenkowski to discuss what Perkins's counter-amendment might do to Chicago's Title I grant. We had a good conversation, with Rostenkowski reminding me of my Chicago roots and telling me how much the city's schoolchildren would suffer if this decrease in funding went through. After I left his office, I reported to Perkins what had been said since I knew the value of loyalty. If this type of pressure was put on me, I could only imagine what else was done to get votes for and against Perkins's amendment.

Other lessons in politics that I learned from this battle were the benefits of being bipartisan and also generous in victory. Perkins had defeated Quie's amendment to use test scores to distribute Title I funds, but he wanted to retain Quie's support for Title I and other federal aid programs. So he sought ways to find common ground with Quie.

In his fight to cap the number of children in families receiving welfare payments—a number that had grown enormously under the Pucinski amendment—Perkins courted Quie to become an ally. The effects of Pucinski's amendment differed by region, state, and urban or rural status, and therefore it was not a partisan issue. Members of Congress "voted my district," as they liked to say. That meant if their districts gained money by leaving the law the way it was, they would vote to maintain the prevailing distribution system. If their districts gained money by changing that method of distribution, they would vote for Perkins's amendment to trim back the effects of the Pucinski amendment. In such a situation, a strong Republican advocate like Quie was beneficial to Perkins. Quie had credibility with many Republicans and could talk to them as Perkins could not. The benefit to Quie was that he became a prominent spokesperson for rural areas, which were often represented by Republicans.

After a hard battle, Perkins won in the education committee and then in the House. He sent me to brief Senator John McClellan, a Democrat from Arkansas, who was going to sponsor the amendment in the Senate because the education committee in that body was weighted in membership toward the northeastern states. The Perkins/McClellan amendment prevailed in the Senate, which essentially ended the battle. There were other differences between the House and Senate ESEA bills, however, that had to be reconciled in a House-Senate conference.

In that conference, the Senate refused to accept some Quie-backed amendments. Perkins turned to me and told me to find some provisions that Quie wanted so that he could argue for them. I came up with two items. The first was to allow a *school district* the option of using test scores instead of counts of poor children to distribute funds among the schools in the district, although the district's Title I grant would still be based on the district's count of poor children. The major opposition to Quie's original amendment was that it would affect the distribution of funds among states and districts, with lesser concern about the more limited effects involved with the use of test scores within a district. The second amendment was to authorize a scientifically based study of Title I. Perkins strongly argued for those provisions, and the Senate-House conferees approved both. Perkins valued working with Quie, and wanted him to leave his imprint on the ESEA even though he had lost his major amendment to shift to the use of test scores for the national and state distribution of funds.

In other words, Perkins did not want to leave Quie empty-handed. He wanted to bring him into the final bill. Such political shrewdness helped to ensure that federal aid would survive for fifty years. ESEA was shaped over time by both Democrats and Republicans, and that helped to maintain it through shifts in political party control of the Congress.

In 1976, Jimmy Carter was elected president, and in anticipation of the 1978 reauthorization, his administration wrote a bill to renew ESEA that included many changes to Title I and other programs. The administration then asked Congressman Perkins as chair of the House education committee to introduce the bill. But, as part of an effort to build a bipartisan base of support for federal aid, Perkins had already agreed with Quie that a bipartisan bill would be introduced in 1978. That bill would be shaped by findings from the scientifically based study of Title I, which Quie had supported and which had been included in the 1974 amendments.

The Carter administration representatives could not understand that and wanted their bill used as the basis for reauthorization. Perkins held his ground, but he told me to find parts of Carter's proposal that he could support so it would not be a complete shut-out. Several changes were selected, including major amendments that resulted in greater funding for school districts with high concentrations of poor children. Those amendments were later added to the bipartisan bill that Perkins and Quie supported.

Perkins's determination to keep his word with Quie was an example of true bipartisanship. To agree to introduce a bill based on a scientific study and then to say no to the president of your own political party requires strength of character. This type of bipartisanship was possible forty years ago and, regrettably, is in short supply in today's Congress.

The ESEA reauthorization that was enacted in 1978 represented the high point of categorical aid. Dozens of new targeted assistance programs were created, only some of which received appropriations and others that appeared as empty words on the law books. In the area of education, most programs are first authorized by one committee—the Education and Labor Committee in the House—and then if the legislation is signed into law, the House appropriations committee decides whether to fund them and at what level of funding. The same process occurs in the Senate. Exceptions are the school lunch program, the federal postsecondary loan programs, and a portion of Pell Grants for college students, all of which must be funded if authorized.

The Education Amendments of 1978 included not only ESEA amendments, but also changes to numerous other federal education laws, such as the Impact Aid Acts, which provided funds to compensate school districts for revenue lost from local property taxes because the federal government did not pay taxes on federal lands for military bases or other activities, even though children of federal employees attended the public schools. Also amended was the Indian Education Act, which provided support to both public schools and Bureau of Indian Affairs schools for the education of Indian children.

In that same reauthorization, the urban members of Congress tried unsuccessfully in the House to reverse their defeat of four years earlier. During the Senate-House conference committee that year to resolve the differences between the two versions of the ESEA reauthorization, Senator Jacob Javits (R-NY), a leader of the urban bloc, openly acknowledged to

Congressman Perkins, the leader of the House negotiators, that Javits and his urban allies had failed in their efforts to reverse the formula changes because "the rural boys had defeated us again."

Nevertheless, Javits worked closely with Perkins on many other issues, such as the anti-busing amendments that will be discussed in part III. In fact, in the same conference committee of 1978, Perkins and I met privately with Javits to find acceptable alternatives to House-passed restrictions on busing schoolchildren for desegregation. At that time, it was not uncommon for members of Congress to work together on some issues and then to oppose one another on other issues, even issues as important as determining how much money they could say they brought home.

This 1978 law marked a high-water point of political support for federal aid up to that time. Although it contained numerous new categorical programs and imposed new administrative burdens on local school districts, it received broad bipartisan support in the Congress. In the House, 98 percent of Democrats and 90 percent of Republicans voted for the final legislation. In the Senate, the vote was 97 percent of Democrats and 86 percent of Republicans.[8]

3

Regulatory Burdens Lead
to Change, 1978–2015

BY THE LATE 1970s it was obvious that congressional support for federal aid to education had grown. Federally funded programs were common in schools throughout the nation, and millions of disadvantaged students received extra services. In the mid-1970s the Individuals with Disabilities Education Act had been passed, and millions of children with disabilities had access to regular public schools, as will be discussed in part III.

The other side of the equation, though, was that school administrators had to comply with a growing number of regulations and undergo an increasing number of audits. The 1978 Education Amendments contained several significant changes to Title I that seemed helpful and even necessary at the time but that eroded support for Title I among school administrators once they were implemented.

For example, parents of children participating in Title I programs had to be given the opportunity to advise the school district about the instructional goals of funded activities; precise rules were set for membership of parental councils in schools serving a minimum number of children through Title I; and funding was authorized to support those councils.[1] Another amendment required school districts to report annually on how their services in Title I schools were comparable to services in schools not receiving those funds. The U.S. Office of Education was given authority to specify the types of information that school districts would have to include in those reports.[2] In carrying out that provision, the Office required detailed data on teachers' salaries and other local school expenditures.

To comply with federal student targeting requirements, school districts adopted a common practice of pulling disadvantaged students out of the regular classroom to be given extra help supported by Title I or similar programs. Further, the funds had to be targeted on students most in need of assistance. Students who made sufficient academic gains while receiving Title I services lost their eligibility for these services.

These features of the program were well-meaning but created administrative problems in schools and classrooms, as will be explained in the next chapter. The effectiveness of Title I was also limited because it could not compensate for the inherent inequities in school quality, funding, and support within and across districts.[3] In particular, Title I grants were too small to make up for the differences in resources among school districts caused by inequitable state and local distributions of financial resources.

In sum, Title I and other federal categorical programs were effective in bringing needed resources and services to schools and particular groups of students, but as they evolved they had their limitations. They were too small to provide major assistance; they were offered in schools with inequitable distributions of experienced teachers and financial resources which they could not overcome; and their requirements led to filling out numerous forms to show compliance.

At some point, a line was crossed, and state and local administrators began to resent the regulatory burdens more than they appreciated the extra financial aid. That was when Ronald Reagan walked onto the national stage. Considering the advantages and disadvantages of federal aid as it had evolved to 1980, but taking a broad view, David Cohen and Susan Moffitt in their book on Title I concluded:

If we consider where America was in 1965 with respect to the education of disadvantaged children, Title I had made significant progress by the end of the 1970s. It delivered funds that were reasonably well targeted to schools with disadvantaged students. It helped to make better education for disadvantaged students a new educational priority. It moved local use of federal funds from diverse and noninstructional services to instruction, and it did these things without losing political support . . . Despite its modest size and grave weaknesses, it also stopped the relative slide in achievement for many of its students and enabled them to make small relative gains in the early grades. That was both indirect evidence of how weak education had been for those students and a success for Title I. That element in its success was modest, but so was the program.[4]

DIMINISHED FEDERAL AID

In the late 1970s and early 1980s, Title I had a "modest" level of funding compared with all spending on public schooling, and the program's attempts to target assistance on the neediest created administrative problems. Nonetheless, it was present in schools throughout the country, and political support in Congress had grown.

During school year 1982–1983, before any effects of the new Reagan administration changes were felt locally, Title I alone provided the following benefits:

- More than 4.75 million children were served each year, including 180,000 in private schools.
- About 3.5 million children each year received supplementary instruction in reading.
- About 2.2 million children each year received supplementary instruction in mathematics.
- Roughly 160,600 full-time equivalent staff members were employed through grant funds each year.[5]

As described in chapter 7, the Bilingual Education Act, the IDEA, and other programs also provided supplementary services. Thousands of children of migratory farmworkers were helped. Children whose native language was not English received instruction in the mother tongue of the United States. Children with physical and mental disabilities were educated in regular classrooms, while youngsters in state institutions for the neglected and delinquent were taught mathematics and reading.

In the early 1980s, about the same time as those benefits were being provided, the new president, Ronald Reagan, fought to implement his philosophy, which held that government was part of the problem, not part of the solution. Since he included in "government" both local public schools and the federal government, he sought to eliminate or to curtail federal aid to public education.

This second major attack on federal aid to education bore some similarities to the first assault initiated by Richard Nixon more than a decade earlier. Reagan proposed combining numerous federal programs into block grants and eliminating most of the regulatory strings on this federal money. Local educators had opposed Nixon's cutbacks and defeated them, but this time it was different because of Title I's increased regulatory burden. In fact, some educational leaders who had worked closely with Congress during the 1970s on amendments to categorical or focused programs switched their allegiance in 1981 and helped the Republicans in Congress write legislation that embodied Reagan's ideas. In particular, big city school administrators from Los Angeles, Philadelphia, and many other districts that received large Title I grants were intimately involved in drafting this legislation.[6] The turning point for them had been the 1978 amendments to Title I, which were so specific about parental advisory councils and imposed time-consuming reporting requirements for local expenditures in both Title I and non-Title I schools.

Although Congress passed a bill that kept Title I mostly intact, the parental council provisions, the expenditure reporting requirements, and other duties that were considered administratively burdensome were removed. That bill also combined twenty-eight small and medium-sized categorical programs into a block grant with few requirements and less money.

After that victory of trimming Title I and eliminating other programs, Reagan continued his efforts to diminish the federal role in education by reducing funding. As Christopher T. Cross, my former colleague and later a high-ranking official in President George H. W. Bush's administration, observed, "Over the course of the Reagan years, the proportion of K–12 education revenue from federal sources fell by about 30%. The constant battles over education spending were the most significant recurring theme of the Reagan years."[7]

After those changes under Reagan, federal aid retained its outward appearance but in a shriveled form. Categorical aid, provided through Title I and similar programs for disadvantaged children, survived, but decreased funding meant that fewer students were assisted. This point is made clear by an analysis done by Wayne Riddle, the former chief expert on ESEA for the Library of Congress's Congressional Research Service, the nonpartisan source of information and analysis for the House and Senate. According to his study, throughout the period of fiscal years 1981–1989, the annual funding level for Title I was $9.3 billion or lower in 2014 dollars. By contrast, in the previous decade, from 1970 to 1980, the funding was higher than this level in all but two years.[8]

THE FEDERAL ROLE CHANGES

Despite limited appropriations for Title I and other federal programs, some supporters of these programs were becoming impatient that student academic achievement was not increasing in schools with concentrations of poor students. They wanted to see more progress after two decades of federal assistance.

The 1988 ESEA reauthorization was the occasion for them to seek change. Congressman Augustus Hawkins (D-CA), the chairman of the House education committee during the last half of the 1980s, was a liberal who represented Watts, one of the poorest parts of the Los Angeles megalopolis. When I was working for Hawkins as chief counsel, I often heard him bemoan the fact that schools in his congressional district received millions in federal education dollars and yet their test results continued to be abysmally low.

Hawkins wanted me to find a solution. Fortunately, we had on the staff a temporary intern, Judy Billings, who was on leave from being the Title

I director for Washington state's department of education. She knew how federal aid worked at the state and local levels and had an idea of how to change federal law to bring about improvement in a workable way. This was an instance of the right person being at the right spot at the right time.

Therefore, in considering ESEA for renewal in 1988, Chairman Hawkins offered an amendment to require school districts to set academic goals for their students. If a school district did not succeed in improving basic and more advanced skills among students based on those goals, then the state had to work with the district on an improvement plan until it showed sustained success. That process served as the template for the implementation of standards-based reforms adopted at the national level in the 1990s.

In exchange for this increased accountability, schools with high percentages of poor children were allowed to use their Title I funds for "schoolwide projects"—a provision that relaxed some of the categorical aid rules to allow schools to fund services that benefitted all of their students instead of limiting services to the most disadvantaged. Examples of these services would be hiring more teachers to reduce class size, or hiring a reading tutor who could help any student regardless of whether he or she would have qualified under the regular rules for Title I that focused assistance on the students who were furthest behind.

The Hawkins proposals were accepted, and consequently the 1988 amendments marked a change in attitude among congressional leaders, characterized by increased demands on educators to show academic results as a consequence of receiving federal aid. These leaders no longer believed, as Senator Morse had stated in the 1960s, that the problem was simply a lack of money. Rather, the belief was growing that schools receiving federal funds should demonstrate that their students were making greater academic progress. Hawkins's amendments laid the groundwork for congressional supporters of federal aid to endorse a standards and testing approach in the early 1990s.

Congressman Hawkins was an African American representing a heavily African American district. His impatience about the lack of improvement in the schools in his area accelerated this change of congressional attitude about what should be expected from federal aid. In retrospect, it was also a precursor to African American impatience with inner city public schools and support by some African American leaders of vouchers for private school tuition and for charter schools. Arguments about the value of public education were beginning to wear thin when minority parents did not see their children getting a good education.

The 1988 ESEA law was titled the Hawkins-Stafford Amendments, in honor of Congressman Hawkins and Senator Robert Stafford, a Republican from Vermont, who was a strong supporter of federal aid to both elementary and secondary education and postsecondary education. That spirit of bipartisanship was reflected in the final vote for the legislation. In the House all Democrats voted for it as did 99 percent of Republicans. In the Senate, all Democrats voted "aye," as did 98 percent of the Republicans.[9]

After the partisan battles of the Reagan years, these votes showed a return to bipartisanship in support of federal aid. A major reason for this near unanimity, registering the highest margins of victory attained by any ESEA bill, was the new accountability features in Title I. It was no longer simply federal grants to school districts to provide extra services; it became grants to improve student achievement, and changes had to be made if no such improvement occurred. Both Democrats and Republicans supported that new approach.

In the 1990s, the push for greater accountability accelerated, but in a way that moved the emphasis of federal aid away from Title I and the other categorical programs. In 1992, President George H. W. Bush proposed national academic standards and national tests, a startling departure from the American tradition of local control of public education. The assumption of the proponents of this new standards/testing reform was that Title I was not effective; a further assumption was that the new reform would make up for the weaknesses of federal programs. Therefore, the attention shifted from Title I to creating a new structure of academic standards and tests.

The first President Bush did not succeed in enacting legislation in this area. The next opportunity for change arose with the regularly scheduled review and reauthorization of Title I, ESEA, and related programs in 1994.

By then, Bush had been defeated by Bill Clinton. The Clinton administration used that opportunity to enact two major pieces of legislation. Goals 2000 was a voluntary program of grants to states to establish a framework of reform based on state academic standards and tests, and ESEA was amended to require states accepting Title I funds to adopt standards and tests.

The 1994 legislation also included other amendments to Title I, which raised the expectations for the educational improvements that would result from federal aid. A prime example was the new purpose of Title I. This aid was now meant to provide opportunities for students to learn the content in challenging state standards and to meet state performance goals. Students were to be given an enriched and accelerated program, to have access to intensive complex thinking and problem-solving experiences, and to receive the same amount and quality of instructional time as students not served by Title I. Accountability for results was also expected to increase, and a reference was made to distributing resources to schools with the greatest needs. Another section of the new law mentioned the goals of narrowing the achievement gap between disadvantaged and other students and boosting appropriations for Title I.[10]

These expectations represented a considerable change from the purpose of the original 1965 ESEA. The 1965 purpose emphasized the need for financial resources but said little about academic expectations and practices. By contrast, the 1994 legislation expected greater results based on challenging standards and academic coursework, as well as reductions in the achievement gap, but paid less attention to inequities in the allocation of local financial resources. In the congressional debates on the 1994 amendments, so many references were made to the need to close the achievement gap that this seemed to be the purpose of Title I. Furthermore, much was said about the need for challenging standards and enriched curricula at the state level.

Clearly, the 1994 ESEA reauthorization demanded much more academically of schools that received federal funds than had been asked in 1965. In addition, the demands for accountability were far heavier than in the original ESEA, as will be discussed in part II.

The other major change to Title I in these 1994 amendments expanded the use of schoolwide projects, which were first authorized in 1978 for schools with concentrations of students from low-income families and were further encouraged in 1988. The 1994 ESEA amendments lowered the threshold for eligibility so that any school in which at least 50 percent of the enrollment consisted of children from low-income families could use Title I funds to improve education across the entire school. These schools were also permitted to combine Title I funds with some other federal grants. This expanded flexibility allowed schools to fund the same types of activities as Hawkins's amendment in 1988, for example, hiring teachers to reduce class size, buying computers for all students and not just for Title I students, and hiring experts in reading and mathematics who could train all teachers to improve.

In 2001, the ESEA was on schedule for another review and renewal. This became the opportunity for President George W. Bush to strengthen the Clinton reforms of 1994 dealing with standards and tests. Title I became the platform for those changes, but the focus was clearly on that new reform and not on Title I and the traditional categorical programs. Bush's amendments to ESEA were called the No Child Left Behind Act (NCLB).

In addition to strengthening standards and test requirements, NCLB further lowered the threshold for schoolwide programs to schools in which at least 40 percent of the enrollments consisted of poor children; this action made many more schools eligible for schoolwide programs (formerly called schoolwide projects). Currently, more than half of the schools receiving Title I assistance can use those funds for schoolwide programs. Since this expansion of eligibility occurred at the same time as the standards/testing/accountability reform was implemented, much of the funding may simply be used to help students meet state performance goals.

In effect, these schools can use funds from Title I and certain other federal education programs as a form of general aid for school improvement. This is close to Senator Taft's original concept of federal general support for public education. A key difference, though, is that the Title I school may still be staffed by less experienced teachers, while more experienced teachers go to more affluent schools in the same district. Also, the district may have less state and local funding available for education than more affluent districts in the state. Thus, while schoolwide programs have more flexibility in using federal funds, they continue to operate within inequitable systems.

Finally, in 2008 President Barack Obama was elected and continued to emphasize new reforms rather than Title I and the traditional categorical programs. Obama took office in the midst of a worldwide financial crisis. For several years, his administration was absorbed with preventing that crisis from becoming an economic depression. The other major goal that absorbed the Obama administration's attention was to achieve the passage of national health care legislation.

Although Obama had promised changes to NCLB/ESEA during his campaign, he put those aside to focus on these other issues. However, as part of the American Recovery and Reinvestment Act of 2009 (ARRA), a measure to stimulate the national economy, Obama and the Congress nearly doubled federal aid for elementary and secondary education. It was made clear, however, that this was a temporary increase due to the economic crisis. Most of these federal funds were sent to the states to maintain the public schools during this crisis since the states had lost so much in revenue. Those funds were incorporated into state funding formulas for aid to local school districts and used to pay for the salaries of teachers and other educators, thereby avoiding massive layoffs. This funding helped public education to survive and averted further damage to the economy by keeping educators employed.[11]

States that received these ARRA funds, however, had to comply with school reform requirements—specifically, to adopt challenging state academic standards, improve their data systems, evaluate teachers more thoroughly, and improve the lowest performing schools.

The ARRA also gave the Department of Education several pots of money to be used mostly at the discretion of the secretary. The most important of these new programs was Race to the Top (RTTT), which became the favorite of the secretary and of the president. Although originally authorized as part of the ARRA to stimulate the economy, the president has continued to ask for yearly appropriations.

The RTTT is a competitive grant program for the states. If they fulfill the requirements and receive high scores on their grant application for pledging to undertake reforms, they can receive substantial funds from the federal government. As of June 2014, from the first competitions for funds, eighteen states and the District of Columbia had received grants, ranging from $25 million to $700 million. To qualify, states had to fulfill certain requirements, including placing no limits on the number of charter schools (public schools freed from some regulations) that could be authorized in their states and instituting evaluations of current teachers using student test scores as a significant factor.

The Obama administration has high hopes that the RTTT states will make major improvements in their systems of education.[12] It is too early to know the results of those grants.

While favoring RTTT and other competitive programs, the administration for the last three years has not asked for significant increases in funding for Title I and other traditional programs. The doubling of federal funding in 2009 was promoted for economic recovery reasons rather than as a sign of faith in the ability of Title I and other traditional programs to bring about improvement. The Obama administration is putting its chips on RTTT and a few other smaller new programs for that.

Before becoming president, Obama lived and worked in a part of Chicago that has public schools attended overwhelmingly by African American students. Those schools could have been in Congressman Hawkins's area of Los Angeles. As the country's first African American leader, Obama seems to reflect the impatience Hawkins and later racial and ethnic minority leaders have had with the quality of education that minority students receive in traditional inner city public schools. That desire for rapid change and improvement may explain Obama's support for new reforms like RTTT and lack of interest in the traditional federal programs such as Title I.

For whatever reason, the Obama administration's actions show how far the spotlight has shifted from Title I and other categorical programs to different ideas for change. Title I has receded into the background, and hope for school improvement is placed elsewhere.

CONCLUSION

The subtitle of this book, "The Politics of Education Reform," certainly describes the fifty-year history of the creation, growth, and shrinkage of federal programs to aid public schools. Title I is central to this story not only because it is the largest federal aid program and has served as the exemplar for other categorical programs, but also because President Johnson and others placed so much hope in its potential to improve education. Title I was the belle of the political ball in the late 1960s and 1970s, but today it is the scorned stepdaughter—a story of Cinderella in reverse. Race to the Top and charter schools are now the favorites of those in power in the government, charitable foundations, and high-tech millionaires. For Title I, what a "riches to rags" saga! What a downfall!

Equally ironic is the shift from general aid to categorical aid and back again. The story started with Senator Taft and the ESEA congressional sponsors who wanted general aid to education but did not get it. This was followed by decades of increased targeting on disadvantaged children. Now, the use of schoolwide programs rejects the targeting approach to improvement, so that most Title I funds are used in a quasi-general aid way.

The standards and accountability movement emerged out of widespread dissatisfaction with Title I and a search for a new way to make schools better. Before moving on to an analysis of that movement, however, let's pause to assess the effectiveness of Title I in improving student learning.

4

Was Title I Effective?

ON ONE LEVEL, the effects of the new federal aid provided by ESEA were—
and are—obvious. Since the late 1960s, millions of children throughout
the country who need extra assistance with their education have received
supplemental services. But has this extra aid raised student academic
achievement? Remember that the authors of ESEA and related programs
thought that the problem was a lack of financial resources, not a deficiency
of knowledge about how to improve education. Were they right?

To help answer that question, Senator Robert Kennedy (D-NY) in the
early days of ESEA successfully amended that law to require evaluations of
the new federal programs. He argued that because so much money was being spent, school districts and states should be able to demonstrate results.

As a consequence, states and local school districts annually evaluated
their programs, but "most districts and states responded in a perfunctory
fashion [because] few had the capability to collect valid data on school
operations or program effects."[1] To address these deficiencies in data, the
federal government required greater uniformity through adoption of a system called TIERS (Title I Evaluation and Reporting System), which had
limited usefulness because it was only a general framework for evaluation
and offered little evidence on teaching and learning.[2]

The Title I evaluation required by the Education Amendments of 1974, discussed in chapter 2, concluded that Title I was successful in delivering additional services to educationally disadvantaged children, and that school districts could create the conditions for increased student achievement, but that not all districts were successful in doing so. The National Institute of Education (NIE), which conducted the study, also pointed out that Congress's objectives for Title I were not limited to increased educational achievement, but also included social and health services to offset the effects of poverty on children eligible for Title I.[3]

That evaluation answered some questions, but the basic issue continued to be raised: did Title I increase student achievement? Therefore, in the late 1970s and early 1980s a national evaluation of Title I focused on that question. The *Sustaining Effects Study* collected data for three years on a nationally representative sample of pupils beginning in grades 1–3. The results, released in 1982, showed that achievement gains for Title I participants were significantly greater than those of disadvantaged nonparticipants in mathematics in grades 1–6, and in reading in grades 1–3, although gains were not significantly different in reading in grades 4–6.[4]

That was the mostly good news. Other results were not perceived as favorable. The achievement gap between disadvantaged and nondisadvantaged students was not reduced because Title I participants improved at the same rate as other students. Lastly, students who participated for shorter periods of time retained their achievement gains, while those who remained in the program—and who were generally the most disadvantaged—did not improve.[5]

Thus, the study identified some successes of Title I as well as some shortcomings. Students in the early grades made significant gains, but they did not exceed the gains made by nondisadvantaged students. Further, the most disadvantaged students did not do well. Overall, these conclusions were disappointing because so much hope had been placed on this program as the way to help disadvantaged students do better.

The *Sustaining Effects Study* became a weapon in the political debate in Congress about federal aid. The year it was released, 1982, President Reagan and a Congress that was more conservative than previous ones sought to decrease the federal role in education. As described in the previous chapter, they succeeded.

During the next decade, several other studies of Title I were released, but none as comprehensive as the *Sustaining Effects Study*. In 1993 the RAND Corporation concluded that on average Title I achieved "modest short-term benefits." Further, although many individual programs achieved outstanding results, this was hidden when results were averaged for programs across the nation.[6]

That same year, the Commission on Chapter 1, created by Congress to report before the reauthorization of 1994 on the effects of Title I (labeled "Chapter 1" for a few years), issued its findings. Chapter 1/Title I was the primary factor, it concluded, in reducing by approximately one-half the gaps between white and Hispanic, and white and African American, pupils on the National Assessment of Educational Progress (NAEP), the highly regarded national test. The Commission also determined that Chapter 1/Title I participants received assistance in improving basic skills but not with more advanced academic skills. A key limitation of both the RAND and the Commission studies was that these reviews did not collect new data; rather, they reanalyzed other research.[7]

Some good news was not good enough. Since these studies did not show great success in raising poor students' academic achievement, dissatisfaction grew with the program as it was then constituted. Therefore, "during the 1980s, Title I began a fundamental shift, away from a program that sent money to schools, toward becoming a program that pressed schools to boost students' achievement scores," wrote David Cohen and Susan Moffitt, noted Title I researchers.[8]

The first evidence for this shift came in the form of ESEA amendments offered in 1988 by Congressman Augustus Hawkins. Those accountability requirements, described in the last chapter, were the precursor to the standards/tests/accountability changes advocated by the four most recent presidents, as will be described in the next chapter.

This shift in Title I was also influenced by the *Prospects Study of Educational Growth and Opportunity*, an important piece of research that involved large numbers of students and collected an impressive amount of data. In 1993, this congressionally mandated study, which analyzed a sample of third- and seventh-grade Title I participants, found only a small gain in academic achievement for seventh graders in mathematics. It also found no evidence of any closing of the achievement gap and no significant differences in the gains made by Title I participants and a "comparison group."[9]

Various studies over many years using different approaches reached about the same conclusion. In a nutshell, the billions of dollars spent on Title I had at best a modest effect on the academic achievement of the disadvantaged students who participated in the program, with the most disadvantaged showing the least effects. Further, if the impact of this federal aid was measured by how much the achievement gap between disadvantaged and advantaged students had closed (which was not an explicit goal of the law until 1994), it had not succeeded by that measure.

Why was this so? Were the authors of ESEA wrong in relying on educators to use the funds wisely?

Several important caveats must be kept in mind when reviewing these results. For example, the researchers involved in *Prospects* pointed out that their conclusions did not address what would have happened to Title I students if they had *not* received any extra services at all. Those students could have fallen further behind.[10] The same observation could have been made about other categorical programs, such as assistance for children of migratory farm workers.

However, the most important factor influencing the outcomes of Title I and similar aid had to do with the nature of these categorical programs. In addition, the amount of funding they received was a crucial limitation. Title I contained requirements meant to target the extra assistance on the students most in need, but heavy administrative burdens and disrupted classrooms were often a side effect. To comply with federal student targeting requirements, school districts adopted a common practice of pulling disadvantaged students out of the regular classroom to be given extra help supported by Title I or similar programs. But this practice also meant that the students who were pulled out were identified as disadvantaged to their peers and missed the subject matter taught in the regular classroom during their absence.

Jesse Rhodes, a scholar who studies federal aid, stated it this way:

Furthermore, federal programs and their recipients were largely isolated
from the regular school program and nonprogram recipients. In part in
order to comply with federal accounting rules, state and local policymak-
ers often designed their compensatory education offerings as "pull-out
programs," in which disadvantaged students were removed from regular classes and provided with separate, special instruction by federally
funded instructors. This approach made it easier for federal regulators
to track federal funds; but it also limited the overall impact of federal
programs on schools, while fragmenting the education of recipients of
federal aid.[11]

Another problem arose because the funds had to be targeted on students most in need of assistance. If a student gained academically while
receiving services, he or she was considered no longer eligible for services.
Thus "each year about 40% of Title I recipients were replaced by new low-
achieving students."[12] But students did not always retain their gains; Title
I assistance was not like being given a shot against polio. Some students
failed again and had to return to the Title I program. This churning was
disruptive, and meant that the evaluations of the programs showed few or
uneven results. In 1978, Congress adopted an amendment to lessen this
effect by permitting a student who showed improvement to remain in the
program for an additional year, but this was of limited help.[13]

These features of the program were well-meaning but created administrative problems in schools and classrooms. The effectiveness of Title I was
also limited by its status as an extra resource; it could not compensate for
the inherent inequities in school quality, funding, and support within and
across districts. Within school districts, Title I schools often had poorly
educated aides and less experienced teachers because more experienced
teachers and paraprofessionals often chose to work at schools serving students from more affluent families.[14]

Furthermore, Title I services were provided in local districts with
greatly varying local and state funding. In other words, the baseline state

and local funding for education was inequitably distributed, and Title I grants were too small to make up the difference in the lower-spending districts.

A current example from two districts in the Chicago suburbs shows that these inequities still exist.

> In Cicero, Illinois, 93 percent of the enrolled students come from low-income families, and the district spent $9,669 per pupil in 2011–12. In Winnetka, Illinois, in the same county, about 0.3 percent of the students are from low-income families, and the district spent $19,663 per student in 2011–12. Cicero received a federal grant of $18 million, while Winnetka received $300,000 from federal sources.[15]

Cicero received about 8.3 percent of its budget from Washington, DC, and Winnetka received almost nothing in terms of its expenditures. But the federal funds Cicero receives do not go far to make up for the vast disparity in spending between it and Winnetka. The original intent of Senator Morse and Congressman Perkins is far from being fulfilled.

Another way to view this important limitation on the effectiveness of Title I is through the level of funding provided by the Congress. Michael Puma, who led the *Prospects* study, concluded that it was unrealistic to expect "Title I to be the single solution to the very difficult task of compensating for the substantial educational deprivations associated with child poverty." A major reason, he noted, was that the Title I appropriation was "a relatively small amount when compared to the total cost of elementary and secondary education." Title I amounted to less than 3 percent of total U.S. expenditures for elementary and secondary education in 1999.[16]

Puma's point about Title I was true in the 1990s, but was also supported when one compares the appropriations for earlier years, such as for 1966 and 1980. The following illustration, from information gathered by Wayne Riddle, uses both current dollars (the face value of the dollars at the time) and constant dollars (amounts adjusted to take into account inflation over the years).

In 1966, Title I received its first appropriation of $969,935,000; by 1980, the appropriation in current dollars was $2,731,651,000, which appears to be a hefty increase. But in constant 2014 dollars, the program received $10,174,976,000 in 1966 and $10,266,372,000 in 1980. In other words, despite the greater political support, the program received almost the same level of funding in 1980 as it did in ESEA's maiden year of 1966, in terms of what the dollars could buy.[17]

Another way to view this is in terms of per-pupil funding. In 1966, $1,321 was provided per poor child. In 1980, $1,445 was allotted per poor child in constant dollars—a very similar amount.[18]

Thus, Title I was not only a relatively small program as measured by the overall spending in the country for elementary and secondary education, but it was also a program that never expanded sufficiently in funding to have the major impact intended by President Johnson and its initial congressional sponsors.

Title I and other federal categorical programs were bringing needed resources and services to schools and particular groups of students, but as they evolved they had their limitations. They were too small to provide major assistance; they did not improve classroom instruction because they were provided as supplements to regular education; and they were offered in schools with inequitable distributions of experienced teachers and financial resources.

These points were relevant to federal categorical aid in general, not just to Title I, but they were most obvious with Title I, the largest federal program. When Title I and these other categorical programs were conceived, they were meant to grow much larger and provide much more assistance than they did, and thereby to have a much greater impact than they did. They never realized their full promise, but they were judged by the original intent.

In the general debates about the results of *Prospects* and other studies, the unique characteristics of Title I were often ignored or downplayed. Also pushed aside were the inequities in the American system of public education in which Title I functioned. The modest results for the program should not have come as a surprise. As Cohen and Moffitt asserted in their study of Title I:

> Given its modest nature and scope, Title I was modestly effective, but the gains seemed small when viewed in light of the gap in achievement. As the gap gained visibility in debates about schools, Title I came to seem less effective. The broader school reform movement reinforced that view, for its advocates held that U.S. schools allowed most students to do pallid work and that the solution was more academic challenge.[19]

Part II

STANDARDS, TESTING, AND ACCOUNTABILITY

NOBODY WANTS THEIR taxes used unwisely. Arguments about the usefulness of government-supported programs have been a constant in the national debate, and so it has been with Title I and other measures aimed at ameliorating the effects of poverty on schoolchildren.

From the 1980s on, the belief grew that federal aid was a failure. Or, to state it more accurately, the perception took hold that poverty-oriented federal aid to education was not sufficiently raising the academic achievement of educationally disadvantaged children. That trend was fed by conservatives who had never reconciled themselves to the concept of national assistance to improve public schools and instead backed policies like tuition vouchers encouraging growth of private schools.

Then again, liberals who had earlier fought for Title I and similar programs also became disillusioned in the late 1980s, and came to believe that major changes in federal aid were needed. Remember that in 1988 Congressman Hawkins, a noted liberal, amended Title I to demand corrective action if a school district did not raise student achievement.

This belief in the ineffectiveness of federal aid merged with the more general criticism that the public schools were failing. For decades, the *nation's* public schools have received low grades according to the PDK/Gallup Poll of the public's attitudes towards the public schools, although *local* schools have not. In 2013, the nation's schools received an A or B from only 18 percent of the public, while their community's schools received that ranking from 53 percent of the public.[1] Possibly, the public is satisfied with the schools they know, but their impression of the country's schools is shaped by what they hear and read in the news media—which is often quite negative. Regardless of reason, the general sentiment exists that the country's schools are inadequate.

Chapter 5 examines the dissatisfaction with both public schools in general and federal aid in particular, and describes how this widespread discontent led to the movement to raise academic standards, which eventually morphed into the type of test-driven reform associated with the 2002 No Child Left Behind Act. Chapter 6 asks the same question about this reform that was asked in the preceding chapter about Title I: how effective has it been?

5

Standards, Testing, and
Accountability Under Four Presidents

A NATION AT RISK, a report released in 1983 by President Ronald Reagan, drew enormous media attention because of its dramatic tone and heightened rhetoric. "If an unfriendly foreign power had attempted to impose on America the mediocre educational performance that exists today, we might well have viewed it as an act of war," the report declared. "As it stands, we have allowed this to happen to ourselves."[1]

Ironically, Reagan's Secretary of Education, Terrell Bell, had convened the commission that wrote the report as a way to divert Reagan's attention away from his proposal to eliminate the newly created U.S. Department of Education.[2] When Reagan released the report, he greeted it as a call to improve American schools through the return of school prayer and the introduction of vouchers for private school tuition, neither of which appear in the document as recommendations.

Regardless, the report touched a nerve in the American public about the condition of the schools. Business leaders expressed dismay that American workers were not educated sufficiently well for higher-level jobs. State governors and other politicians voiced the fear that other nations were overtaking the United States in the international marketplace due to the disappointing level of American education.

The political right wing spread stories about the sorry condition of public schools, since they too wanted government support for private schools in the form of vouchers or tax credits. But, as noted by Patrick J. McGuinn, a professor who monitors federal aid:

> Republican efforts to draw attention to the failure of federal policy to improve the performance of public schools had in many ways backfired. They succeeded in expanding media coverage of education and in ensuring that the media would generally portray schools in a negative light. But rather than resulting in increased public support for a reduction in the federal role in education, Republican rhetoric increased the salience of education in national politics and among the electorate and helped to generate momentum for increased federal leadership in school reform.[3]

The view that Title I and other federal aid programs were not doing enough to improve the education of disadvantaged students buttressed this concept that public education was failing. The message became this: the schools are doing a poor job, and federal aid is ineffective and not helping. Another answer had to be found, and it turned out to be the standards/testing/accountability movement.

The tale of how this new reform was incorporated into federal legislation and became national policy involves four presidents—two Republicans and two Democrats, each with his own contribution to make to this major change in American education. In general, they used the existing federal education structure of Title I and layered this new set of requirements on top. The traditional federal programs continued, and the testing and accountability requirements were added.

GEORGE H. W. BUSH AND NATIONAL STANDARDS

After George H. W. Bush, Reagan's vice president, became president in his own right in the elections of 1988, he abandoned Reagan's laissez-faire attitude toward federal involvement in the schools. In 1989, Bush convened in Charlottesville, Virginia, an unusual summit of the nation's governors to discuss how to improve the public schools.

Bill Clinton, then governor of Arkansas, attended that meeting, and afterwards worked as the lead Democratic governor on a bipartisan basis with other governors to write national education goals. Clinton later explained that the governors expected these goals to lead to the establishment of national standards and national tests.[4]

The symbolism of that work was extraordinary. Democratic and Republican governors were saying that although they had labored to improve the schools within their states, they needed a larger federal role to assist them. State governors are known for being very protective of state rights, and so for them to be asking for national attention and intervention was a sea change. They would not have asked for that change in federal-state relations unless they thought it was needed.

The national education goals set aspirational targets for improvement in the schools; for example, one goal called for the United States to become first in the world in mathematics and science achievement by the year 2000. Those objectives were not achieved, but they served as a building block toward creating a new national school reform movement based on high academic expectations. Meanwhile, various groups were calling to raise academic rigor.

In the late 1980s the country's mathematics teachers, working through the National Council of Teachers of Mathematics, developed national standards for what students should learn in math and released them in the early 1990s. In 1991, a presidential advisory committee composed of businesspeople and educators recommended to the first President Bush the adoption of national examinations for elementary and secondary education students—a novel step in American education. Paul O'Neill, the chair of that group and the CEO of ALCOA who would later become the Secretary of the Treasury, asserted that teachers should teach to a set of standards and that national tests would be the only way to reach the goals of school improvement. A few weeks later, an education group headed by the Republican governor of New Jersey, Thomas Kean, proposed that all high school seniors be required to take a national examination of their knowledge and skills.[5]

Influenced by these ideas, in the early 1990s President Bush proposed the creation of national academic standards in core academic subjects and national tests to determine students' progress. As a first step to implement this plan, the first Bush administration entered into contracts with groups to write national academic standards using federal funds from the Department of Education, the National Endowment for the Humanities, and other government sources.

Bush did not include the Democratic-controlled Congress in the development of these standards, but he did submit a small bill to Congress that would fund the creation of a model school in each Congressional district. The House Education and Labor Committee rejected that approach, and Chairman Bill Ford (D-MI) asked me as the committee's education counsel to suggest an alternative.

Ford, a congressman from Michigan, was very close to the unions and to public school administrators. He shared with those groups skepticism about Bush's proposal for national academic standards and tests. He was first elected in the Johnson landslide of 1964, and the first Congress he served in wrote ESEA. His political philosophy was similar to that of Senator Morse, Congressman Perkins, and other creators of federal aid in the 1960s: educators generally knew what they were doing, and they were limited only by a lack of sufficient funds to do the job.

In looking at alternatives to Bush's proposal, I was impressed by the Consortium for Policy Research in Education's study of several state efforts to adopt comprehensive reform, not isolated change measures.[6] A paper prepared by Marshall Smith and Jennifer O'Day was the intellectual basis for this new approach to improvement. In reviewing ten years of school reform, Smith and O'Day found a lack of policy coherence at the state level and also an emphasis on developing basic skills in students, not more advanced skills. They proposed that states adopt instructional standards emphasizing higher-order skills, and tie other reforms to those standards. In other words, within states, school improvement involving professional development, training of new teachers, textbooks, and other aspects of schooling would be anchored in instructional objectives to improve classroom teaching and learning.[7]

Although Ford was skeptical about this approach, he knew that the education committee had to have an alternative to the administration's proposal. Therefore, as chairman of the committee, he introduced a bill to provide grants to the states for the purpose of systemically improving their schools. This legislation passed the House and Senate in lieu of Bush's bill, and was accepted by a conference committee. The House then approved the final bill, but Senator Jesse Helms (R-NC) and other conservative senators, who opposed any increase in federal influence in education, killed the agreement by mounting a filibuster against it. Helms and his allies, however, could not obliterate the concept of federal assistance for comprehensive reform. In the next Congress, that approach became the basis for President Bill Clinton's proposal for states to use academic standards and tests as the underpinnings for broad improvement.

In the short term, though, Bush lost his legislative proposal because of opposition of congressional conservatives. In addition, the administration's actions to create for the first time national academic standards in several disciplines crashed. As would become increasingly clear, reaching a consensus on such standards was a difficult task. Emotionally charged disputes arose, in particular, about the content of the history standards. Lynne Cheney, the former chairwoman of the National Endowment for the Humanities, which helped finance those standards, asserted:

> Imagine an outline for the teaching of American history in which George Washington makes only a fleeting appearance and is never described as our first president. Or in which the foundings of the Sierra Club and the National Organization for Women are considered noteworthy events, but the first gathering of the U.S. Congress is not.[8]

After initial criticism of those standards, the authors revised them to bring better political balance to them, but it was too late. Conservative opposition to the idea of national standards had congealed. There were also problems with the reading standards, which conservative critics said did not give the teaching of phonics its proper due. Ironically, Bush lost both his legislative proposal and the concept of national academic standards because of the opposition of Republican conservatives, including some who had served in his administration, such as Cheney.

Although he was unsuccessful in passing legislation and gaining acceptance of the new national academic standards, George H. W. Bush's actions were significant in that a conservative Republican was proposing to improve public education through adopting national academic standards and tests. That was a revolutionary concept in a country in which education was dominated by local school boards for its first two centuries and every politician seemed to endorse local control of public education. Bush was backed by business leaders who claimed that the United States was slipping economically in the world, and that one of the reasons was a poorly educated workforce.

The first President Bush thus opened the door to a discussion of whether the content taught in local schools should be affected by the national government. In other words, he challenged the concept of local control of curriculum. He also talked of improving all schools from the federal level. The traditional federal approach had been to target assistance on particular children, but Bush proposed raising the academic achievement of *all* American students.

BILL CLINTON AND STATE STANDARDS

In 1992, Bill Clinton defeated President Bush in his bid for reelection. Clinton had campaigned promising a comprehensive agenda for education. As part of that plan, he wanted to continue with the idea of adopting academic standards, but he had seen Bush's unsuccessful attempt to create national standards and tests. So, once he was elected president, Clinton proposed a different strategy, and he succeeded where Bush had failed.

Clinton sought to shift responsibility for developing standards and tests to the states, rather than to national groups or the federal government. His Goals 2000 legislation, which authorized seed money to states to create these standards and tests, became law, and later amendments to

ESEA essentially required states to implement such systems of standards and tests if they wanted to remain eligible for Title I assistance.

Although Clinton won by removing the federal government from the standards-writing business, it was still extraordinary that states were encouraged to develop state academic standards. Earlier, we discussed how state governments traditionally limited their influence over public schools to enacting formulas for distributing state funds to local school districts. The move to set state academic standards was a major departure from the centuries-old tradition of local control of public schools. It may not have been federal control, but it was federally-encouraged state control of the content to be taught in classrooms. And this development came about through federal legislation. "The significance of the 1994 bill is hard to overstate," noted Christopher T. Cross. "A major corner had been turned: the federal government was now firmly involved in the education program of what was happening in almost every district in the nation through Goals 2000 and the ESEA requirements for new standards and assessments."[9]

Clinton's success was marred, however, when a key concept called "opportunity to learn," or OTL, was effectively jettisoned from the Goals 2000 bill while it sat before Congress. OTL was predicated on the idea that if all students were going to learn the content in the standards, which were meant to be more rigorous than what was then being taught, they needed access to well-trained teachers, high-quality instructional materials, and other resources associated with a good education. The states would develop OTL standards to accompany their academic standards.

Initially, President Clinton argued for higher academic standards and tests and said little about OTL. Only after Democratic members of Congress insisted that this concept be included in any legislation did he agree to endorse the idea. But then, when the Congress considered the bill, Representative Jack Reed (D-RI) went a step further and successfully offered an amendment requiring states to take corrective action if the OTL standards were not being carried out in local school districts. That action triggered a maelstrom of opposition from Republicans, who said they would not support any legislation with such a provision. As a result, Clinton changed his mind again and went along with the Republicans; the final legislation did not require states to implement OTL standards. Grudgingly, Reed and other Democrats supported the bill.[10]

Killing OTL was a fatal error, although it may have been politically necessary. It eliminated from consideration the local ability to implement higher standards. Likewise, it removed from state and local officials any responsibility to ensure that teachers were prepared to teach the higher-level content in the standards and that schools were able to implement higher standards. The absence of OTL left the pressure on schools and teachers to raise test scores without any acknowledgement of whether they had the resources and training needed to succeed. The lack of OTL also removed the duty of elected officials to provide those resources.

GEORGE W. BUSH AND NO CHILD LEFT BEHIND

The third president who played a role in standards-based reform, George W. Bush, built on Clinton's success. Bush's support for national legislation to expand the standards/testing movement was a surprise to some, because congressional Republicans had turned against this reform and tried to repeal and then defund Clinton's laws.

President Bush's advocacy for education reform from the national level was, in part, politically motivated. Bush knew that the Republicans needed to make education their issue if they wanted to win votes. In 1996, Bush, then governor of Texas, was quoted in the *Washington Post* as explaining the reelection of President Clinton: "There is no question that from a political perspective, he [President Clinton] stole the issue and it affected the women's vote . . . Republicans must say that we are for education."[11]

Bush was also used to the standards/testing format since Texas had had such a system since the 1980s. So politics and familiarity mixed, and the new President Bush proposed as his first bill the legislation that became the No Child Left Behind Act.

It was difficult for congressional Republicans to pivot from opposition to Clinton's laws to support for Bush's, but they did it out of loyalty to Bush and because they were told it was politically necessary. Congressman John Boehner (R-OH), then-chair of the education committee in the House of

Representatives, was a prime example of this political flexibility. In the Clinton years, he opposed those laws and cosponsored a bill to send federal funds to states with few conditions. Now, he was the author and main proponent of NCLB, the strongest federal legislation ever enacted affecting all public schools in America.

NCLB, as signed into law in 2002, required states to bring all of their students to proficiency in reading and mathematics by 2014. States could set their own levels of proficiency and could use their own tests in reading and math, but each state had to establish a schedule of gradually rising targets for the percentages of students reaching proficiency each year, and to set out penalties for schools that did not meet those annual targets for their students overall and for designated subgroups of students. The subgroup accountability was especially noteworthy. It meant that racial groups, ethnic groups, children in poverty, children learning English, children with disabilities, as well as the entire school enrollment would have to meet the state's testing targets. This proved to be a difficult goal for many schools.

During debate on Clinton's ESEA amendments, some members of Congress, especially Republicans, were concerned that students who did not receive federally funded services would be affected by federally required academic standards. But Bush's NCLB applied state standards and testing requirements to all students in the public schools of a state, even students in schools not receiving federal funds. The boldness of NCLB in 2001 surpassed the Clinton laws of 1994 in their breadth and forcefulness. Yet congressional conservatives voted for NCLB after they had opposed Goals 2000 and the 1994 ESEA amendments as federal intrusions into local schools.

NCLB was also more powerful than Clinton's legislation because of the preciseness of the proficiency goal, the timelines, and the penalties. The only wiggle room was that states set their own standards for proficiency and determined their own year-by-year schedules for students to reach that level of proficiency. In other words, NCLB was very precise on process but loose on content.

Clinton's legislation and Bush's law marked a major shift in the federal role in education. No longer was the principal federal interest limited to particular students who needed extra services. Now, federal policy sought nothing less than to raise the academic achievement of all American public school students. Patrick McGuinn described the significance of NCLB in this way:

> The passage of No Child Left Behind in 2002 fundamentally changed the ends and means of federal education policy from those put forward in the original ESEA legislation and, in doing so, created a new policy regime. The old federal education policy regime, created in 1965, was based on a policy paradigm that saw the central purpose of school reform as promoting equity and access for disadvantaged students . . . The policy paradigm at the heart of the NCLB regime is centered on the much broader goal of improving education for all students and seeks to do so by significantly reducing federal influence over process and inputs while replacing it with increased accountability for school performance. The adoption of tough new federal timetables and accountability measures in NCLB was seen as essential to force states to comply with the standards and testing reforms introduced in 1994.[12]

McGuinn was correct about the importance of the shift in the federal role from a focus on helping disadvantaged children to a broader goal of improving education for all students. But his second point about reducing federal influence over process and replacing it with accountability for performance needs some clarification.

The rhetoric surrounding NCLB asserted that the law would increase local flexibility. For instance, the eligibility for schoolwide programs was broadened to include schools in which 40 percent or more of the student enrollments consisted of children from low-income families. Some other federal requirements were also eased. At the same time, that increased flexibility in Title I and the other aid programs was more than offset by imposing very precise requirements for accountability, such as annual testing for most students. Therefore, I doubt if many local educators associate NCLB with greater flexibility. The overall administrative burden was heavier after NCLB than before, despite the speeches of the politicians.

How did such a strict law make it through Congress?

The atmosphere of the times was a factor. During the summer of 2001, the legislation became bogged down, and then the events of September 11th occurred. After the attacks on New York and Washington, DC, the spirit of patriotism was high, and political leaders tried to work together. That helped to move a compromise on the legislation.

Other factors were also involved. Paul Manna, a professor and expert on federal aid, cited several reasons:

> Even though some Republicans in Congress loathed a growing federal involvement in the nation's schools, these critics could not complain about the political results. In May 2001, for example, Senator Mitch McConnell (R-KY) reminded his fellow Republicans that Bush "has taken us [from] a 20-point deficit on education to a point in which we lead on education." In an interview the following month, Sally Lovejoy, who was Boehner's top staffer on the House education committee, concurred in a personal interview. She described to me the president's influence in light of the party's experiences during the 1990s: "Back in 1994, we [Republicans] came in and cut the crap out of education. We were against the existence of the Department of Education. Battles over education spending were part of the government shutdown. So, those were the positions of the hard-core conservatives. We didn't dig ourselves out of that hole until Bush. He got the Republican Party out of this slump on education."[13]

These themes from Republicans were repeated in meetings in 2003 on Capitol Hill convened by the Center on Education Policy, which I headed at the time. We interviewed three of the six Democratic and Republican congressmen and senators most intimately involved in writing NCLB, and knew the opinions of one of the other key senators because we had briefed him on the effects of NCLB several times around the same period. We also interviewed key Republican and Democratic staff members from both the House and Senate whose work included writing NCLB. The elected officials and the staff people were known to us through our long-time work on the Hill, and therefore they were forthright in expressing their opinions. To ensure that these people would be completely open, we promised them anonymity.

Many of these interviewees said that Republicans supported the bill because they were "boxed in" and had to follow the president. Although that was clearly a factor, one interviewee also pointed out that by writing NCLB, the Republicans had been able "to seize the education issue which they lost a while back."

Several Republicans expressed the belief that federal aid had not been successful, or as one interviewee put it, "A lot of money has been dumped into Title I with no results." The same person asserted that if this attempt with NCLB did not succeed, then there should be no such federal aid. Another said that the mindset about federal education funding needed to change, and added that the federal government is "ponying up as much as it can."

Democrats said that their involvement with NCLB was meant to motivate states and local school districts to improve the quality of public education, "to put some pressure on them" to do better, as one elected official said. They wanted to send a message, he added, that if "you want the federal dollars, we expect some improvement." Others agreed with that sentiment.

Democrats were particularly distressed that children from low-income families were not being well educated and that federal aid had not helped them. They cited the news media, research, and data showing that schools with poor students, whether urban or rural, were doing a bad job of educating those students.

A key staff member observed that during the writing of NCLB a competition had developed between Republicans and Democrats to see who could require more accountability from schools. Another interviewee acknowledged that some congressional Republicans and Bush administration officials wanted to use NCLB to show that the public schools were not working, and that this would lay the groundwork for vouchers.

Many of the people we talked to said that NCLB would not be open for amendment for some time. They wanted the law to settle in and become part of schooling. This was a grave error—on the same level as dumping

OTL. Teachers, state leaders, and others who had complaints had no way to let off steam, and so resentment against the law intensified.

Like his father, George W. Bush pushed the envelope of federal education policy. As conservatives, they proposed a large expansion in the federal role in education: first, national standards and tests, and then strict accountability to force increases in student test scores. If a liberal president had been the first to propose either of those concepts, the political right would have raised a storm of protest about federal takeover of the schools. The right held its collective tongue since the proposals came from their side.

NCLB made a mark on American education, both for good and bad. In 2015, it is still the law of the land, and the standards/testing/accountability movement is a daily presence in the schools. Through that law, President George W. Bush had greater influence on the schools than any president since Lyndon Johnson.

BARACK OBAMA AND RACE TO THE TOP

President Barack Obama is the most recent of four presidents to be involved in the standards/testing/accountability movement. His actions show him to be a supporter of this movement, rather than an opponent.

When he ran for the presidency, Obama promised to address NCLB's shortcomings, but he did not reject its basic philosophy. Dealing with the economic crisis caused a delay in changing NCLB; but during that period, President Obama and Secretary of Education Arne Duncan found time to institute other programs that, in the eyes of NCLB's opponents, especially teachers and school administrators, poured salt on the wounds in their heavy reliance on the use of student test scores. The biggest offender to these NCLB critics was the Race to the Top program, which received from the American Recovery and Reinvestment Act about $5 billion over several years to help states to bring about broad, systemic improvement in their schools.

Nearly every state applied for RTTT because additional federal funding was very attractive in the midst of an economic recession. The Obama administration made it clear that to improve their chances of getting a grant, states should use accountability measures in teacher evaluation systems and remove state-legislated caps on the number of charter schools that could exist in a state. As a result many states did just that. Ultimately, eighteen states and the District of Columbia received RTTT funding.

Another Obama initiative that received funding from ARRA was a program of grants to spur improvement in the lowest performing schools within a state. Again, as administered by the Department, that program relies heavily on test scores to determine which schools are eligible for assistance. Unlike RTTT, which is a competitive grant program, this funding is distributed to the state by a formula; and so, all states are participating.

Only after Obama was in office for two years and had lost control of the House of Representatives to the Republicans did his administration get serious about changing NCLB. By then, the political situation was not conducive to reauthorization. The Democrats lacked unity on how to change the law, but more important was the attitude of the Republicans. Senator McConnell, the Republican leader in the Senate, summed it up in this way: "The single most important thing that we want to achieve is for President Obama to be a one-term president."[14] Therefore, the Republicans did not want to give him any legislative victories, such as revising NCLB.

Since there was no congressional agreement on NCLB, the Obama administration resorted to giving waivers to most states of provisions of the law. Since each waiver differs, this means the law is being changed piecemeal, without the public knowledge that congressional passage of amendments brings. Secretary Duncan has also gone beyond merely waiving provisions of the law; he has required new obligations of the states if they wished to receive waivers. These conditions are similar to the requirements states had to fulfill several years earlier to receive ARRA funds: adopting high academic standards, enhancing state data systems, changing their teacher evaluation systems, and improving the lowest performing schools.

As of May 13, 2014, forty-two states and the District of Columbia had been granted waivers.[15] The overwhelming majority of these states believed that these waivers would help them with some of the problems created by NCLB, but they were concerned about what would happen in the long term—would waivers be continued, would a reauthorization adopt different methods than were permitted by the waivers?[16]

It is too soon to know whether the Obama initiatives will be successful. States so far have not shown great success with Race to the Top or with the program to improve a state's lowest achieving schools. States are implementing their revisions to teacher evaluation systems, but it is too early to judge the results. Further, several lawsuits have been filed against that reform from disgruntled teachers and their unions.

While the jury is out on deciding the effectiveness of the Obama programs, the judgment is clear that the extensive use of waivers and the lack of congressional action to amend or replace NCLB show a breakdown in the process of deciding national policy as envisioned in the U.S. Constitution. The president is supposed to propose, and then the Congress disposes—as the saying goes. That means that decisions are made on policy by the president and the Congress, and those decisions are the rules that govern our society.

That process has not been followed in recent years in the area of national policy for elementary and secondary education. The Republicans in the House are mostly to blame because of their refusal to deal with President Obama, and Senator McConnell and other Senate Republicans also share the blame for their political motivations of wanting to defeat or wound Obama by not giving him any victories. But the Democrats also share some of the blame. Obama and Duncan should have pushed for congressional action in the first two years of Obama's first administration, and the congressional Democrats ought to have moved on NCLB legislation. This negligence has resulted in policy by waivers, not by open general rules. That is not good for the country.

In conclusion, four presidents have advocated for the standards/testing/accountability reform. As a consequence, it has become the nation's primary education policy, embedded in federal law, and affects on a daily basis the schooling of millions of American students.

The question is whether that reform has improved American education.

6

Has the Standards, Testing, and Accountability Movement Been Effective?

AT THE END OF PART I we asked how effective Title I, as originally envisioned, had been, and concluded that the additional aid was modestly effective in improving the achievement of disadvantaged students with limited dollars and within an inequitable system of public education. To put it another way, providing additional aid to students without changing the fundamentals of ordinary teaching and learning has had modest positive effects on their educational achievement.

Now the same question must be asked about the theory of change adopted as a result of the perceived failure of federal aid and of the public schools. Has the introduction of state academic standards, state assessments based on those standards, and accountability measures to back up those higher academic expectations been effective?

The answer is that there is no conclusive evidence that NCLB has resulted in a broad increase in academic achievement among American schoolchildren. This is true even though attaining such an increase was the original promise of NCLB thirteen years ago. Apart from the question about academic achievement, the standards/testing/accountability movement has brought some good practices into education, as well as some bad ones. It has been a mixed bag.

To see how these conclusions about practices and student achievement were arrived at, we need to go to the research and evaluations. A good place to start is the comprehensive and long-term work done by the Center on Education Policy. NCLB has been controversial from the day it took effect in January 2002. Based on my then-nearly three decades of experience with federal programs, I knew that would be the case. As president of the Center on Education Policy, I sought funds from charitable foundations to undertake an objective, multifaceted review of NCLB's effects. Fortunately, CEP received that funding and began its work several months after President Bush signed the law in January 2002.

Since then, CEP has monitored the effects of the law through surveys of states and school districts and through case studies of both. The early research included a series of annual reports entitled *From the Capital to the Classroom*. That research not only looked at how educational practices changed as a result of NCLB, it also sought an answer to the question of whether an increase in student achievement had been accomplished through that law. The latter research involved the cooperation of all fifty states and the District of Columbia and encompassed a massive compilation and analysis of state and national test data under the direction of a bipartisan expert panel.

CHANGE IN PRACTICES

This work produced the following *general* conclusions about how practices changed in schools as a result of NCLB. This policy of standards/tests/accountability produced a mixture of general improvements and impediments to a good education.

Among the most positive accomplishments of NCLB has been the focus on students who were frequently overlooked because they were more difficult to educate and on schools with concentrations of struggling students. Due to the law's emphasis on accountability for all major groups of children—such as African American and Latino students, students learning English, and students with disabilities—the achievement level of each group was a factor in determining whether or not a school was making sufficient progress. Too often in the past, the lack of achievement of these students would be masked in a school by the overall achievement trends for the entire student body. Now, disappointing results for a particular group would become obvious. The school was responsible for each group of students. The school district, in turn, was held accountable for each school; and so, there was no way to bury the poor performance either of subgroups of students within schools or of poorly performing schools within school districts.

NCLB's main fault was that it placed too much weight on state accountability tests. Teachers tried to teach to those tests, days were spent preparing students for anticipated questions, and subject areas not tested were relegated to secondary importance. These shortcomings were more pronounced in schools with concentrations of children from low-income families because those were the schools with the lowest test results. More-affluent schools had fewer problems meeting state achievement targets, except for students with disabilities and English language learners.

So it truly was a mixed bag. The spotlight was directed on groups of students whose low performance could have been concealed in the past, and districts were held accountable for every school. The weakness, though, was that tests do not a good education make. In other words, student achievement is not always fully or fairly measured by a standardized state test administered once a year. So, the means to bring about the good ends were defective.

A short summary of NCLB's *particular* effects on school practices illustrates this mixed picture.

- Students are taking many more tests.
- Many schools, especially those with concentrations of children from low-income families, are spending more time on reading and mathematics, sometimes at the expense of subjects not tested.

- The lowest performing schools, which have received extra assistance, have not consistently shown greater improvement.
- Most teachers are "highly qualified" as defined by the NCLB requirements, but considerable skepticism exists about the value of that designation.
- Schools are paying much more attention to aligning curriculum and instruction to state standards, and are analyzing test score data much more closely.
- Schools are paying much more attention to achievement gaps and the learning needs of particular groups of students.
- The federal government, state governments, and local school districts have all expanded their responsibilities, but funding is inadequate at the state and local levels to fully carry out these duties.[1]

This short list shows the mixture of good and bad effects of NCLB. Better and more frequent use of data to change instruction is obviously an improvement, but taking many more tests is not good practice when education becomes test-driven and blocks of time are diverted from instruction into test preparation.

Practices for implementing Title I and the targeted assistance programs have also undergone changes in schools. For example, schools often used to pull an educationally disadvantaged student out of the regular classroom for specialized instruction to improve reading or math, but the effects of this instruction were limited to participating students. With NCLB, whole schools are affected by the policy. All students now have to be brought up to proficiency in mathematics and English language arts, and the whole school's enrollment, not just subgroups of students within the school, must reach certain targets for the percentages of students achieving proficient scores on state tests every year in order to reach the goal of full proficiency by 2014. Those broad requirements have meant that the changes in instructional practice caused by NCLB have had a wider effect than those resulting from Title I and other categorical programs.

Essential to that wide impact was NCLB's goal that *every* student by 2014 would attain proficiency in mathematics and English language arts.

That goal was not reached that year, and it has been waived as a requirement in many states by the Department of Education. It is ironic that the failure to reach that goal has been little discussed in the general news media. That objective was the centerpiece of NCLB so that the title of the law could be achieved: no child would be left behind. Obviously, many have been. The question, though, is: was that the proper goal, and were the means intended to attain it useful ways of raising student academic achievement?

ACCOUNTABILITY SYSTEM

NCLB placed great weight on a precise accountability system to encourage an increase in student achievement. The main components of this system included this goal of bringing all students to proficiency in reading and math by 2014, state-determined targets to measure progress toward this goal, and consequences for schools that did not make "adequate yearly progress" (AYP) toward those targets for their entire student body as well as for specific subgroups of students.

That accountability system has resulted in a vast number of schools missing the mark. By 2010–2011, nearly half of American schools were considered as "needing improvement" under NCLB because they had fallen short for multiple years of their state's yearly targets for the percentage of students who were expected to reach proficiency.[2]

Does this mean that half of the schools are failures? No. What this shows is that NCLB has a clumsy way of determining success; its instrument (AYP) was too crude. Forty-two states shared that opinion, and have received waivers of those and other NCLB requirements from the Department of Education. When it came to appropriately measuring student progress in school, NCLB got it wrong.

STUDENT ACHIEVEMENT

Putting aside this imprecise AYP system, the important question is whether student achievement increased significantly under NCLB. To answer that question, we will look at three sources of data: state test scores, main NAEP (National Assessment of Educational Progress), and longitudinal NAEP. These three assessments were created using different assumptions, and therefore yield varying results. That variance leads to a sometimes confusing discussion of testing's effects and of the status of student academic achievement. Another factor that sometimes leads to questions or confusion is that different sets of NAEP data compare different years to determine trends over time. This is because certain NAEP tests are only given in certain years, and so those years must form the basis for comparisons.

While I recognize that the following analysis of test results is complex, it is intrinsic to any consideration of student achievement under NCLB. To obtain a full picture of the effects of NCLB, we will first review data from *state tests*, which are administered in grades three through eight and once in high school, for students overall and for subgroups of students in the two subject areas of reading and mathematics. Next we will compare those results on state tests to results on the *main NAEP* to see if the latter data independently confirms the trends from state tests for students overall and by subgroups in the two subject areas. Then we will look at the main NAEP results themselves. Finally, we will consider results from the *longitudinal NAEP*, which shows certain national trends that the main NAEP does not, even though the longitudinal NAEP cannot produce results by state. We will include some information to show the progress, or lack of progress, in narrowing the achievement gap between different groups of students.

The challenge is to reach general conclusions from such massive amounts of data from three different testing systems at various grades and ages, for students overall and for student subgroups, in two academic subjects. One could drown in all this information.

Since NAEP is interwoven into all this analysis, it is important to know what it is and what it shows. When I started work on Capitol Hill in 1967, there was no valid way to measure student academic achievement, either in general for the whole country or for most states. In 1970, that began to change with the establishment of the National Assessment of Educational Progress. NAEP is a federally funded assessment system that started out measuring reading and mathematics achievement, and expanded over time so that it now also measures other subject areas. One part of the NAEP system, the longitudinal NAEP, measures reading and math from the early 1970s using basically the same academic content, and therefore provides valid longitudinal data showing results in reading and mathematics that can be compared over time. It uses a 500-point scale to measure results.

Another part of NAEP, the main NAEP, began in the 1990s. It measures achievement on a curriculum that has been updated over time, and describes students' performance in terms of three achievement levels as well as in point scale scores. This part of NAEP has been called aspirational because the proficient and advanced standards have been criticized as having been set too high to be realistic about fairly measuring what students are achieving. Instead, they measure what we hope students will know eventually.

In the late 1960s, when debate about the need for NAEP began, the states fought its establishment, and the compromise was reached to assure states that no state's individual results would be identified. In the 1980s that changed, and now there is state-level data, but only for the main NAEP.

Rather than testing all students nationwide, both main and longitudinal components test representative student samples, but the two components test somewhat different populations. The longitudinal NAEP tests are given every four years to students at ages nine, thirteen, and seventeen. The main NAEP tests students in grades four, eight, and twelve. The main NAEP administers tests every two years according to a schedule measuring different academic subjects at regular intervals. Both NAEP components report their data by major racial and ethnic student groups, gender, and poverty status and for students with disabilities. Another, more recent component of NAEP, the Trial Urban District Assessment, reports district-level results for the nation's largest urban school systems.

The National Assessment Governing Board, which is appointed by the Secretary of Education, sets policies for NAEP, including the schedule for administering both parts of NAEP and the subject matter to be tested.

Despite its limitations, NAEP provides an invaluable source of information on student achievement in American elementary and secondary public schools. It is often referred to as the "gold standard" of assessment because it is the largest nationally representative and continuing assessment of what America's students know and can do in various subject areas.[3]

State Tests and Main NAEP

To begin its analysis of state tests, CEP collected from all the states and the District of Columbia their student test score data from the state assessments used for NCLB accountability from 2002 through 2009, as well as earlier years' test results from some states. It is important to understand that under NCLB, each state established its own academic standards for the content students should learn, its own state assessment based on those standards, and its own definition of proficient performance on its test. For these reasons, results from one state's test were not comparable to results from another state's test. Therefore, CEP did not compare one state's test scores to another's, but rather analyzed the general trends within each state on its own tests—had they increased, decreased, or remained the same over this period? CEP then compared trends in each state's test scores with trends for the same state in scores on the main NAEP, a common national test. (The longitudinal NAEP could not be used for this purpose because it does not yield state-level data.)

Based on this analysis, CEP reached several conclusions. Since 2005, state test scores had increased in most states with comparable data. Trends on state tests had moved in the same direction as trends on NAEP in some, but not all, states. Gains on state tests tended to be larger in size than gains on NAEP.[4]

State test results also showed some narrowing of achievement gaps between different groups of students, but this occurred unevenly across states, grades, and subjects and was not the case for all student groups. Even when gaps narrowed, they often did so at a rate that meant it would take many years of similar progress to close the gap. And there was little agreement between trends in achievement *gaps* on state tests and NAEP. Trends in achievement gaps on state tests were confirmed to only a modest degree in reading, and often conflicted with NAEP trends in mathematics.[5]

There are some good reasons why the results from state tests are generally more positive than NAEP trends. Students in a state are taught the subject matter that state tests measure, and teachers take the state tests seriously because of the high-stakes consequences under NCLB. On the other hand, almost no state bases its instruction on the content measured by NAEP, and the test is low-stakes with no consequences for students or teachers.

Nonetheless, the lack of congruence between state test and NAEP results throws into doubt the ability of NCLB's accountability provisions to raise general student achievement, when measured with an objective yardstick. To dig further into this question, we should look at the main NAEP results without reference to the state tests.

Main NAEP

Secretary Duncan and others refer to some results from the main NAEP to show progress in raising test scores, and thus they infer some success for the NCLB accountability reforms. As mentioned above, the main NAEP began in the 1990s and uses the proficiency levels and point scale scores.

The main NAEP shows improvements in test scores both before and after NCLB was put in place. Further, the gains were not uniformly greater after 2003 than before. It is a mixed picture.

Table 6.1 compares gains from approximately the decade before and the decade after NCLB took effect. The precise years in the table—1992, 2003, and 2013—are used because those are years in which NAEP was given.[6]

The data in this table show that the results for all students were different in reading and math; students did better in reading after 2003 than before, and in math the opposite. Of the subgroups, in reading, four did better after 2003 than before, two did the same, and two did worse. In math, six subgroups did worse after 2003 than before, and two did better.[7]

In sum, gains in achievement on the main NAEP show increases both before and after NCLB became the established policy in schools, which is reassuring. American students are doing better, especially if results are considered by subgroup which will be explained in the next section. But, the question is: are students doing better once standards/tests/accountability reform took effect after 2002 than they were doing before? On balance, these results do not show the kind of clear trend that proponents of NCLB

TABLE 6.1

Achievement gains between 1992–2003 and 2003–2013 on main NAEP reading and mathematics assessments (0–500 point scale)

	Reading		Mathematics	
	1992–2003	*2003–2013*	*1992–2003*	*2003–2013*
Grade 4				
All students	+2	+4*	+15*	+7*
White	+4*	+4*	+16*	+7*
Black	+6*	+8*	+24*	+9*
Hispanic	+5	+7*	+20*	+9*
Asian/Pacific Islander	+10*	+10*	+15*	+12*
Grade 8				
All students	+3*	+5*	+9*	+7*
White	+5*	+4*	+11*	+7*
Black	+8*	+6*	+16*	+11*
Hispanic	+5*	+11*	+11*	+13*
Asian/Pacific Islander	+1	+10*	-1	+17*

*The score difference is statistically significant ($p < .05$).

Note: Testing accommodations were not permitted on the NAEP mathematics test prior to 1996 and on the NAEP reading test prior to 1998; this should be considered when comparing scores over time. Scores are given for students in public schools since NCLB only applies to such schools.

Source: U.S. Department of Education, Institute of Education Sciences, National Center for Education Statistics, National Assessment of Educational Progress (NAEP), various years, 1990–2013 Mathematics and Reading Assessments.

would need to prove its effectiveness; rather, they raise questions about the wisdom of NCLB's demands for accountability.

Longitudinal NAEP

The longitudinal NAEP spans nearly the entire period of modern federal aid, and therefore is better for our purposes to see long-term results. These tests were first administered to national samples of students in the early 1970s. The latest test was administered in 2012, and the results appear in table 6.2.

In a nutshell, the longitudinal NAEP shows that student academic achievement has increased since the early 1970s, and the achievement gap has narrowed between white and black, and white and Hispanic, students (the terms for groups tested since the early 1970s). This is good news but it looks even better when considered more carefully.

The higher test scores for students overall are notable, though not huge. But there are significant increases for all three major racial/ethnic groups with disaggregated test data—white, black, and Hispanic students—and the gains made by each group are generally larger than the overall gains.

TABLE 6.2

Changes in longitudinal NAEP scores between 1973–2012 and 2008–2012

	Score changes from 1973			Score changes from 2008		
	Age 9	*Age 13*	*Age 17*	*Age 9*	*Age 13*	*Age 17*
Reading						
All students	+13	+8	–*	–	+3	–
White	+15	+9	+4	–	–	–
Black	+36	+24	+30	–	–	–
Hispanic	+25	+17	+21	–	+7	–
Mathematics						
All students	+25	+19	–	–	+4	–
White	+27	+19	+4	–	–	–
Black	+36	+36	+18	–	–	–
Hispanic	+32	+32	+17	–	–	–

*A dash means no significant change in 2012. Asians and Pacific Islanders are not included since they were not in the chart prepared by the U.S. Department of Education.

Source: National Assessment of Educational Progress, 2012 Long-term: Summary of Major Findings, Institute of Education Sciences, National Center for Education Statistics, U.S. Department of Education. Data downloaded August 14, 2014, from http://www.nationsreportcard.gov/ltt_2012/summary.aspx.

Further, the gains made by black and Hispanic students generally outpace those of white students.

This odd result of a lower general increase and higher increases for each of the constituent groups occurs because student demographics in U.S. schools have changed dramatically. White students, who score higher on average, have substantially declined as a percentage of the student body, while Hispanic and black students, who have traditionally scored lower, have increased as a proportion of the student body. Although Hispanic and black students have generally improved their test scores at a greater rate than white students, those higher scores have not been sufficient to offset the decreased percentage of higher average scores from fewer white students.

Table 6.3 helps to explain the changes in student populations.

As shown in table 6.2, the long-term NAEP results showed gains, especially for black and Hispanic students, until 2008. A disturbing finding, though, is that since 2008, achievement has not increased for students except for 13-year olds, nor have the achievement gaps narrowed between racial/ethnic groups.

An important caution with data in tables 6.1 and 6.2 is that NAEP test results cannot be causally linked to particular changes in education. Not enough data has been collected to permit one to arrive at conclusive

TABLE 6.3

Percentage distribution of 13-year-old students assessed in NAEP mathematics by race/ethnicity, 1978 and 2012

Racial/ethnic Group	1978	2012
White	80%	56%
Black	13%	15%
Hispanic	6%	21%

Source: National Assessment of Educational Progress, 2012 Long-term: Summary of Major Findings, Institute of Education Sciences, National Center for Education Statistics, U.S. Department of Education. Data downloaded August 14, 2014 from http://www.nationsreportcard.gov/ltt_2012/summary.aspx.

reasons for the more positive long-term results or for the possibly disturbing short-term results. Even if there were more data, firm conclusions would still be hard to reach because there were too many other things going on. That is just a limitation of social science research.

After stating that caution, though, one can lay out some hypotheses. Since the federal categorical programs, such as Title I and IDEA, encouraged greater attention to the needs of disadvantaged students in the decades of the 1960s and 1970s, it is logical to speculate that this prolonged focus contributed to the gains in both reading and mathematics made by poor children. And, in fact, black and Hispanic children, who are more likely than white students to come from families with lower incomes, had greater test score gains than white students. Other factors were also involved in the increases, such as minority parents obtaining better jobs and improving their economic situation, according to a study by David Grissmer.[8] Thus, civil rights laws that removed barriers as well as a better economy were some other factors that affected educational performance.

On the other hand, the recent short-term stalling of progress on NAEP since 2008, in terms of both general achievement scores and achievement gaps, suggests problems with the NCLB accountability approach. Although NCLB is a forceful statute, it has not been able to forestall the slowing in the rate of student achievement.

We are left with this question: was the analysis of the effects of the categorical programs, which were used to justify NCLB-style accountability, wrong? It is ironic that from the 1970s to the early 2000s, achievement generally rose and achievement gaps generally narrowed, which would seem to refute the Title I evaluation results used to support the shift to test-driven reform.

It is likewise ironic that in the years after test-driven reform was implemented, NAEP scores, depending on which version of NAEP is considered, have either not increased uniformly and broadly, or else the gains were greater before NCLB was embedded in schooling than they were afterwards. Were the arguments used for that reform fallacious?

To sum up, NCLB has not proved to be the solution to the weaknesses of Title I and the other categorical programs or the way to raise student achievement in general. The primary justification for NCLB was to raise student achievement, and since it has not been shown to do that, it is time to pull the plug. The bad effects of NCLB outweigh the good. NCLB has outlived its usefulness and ought to be repealed.

That assertion, however, should not be interpreted to mean that everything about that movement ought to be done away with. Worth keeping is the work that has been done on developing more demanding academic standards for American students, as well as some other aspects.

COMMON CORE STATE STANDARDS

The Common Core State Standards for reading/English language arts and mathematics, which are being implemented in most American school districts, represent an advance in American education, as do the new national standards for science, called the Next Generation Science Standards. These three sets of standards have the potential to raise both the quality and rigor of what is taught in public schools.

The Common Core State Standards were state-initiated and privately funded. The National Governors Association and the Council of Chief State School Officers organized and led the effort to write these standards. The Bill and Melinda Gates Foundation was the chief funder.

Curriculum specialists and other experts developed these standards by first identifying what students should know by the time they complete high school so they can get a job or continue with postsecondary education or training. Then, the sequence of what students needed to learn at each grade was set out, going back to the beginning of elementary school. The acquisition of knowledge and skills in reading and math builds on itself beginning in first grade and extending through high school graduation.

As of May 2014, forty-four states and the District of Columbia had adopted these state-created and privately funded standards. Meanwhile, opposition to the standards arose from political conservatives who alleged that the Obama administration was orchestrating this change, and from parents and others who opposed the standards mostly out of concern about the influence of tests. Indiana and South Carolina have subsequently withdrawn from using the standards, and several other states have been grappling with whether to drop the Common Core.

Teachers throughout the country are becoming more familiar with the standards, and curricula and other materials are being developed to support them. A poll of five hundred school administrators conducted by the American Association of School Administrators and released in June 2014 showed overwhelming support for the Common Core coupled with concern about the fast implementation that hampered teacher preparation.[9] In July 2014, a Gallup poll of 1,800 school district superintendents found that two-thirds of them believed that the Common Core would improve the quality of education in their communities, while 22 percent said the standards would have no effect. Two-thirds also believed that the standards were "just about right" in terms of difficulty for students.[10]

Obviously, new assessments based on those standards are necessary, since currently used tests are geared to the fifty states' varying standards for reading and math. The ARRA provided $350 million to the U.S. Department of Education to fund these new assessments. Secretary Duncan held a competition for this funding and specified that at least two entities would receive grants to allow states some choice of assessments. Two state consortia won that competition and have been developing new systems of assessments, including two different types of tests: those to inform states about whether students have learned the content (summative tests), and those to help teachers to improve their instruction (formative tests). Both assessment groups have had difficulties with the amount of testing their systems may require, with the costs to states, and with the lack of access to sufficient computers and broadband in some school districts to administer the computer-based components of these new systems.

To complicate the situation, ACT (the college entrance exam sponsor), Pearson (a large international company with an education division), several other companies, and some state governments are developing their own tests based on the Common Core. Most states originally showed an inclination to adopt one of the two federally funded assessment systems, but several states have since said they would rather choose one of these other options. Some states have dealt with political pressure against the

Common Core by dropping the federally funded assessments while keeping the new standards.

The Next Generation Science Standards were developed with the support of science teachers and with private foundation funding. As of October 3, 2014, twelve states and the District of Columbia had adopted those standards as their state science education standards, according to Achieve.

A Bad Decision

As resistance to NCLB grew in recent years, it would have been helpful if Congress had amended the law to resolve some of the disputes about its provisions. Since that did not occur, resistance has spread to the Common Core State Standards and related new assessments, and may well spread to the science standards.

The seeds of discontent about the standards/testing/accountability movement were sown when complaints started coming from educators, administrators, and parents. Unfortunately, those criticisms were mostly ignored. Not only is NCLB unique among federal education laws due to its forcefulness, it also stands out because not a single word of the law has changed in its thirteen years of existence. Usually, during the last fifty years, a technical bill would be passed the year after a major education bill was enacted in order to straighten out some problems. In addition, the normal schedule was to reconsider the legislation and pass a renewal and set of amendments every five to six years. No wonder the resistance against NCLB and related developments is growing. What the Congress has sown it is now reaping.

A WORD ABOUT CHARTER SCHOOLS

Charter schools have been favored as a means of school reform by the last three presidents—two Democrats and a Republican—as well as by charitable foundations, new tech millionaires, and others. These schools have the aura of being a new and innovative type of institution.

It is important to understand that the characteristics of charter schools vary greatly by state. Some states have strict laws for their oversight; some have weak laws. Some states make it difficult to create them; some states spawn them like minnows. A few generalizations about charters can be made, however.

Charter schools are public schools, not private schools, but their unique features tend to blur the boundaries between public and private. They receive public tax revenue to operate like regular public schools, but states have different ways of providing them with funds. In some states, they receive less per student than regular public schools; in other states, they receive the same amount. However, many charter schools also receive considerable amounts of private funding from charitable foundations and others, which does not occur with the usual public school.

Charter schools operate free of many rules that apply to regular public schools. Most often, they are independent of local school boards and are run by their own boards, which are not elected by the public. Depending on the state law, profit-making companies, as well as nonprofit entities, are permitted to manage these schools. State governments, local charter boards, and universities are among the diverse set of authorizers of charter schools, again varying by state.

Since these schools are public, they must follow some federal education laws and regulations. Of particular note, the provisions of NCLB apply to charter schools; for example, their pupils must be tested, and the results of these tests must be used to determine school performance and impose interventions for underperforming schools.

When discussion began twenty-five years ago about creating charter schools, proponents argued that these schools would be able to be innovative because they would be free from many rules, including limitations rooted in teacher contracts. The hope was that regular public schools would then adopt the best innovations for their own improvement. Another argument for these schools was that they would be able to raise student achievement to higher levels without all the regulatory and contract restrictions.[11]

Originating in the 1990s in Minnesota and California, charter schools have spread to other states over the past two decades. Parents in many large cities have found charter schools an attractive alternative to the typical inner-city school, and in these urban settings, charters usually serve a high proportion of minority students.

Charter schools were first advanced by liberals, who viewed them as a way to improve education for disadvantaged students. Then conservatives saw them as a way to diminish the power of the teacher unions, since teachers in charter schools would not have to be union members. Today charters are supported by some liberals, who see them as a way for inner-city minority parents to get a better education for their children, and by many conservatives, who see them as a way to introduce free-market principles into the education landscape.

A common controversy about these schools is that they generally do not have unionized teachers. Therefore, teachers can be paid less than teachers covered by a contract between the local school board and the teacher union. Teachers in charter schools can also be paid at differential rates, and can be made to work longer hours than usual, both of which are not normally permitted under union contracts.

Not surprisingly, local teacher unions often oppose the introduction or expansion of charter schools in a school district. This opposition has not stopped the spread of these schools. By 2011, legislation authorizing charter schools had been passed in forty-one states and the District of Columbia. From 2000 to 2011, the number of students enrolled in charter schools increased from 0.3 million to 1.8 million. During the same period, the percentage of all public schools that were charters increased from 2 percent to 5 percent.

Charter school enrollment tends to be concentrated in certain cities or states. In 2011, California enrolled the most students in charters, and the District of Columbia enrolled the highest percentage of students in charters—38 percent.[12] New Orleans also has a high percentage of students in charter schools.

Several federal programs encourage the establishment of charter schools, and funding for these programs is substantial. In the fiscal year 2014 appropriations granted by the Department of Education, the Charter School Grant Program received funding of $241,500,000 and the Credit Enhancement for Charter School Facilities Program received $91,600,000. By comparison, Title I received nearly $15 billion and IDEA nearly $12 billion. However, both of those large programs give grants to most American school districts, so while federal charter school funding is lower than the appropriations for the large federal programs, the pool of recipients for the charter grants is much smaller, which makes these forms of aid important for charters. Those schools can also receive regular federal aid, such as Title I grants.

President Obama is the latest presidential booster of charters through such programs as the Race to the Top, which contains several provisions in support of expanding high-quality charter schools. Despite that support from Obama and his two predecessors, and large grants to establish charter schools from the Walton Family Foundation, the Gates Foundation, and others, the record of charter schools in outperforming regular public schools is, on whole, not impressive.

Two major national studies of charters were conducted by CREDO, a research group associated with Stanford University. The 2009 study found that in mathematics just 17 percent of charters outperformed traditional public schools, and 37 percent performed worse. Forty-six percent had results that were not significantly different. In reading, charter students on average realized growth that was less than public school counterparts but was not as statistically significant as the differences in mathematics, according to the researchers.[13]

The 2013 study released results that were somewhat better for charters. In mathematics, twenty-nine percent outperformed traditional public schools, and 31 percent performed worse. Forty percent had growth that was not statistically significant. In reading, 25 percent of charters did better than typical public schools, and 19 percent did worse. The remainder had results that were not significantly different. This record certainly does not support a contention that charter schools are superior.[14]

Some charter schools have had outstanding success educating difficult populations of children, especially in large urban areas, but until we perfect the way charters are authorized and monitored, too many weak ones will be allowed to continue. The early rhetoric held that it would be easier to eliminate a bad charter school than to close a bad regular public school. That intent ought to be realized.

Another early argument for charters has not been fulfilled as hoped. In general, there is no evidence that charter schools, with their freedom from regulation, have produced innovative ways to educate students that have been adopted by regular schools. The Gates Foundation is therefore supporting an effort to get the two types of schools to cooperate more closely.

Charter schools are now part of the American public school system, and they offer hope to many inner-city parents who want to secure a better education for their children. It is the duty of those responsible for charter schools to provide that good education. That means that the charter authorities ought to deal with their problems, such as closing schools that are not performing—as originally promised—or working to improve them. Charter authorities also have a responsibility to educate their fair share of difficult-to-educate students, such as children with disabilities and children learning English. Various reports have documented the reluctance of charter schools to meet the needs of those students. If they do not, then the charges of the critics will be accurate, and regular public schools will be left to educate most of the students who need extra attention.

Charter schools are not a magic answer to all our education problems, but they can help some to do better. Even if they are successful for some students, however, the problem still remains of how to increase the quality of education for all children, including the vast majority who attend regular public schools.

Part III

OTHER FEDERAL POLICIES, AND A SUMMARY

PUBLIC EDUCATION IS WOVEN into the fabric of American society. Schools are located in nearly every neighborhood. Teaching and other school-related jobs employ millions of Americans. Nine out of ten youngsters attend public schools.

Over the last fifty years, federal support for education has reflected this breadth of the schools' involvement in society. Title I programs for disadvantaged children, as described in Part I, and NCLB-required student testing, treated in Part II, are the best-known examples of this federal engagement in education and society, but the federal government also provides other types of assistance to elementary and secondary schools.

Teachers receive professional development through Title II of the Elementary and Secondary Education Act. Science and mathematics teachers benefit from specialized training through the National Science Foundation. The U.S. Department of Agriculture nutrition programs provide partially subsidized school lunches for every participating child and free or reduced-price lunches and breakfasts for children from families with incomes below or slightly above the poverty threshold. Indian children and dependents of military personnel are educated in federally supported schools.

The depth of federal involvement in education, however, is not as great as the breadth. Only about 10 percent of the total expenditures for public schools comes from federal sources; the rest comes from state and local sources.[1]

In addition to supporting education through grant programs, Congress has sought to influence how other issues are dealt with in society, such as through encouraging prayers in the schools and banning guns from school premises. Indeed, when the House and Senate consider comprehensive legislation to amend ESEA and other programs or create new programs, these bills have often become magnets for amendments concerning social issues.

Grant programs and the conditions placed on the receipt of those funds are just one way that federal education policy is made. Rulings of the U.S. Supreme Court and lower federal courts, regulations developed by federal departments and agencies, and executive orders of the president are other routes to creating national policy for the schools.

Part III describes the complex ways in which federal education policy is enacted and how it has become enmeshed with broader social issues. The five case studies described in these chapters also illustrate the variety of social forces, motives, and political dynamics that have led to the creation of federal policies in education.

The Individuals with Disabilities Education Act (IDEA) enjoys wide political support even though it is very forceful, and reflects the influence of court orders requiring the education of children with disabilities. Bilingual education became a prevalent method of teaching English due to the availability of federal funds; however, over the years, that method attracted considerable controversy. Political criticism ultimately led to a curtailing of this approach. These grant-funded programs are described in chapter 7.

Chapter 8 addresses national policies based on federal court decisions and legislative prohibitions. These include busing of school children as a remedy for segregation; Title IX's prohibition of discrimination based on sex; and the development of legislation permitting both student prayer groups and gay/straight alliances to meet in public schools.

The final chapter in this section summarizes the lessons to be learned about the creation and implementation of federal policies in education and lays the groundwork for the recommendations that will follow in part IV.

7

IDEA and Bilingual Education

IN 1975, CONGRESS ENACTED legislation for educating students with mental and physical disabilities, the Education of All Handicapped Children Act or Public Law 94-142. This law was unique among the equity-oriented initiatives created in the 1960s and 1970s because, although it was unusually forceful, it encountered less opposition from many people who ordinarily objected to other federal programs on the ground of interfering with local control of the schools.

This law, which eventually became known as the Individuals with Disabilities Education Act, or IDEA, has its roots in advocacy campaigns to help children with disabilities and in litigation that forced school districts and states to educate these children. In particular, landmark judicial rulings in Pennsylvania and the District of Columbia required education for children with disabilities under the equal protection clause of the 14th Amendment.[1] Those cases, however, were never appealed to the U.S. Supreme Court, and so there was no court ruling about the education of these children that had a nationwide effect.

In terms of federal funding for public schools, IDEA is the second largest program after Title I. The provisions of IDEA, however, are far stronger than those of Title I or any other federal education law before the signing of NCLB in 2002. It can be argued that in its own way IDEA is at least as potent as NCLB.

The forcefulness comes from its precise civil rights guarantees to ensure that children with disabilities have access to schooling, generally in the regular classroom. To secure this objective, schools must develop an individualized education program, or IEP, for each such student, which specifies the services that will be provided to meet the particular needs of that child. Then the local school district must deliver those services, regardless of whether there is enough federal aid to pay for them. Parents of children with disabilities are included in these IEP consultations, and they have a right to sue if they believe that the needs of their child are not being met. The legal remedies include sending the child to a private school with the costs paid by the local school district.

The IDEA authorizing law set a target that the federal government would pay for 40 percent of the extra costs of educating children with disabilities, but the actual federal appropriations have never come close to fulfilling that promise. A major reason for this shortfall is the IDEA requirement that all services outlined in the IEP must be provided regardless of the level of federal funding. Consequently, if Congress shirks its responsibility to pay, children with disabilities still receive the full range of services, but at the expense of local and state governments. While this is good for these students, it creates resentment at the state and local levels. Thus, this guarantee of services is a two-edged sword.

Another federal law, section 504 of the Rehabilitation Act of 1973, has proved to be a useful complement to IDEA. Section 504, considered the first civil rights statute for individuals with disabilities, bans discrimination against these individuals in any activity receiving federal assistance. Section 504 is broad in its reach, most notably in employment but also in ensuring access for individuals with disabilities to public transportation and buildings. It is therefore used to ensure that students with disabilities have access to public schools. For example, a child who uses a wheelchair cannot be denied access to AP Chemistry as a result of the lab being placed on the second floor of a building without an elevator. Moreover, at times, a child will have a Section 504 plan instead of an IEP under IDEA because the student needs noneducational assistance, such as insulin shots for diabetes, rather than specific educational services.

This broad coverage of section 504 also serves as a backup for IDEA by affecting some activities not directly included in the education statute. For instance, colleges and universities became accessible to students with disabilities after section 504 was invoked. This law also covers issues outside of the school day that are not covered by IDEA, such as extracurricular activities, sports, and afterschool care.

Section 504, IDEA, and several other federal laws laid the groundwork for erecting the legal pinnacle of nondiscrimination policies for individuals with disabilities—the Americans with Disabilities Act of 1990 (ADA). That act, signed into law by the first President Bush, broadly prohibits discrimination against people with disabilities in the private sector.

It has been remarkable how these federal statutes have helped Americans with disabilities to do better in life. When I was in law school, I became involved in politics, and several times a year I went from door to door in my family's neighborhood to become better acquainted with voters so that when election day came I could ask them for support of my candidates. One evening, a family who lived nearby and whom I thought were very private let me into their house for a chat. There, I learned to my great surprise that they had a teenaged child who had a nerve disease and whom they hardly ever let out of the house. They were embarrassed by his disability and somehow felt responsible for it. They hid their guilt by hiding him. That situation was not that unusual decades ago.

The federal laws have changed that attitude. Twenty-five years after IDEA passed, a majority of children with disabilities were in neighborhood schools in classes with their nondisabled peers. Children with disabilities increased their graduation rate from high school by 14 percent from 1984 to 1997. Postsecondary employment rates for students served by IDEA were twice as high as they were for those persons with disabilities not benefiting from that law. These accomplishments are even greater today, and would not have been possible unless IDEA had opened the classroom doors to persons with disabilities.[2]

IDEA is not without its flaws: too much paperwork and administrative burden, too little federal funding to pay for guaranteed services, too much money spent on lawsuits, and too much money spent on placements in private schools. But these deficiencies, in my experience, have not generated the intense opposition targeted at some other federal policies discussed in this book. These IDEA provisions were not subject to long, multiyear debates or barrages of amendments, as happened with other equity programs.

The reason is that over the years of its existence IDEA has enjoyed bipartisan support from both liberal and conservative members of Congress. For instance, Congressman Al Quie (R-MN) fought against and voted against the original ESEA, but he helped to draft the initial IDEA legislation and became a strong proponent of it.

A telling example of the deference given to IDEA from those who often oppose other federal education legislation occurred in 1981, when President Reagan had control of the Congress and could pass nearly anything he wanted. His administration suggested a consolidation of Title I and IDEA, which could have eliminated some provisions to "simplify" the combined laws and also could have reduced funding because there might be a "lesser administrative burden" with one program instead of two.

Reagan's proposal ran into opposition from his own party. Conservative Republicans opposed that concept as being in the "wild blue yonder,"[3] in the words of Charles Radcliffe, chief counsel for the Republicans on the education committee. Congressman John Ashbrook (R-OH), the leading Republican on the education committee and one of the most conservative members of the House, refused to even introduce Reagan's bill. Ashbrook and other congressional Republicans thought that a good argument could be made for the administration's draft, but, as Radcliffe has noted, "the political reality was that it drove major constituencies right up the wall to the point that there was almost no support for it in Congress even among Republicans."[4]

This less emotional tone surrounding debates about IDEA and related federal legislation is due to the fact that people with disabilities come from all walks of life—from high, middle, and low income levels, from all ethnic and racial backgrounds, and from all political persuasions. For instance, a Republican millionaire with a disability who was a prominent supporter of the Americans with Disabilities Act sat next to the first President Bush as he signed that antidiscrimination law.

IDEA is a success story of federal aid to education. Millions of lives are better as a result of that law. By contrast, other equity programs have attracted more heated debate because they helped a particular subset of the population—and often the groups with the least political influence, such as racial or linguistic minority students or children from low-income families. For example, bilingual education was meant to teach English primarily to Spanish-speaking students using their native language, and these children differed from the majority population in ethnic origin and often in their families' level of income. In addition, it became a lightning rod for political controversies that had little to do with education.

THE BATTLE OVER BILINGUAL EDUCATION

Bilingual education is an approach to teaching students who enter school without proficiency in English that begins by providing instruction through the medium of the native language, moves on to using both the native language and English, and ultimately provides instruction in English only. For decades, the federal government encouraged this approach to help children with limited English proficiency. Since the United States from its inception has been a magnet for immigration from other countries, a serious need has always existed for educating such children.

This education issue, however, became a battleground between those who sought to maintain the Spanish language and Latino culture in the United States and those who fought to keep English as the country's sole official language and opposed "multiculturalism." The outcome of this controversy can be seen in the change in name of the relevant federal law that authorizes programs to help students learn English. Originally enacted as the Bilingual Education Act of 1968, the program became the English Language Acquisition, Language Enhancement, and Academic Achievement Act in 2001, with no reference to bilingual education in the current title.

The story told here is about creating and maintaining a federal policy to meet the needs of children with limited English proficiency, and it begins in 1968 with the passage of the Bilingual Education Act as an amendment to ESEA. That legislation, the first official federal recognition of the needs of these students, had its origins in a bill drafted by Senator Ralph Yarborough (D-TX). The Texas senator's bill would have provided, through a competitive process, grants to school districts to teach Spanish as a native language and English as a second language, and to encourage an appreciation of the ancestral language and culture of the students for whom English was a second language. When the final version of the Bilingual Education Act was written, it broadened coverage to make grants available to help students from any language background. Further, the act did not explicitly require bilingual instruction or the use of the students' native language; rather, it encouraged innovative programs to teach students English.[5]

In 1974, the Supreme Court in *Lau v. Nichols* ruled that children in U.S. schools who could not speak English had to be given instruction to learn English so they could benefit from public education. The suit was brought on behalf of a group of Chinese American students living in California. In its opinion, the Court noted that simply providing these students with the same resources as other students was insufficient:

> There is no equality of treatment merely by providing students with the same facilities, textbooks, teachers, and curriculum; for students who do not understand English are effectively foreclosed from any meaningful education. Basic English skills are at the very core of what these public schools teach. Imposition of a requirement that, before a child can effectively participate in the educational program, he must already have acquired those basic skills is to make a mockery of public education.[6]

That same year, the Education Amendments of 1974 contained the congressional response to *Lau*. Both a civil-rights-based law and a grant program were included. The beneficiaries were meant to be all children with a limited ability to speak English, not just the Chinese children who were the objects of the Court's decision.

The Bilingual Education Act was amended to create a larger and more specific grant program for language instruction than the small program of 1968. Further, the new law declared that it was the policy of the country to encourage programs using bilingual education practices because "a primary means by which a child learns is through the use of such child's language and cultural heritage."[7] The purpose of the grants for school districts under that law was to demonstrate effective ways of providing limited-English-speaking children with instruction using their native language as a means to learn academic content and achieve competence in English. The law also directed that instruction must be given with appreciation for the cultural heritage of such children.

The Education Amendments of 1974 also contained a civil rights measure, the Equal Educational Opportunities Act, which required the removal of language barriers that prevented students from being able to participate equally in classes taught in English. In carrying out that provision, in 1975 the U.S. Office of Education issued regulations called the *Lau* Remedies to determine local compliance with that new law and offer guidance in developing adequate education plans to fulfill its intent.[8] Although neither the Supreme Court decision nor the governmental regulations specifically required schools to use the bilingual education method—rather, it was optional—these events gave impetus to an expansion in the use of that particular approach to learning English.

Bilingual education classes engendered some opposition as they became established in schools throughout the country. Conservatives were especially concerned that children would be taught in Spanish, and that English would lose its primacy as the language of the United States. They were also concerned that teaching children an appreciation of their Mexican heritage, for example, and the history and culture of Mexico, would lessen their commitment to the United States.

Chester E. Finn Jr., former president of the Thomas B. Fordham Institute and a former assistant secretary in the first Bush Administration, recently described in this way the criticisms of bilingual education after the 1974 Amendments:

> Although the ostensible rationale for this change was to ensure that youngsters could continue to learn math and science and other things before achieving fluency in English, in reality bilingual education emerged—not unlike special education . . . as a separate fiefdom within school systems and began to be accused of such sins as retarding immigrants' acquisition of English and nurturing constituencies for politicians who shared their ethnic and linguistic origins.[9]

Kenji Hakuta, a prominent expert on language acquisition, and other researchers in the area, were frustrated by such criticisms because they ignored the scientific basis for bilingual education and instead obfuscated the issue by directing attention to perceived administrative "failures" out of a fear of changes in the ethnicity of the citizens of the country. According to Hakuta, the debate should be on the science and not driven by ethnic fears:

> The debate over bilingual education in the United States is framed in terms of curriculum, effectiveness, and other traditional educational criteria. Answers to many of the objections about bilingual education are available, and research largely supports the contentions of the advocates of bilingual education. Objective data on bilingual programs are ineffective in resolving the underlying issue of the debate, however. Most of the emotional heat over bilingual education is generated by the official recognition of ethnicity as a special status in public education.[10]

Ethnicity was indeed at the core of the debate, and critics did not want to have Spanish recognized as a legitimate medium through which children could learn. During the 1960s and 1970s, the great majority of limited-English-speaking children in the schools were from families that spoke Spanish at home. Most of the bilingual teachers were also Spanish-speaking. So the criticisms of bilingual programs were generally directed against children and teachers of Spanish-speaking origins.

During the 1980s and 1990s, the immigration patterns of the country changed. People came to the United States increasingly from nations that spoke languages other than Spanish. In the late 1990s, for instance, the countries sending the greatest numbers of children were in strife-torn areas such as the former Yugoslavia. Today, it is not at all uncommon for teachers to say that their schools have students from twenty to thirty countries. Unlike Spanish, it is very difficult to find teachers for all these other languages to teach students first in their native language, as bilingual education proposes. This is not to say, however, that bilingual education would be impossible to offer in many communities with concentrations of students from a single-language background and available qualified teachers.

The criticisms against the program and the demographic changes in the student body combined to diminish the primacy of the bilingual education approach. This shift began during the Reagan administration, when the law was changed to permit funding of methods for teaching English other than bilingual education. Opponents of bilingual education used the rationale that teachers fluent in the many native languages spoken by immigrant children were not available, and, therefore, school districts needed flexibility to use methods other than bilingual education. But most of the controversy about bilingual education was over the use of the native language for instruction. In 1981, that was the reason President Reagan gave in explaining his opposition to bilingual education:

> But I have to say—and I think that the Federal Government has a part
> that is played in this, and not a good part—that we have come to the point
> where we're talking about teaching both languages and teaching students
> in their native language, instead of what the move should be if they're
> going to be in America: They have to learn our language in order to get
> along. And I will do anything that I can to help to get rid of any Federal

interference that is trying to force local school districts to continue teaching students in their native tongue. Their job is to teach them English.[11]

The next movement away from bilingual education reflected Reagan's point of view. Studies showing the benefits of bilingual education were swept aside. Political critics, not educational researchers, ruled the day. The Education Amendments of 1984 permitted up to 10 percent of the funds to be used for alternative programs that provided English language instruction and other special services but were not required to use the students' native language. Despite these changes, critics continued to charge that bilingual education was divisive.

The rising number of immigrants who spoke languages other than Spanish was again brought into the debate. As a consequence, the Education Amendments of 1988 increased to 25 percent the amount reserved for alternative approaches to bilingual education. Also included was a limitation that no child should remain in bilingual education classes for more than three years, and under special circumstances, for up to two additional years. The opponents of bilingual education ignored the conclusion of the General Accounting Office, a research and investigative arm of the Congress: "The research showed positive effects for transitional bilingual education on students' achievement of English-language competence."[12]

In 1994, the law was amended to encourage a further move away from bilingual education. A "priority" was placed on the funding of bilingual education programs, but that meant that far less could be spent on those programs than the 75 percent available under the previous law. Further, several new provisions urged school districts to consider approaches other than bilingual education to teaching English. This so-called priority was really the last gasp for bilingual education, which had been a principal instructional method eligible for funding under the original laws of 1968 and 1974.

These developments were frustrating to researchers, as they had been earlier. Jay Greene, who conducted a meta-analysis of studies on English language acquisition, concluded in 1998:

Children with limited English proficiency who are taught using at least some of their native language perform significantly better on proficiency tests than similar children who are taught only in English. In other words, an unbiased reading of the scholarly research suggests that bilingual education helps children who are learning English.[13]

The next set of policy changes involved the No Child Left Behind Act of 2001 which was very important for English language learners. First, it focused attention on ensuring that these children were learning subject matter content and not just learning English. Second, schools and school districts had to demonstrate that students as a whole, as well as English language learners and other student subgroups, were meeting performance benchmarks on state tests that would lead to all students scoring proficient in both English language arts and mathematics by 2014. Schools and districts that missed state achievement targets for either their students overall or for any major subgroup of students would face penalties.

NCLB also greatly changed the federal bilingual education program. In fact, as noted above, the term "bilingual education" was removed from the title of the program that had been created to encourage that approach a half century earlier. Instead, a rather cumbersome title was adopted making clear that English language acquisition was the primary purpose of the funding. There were no references in the act to the value of using the native language to learn English and subject matter content or emphasizing a student's ancestral culture to reinforce learning.

School districts could still choose bilingual education as their approach, but it was more difficult to do that. A series of provisions in the law empowered parents to question why their child was placed in a program for English language learners, which methods were used to make that decision, how the program would meet their child's needs, what alternative approaches were available, how the child could leave the program, and what the expected high school graduation rate was for participants in the program. School districts were also required to give parents written guidance about the means available to them to immediately remove their child from the program, the option to decline to enroll their child in the program, and assistance for parents to choose which English language acquisition program to use if there were alternatives.

NCLB therefore represents a fundamental shift away from bilingual education and from teaching about other countries' cultures and histories as students learn English. The opponents of "multiculturalism" have won the battle against bilingual education, and have moved the education of English language learners in the direction of a child rapidly learning English with little or no use of the native language. At the same time these controversies were playing out at the national level, California, Arizona, and Massachusetts placed legal restrictions on bilingual education in their state programs, although Colorado voters rejected a similar proposal in that state.

It is ironic that NCLB also directs unparalleled attention to the academic progress of English language learners by holding schools accountable for bringing these students to proficiency in English and mathematics. While this has resulted in improvements in test scores for many students, it has created other problems. For instance, some students who did not know English well were tested only in English.

To conclude, the bilingual education debate is an example of how a grant-in-aid program became the object of intense debate on how to meet the Supreme Court's directive to provide additional educational services to children who were not proficient in English. It is also a noteworthy example of the federal government becoming involved in curricular issues, or what was taught and how it was taught in the schools. Those in favor of using the native language to learn English prevailed for a while, and now those who believe in English language immersion and other instructional approaches that overwhelmingly emphasize English are having their way. The pendulum swung one way, and then the other.

Bilingual education also became a lightning rod for fears about changes in American society, such as the fear of losing English as the primary language of the country, shifting jobs from current citizens to newcomers who would work at lower wages, or losing an "American identity" due to the arrival of millions of new immigrants.

In a final irony, support for bilingual education is again growing, at least at the state level. In California, voters may soon have the chance to reverse Proposition 227, which was supported by voters in a 1998 state referendum as a way to end bilingual education in California schools. The California state senate has approved a bill to have a referendum on the issue of restoring bilingual education. Senator Ricardo Lara sponsored the bill, undoubtedly influenced by the tremendous growth in the Latino population in the state.[14]

8

School Busing, Title IX, and Free Speech in Schools

IDEA AND BILINGUAL EDUCATION, discussed in the previous chapter, are both grant-related programs, but federal court decisions and legislative prohibitions have also played an important role in federal education policy. Here too, the outcome of federal policy is heavily influenced by social and political pressures—with lasting and sometimes unexpected results.

The fierce battles over the use of school busing as a means to desegregate the public schools is an example of federal policy making based primarily on court rulings and statutory limitations of activities. In these controversies, federal court decrees to desegregate the schools by means of busing school children clashed with legislative prohibitions against the use of school busing for that purpose. This interplay—or more often confrontation—between the federal courts on one side, and presidents and Congresses on the other side, lasted for several decades, from the 1960s through the 1990s.

The policies limiting busing ultimately prevailed and had various effects, most notably the significant segregation of students by race and ethnicity.

They also had a major political impact, since Republican presidents used the busing issue as part of the strategy of moving the southern states from being solidly Democratic to being as solidly Republican. In other words, a realignment of the political parties was another result of these battles.

Prior to the enactment of ESEA, one of the major obstacles to federal aid to education was opposition of members of Congress from southern states who feared that federal education aid would lead to the end of racially segregated schools. The 1954 *Brown v. Board of Education* decision of the Supreme Court had ruled as unconstitutional laws that required the segregation of school children by race, but the southern states dragged their feet in complying. The South feared that federal aid to education would have strings tied to it that would require action to comply with *Brown*. In 1964, President Johnson got through Congress the Civil Rights Act, which authorized lawsuits and cut-offs of federal funds as tools that could be used to force the southern states to desegregate. With those enforcement tools in place, there was little point in southern members of Congress continuing to oppose aid to education, which would bring to their states so much new money.

However, Johnson's victory in overcoming that obstacle and in getting ESEA through the Congress was not the end of southern intransigence on desegregation. The supporters of segregation found other ways to obstruct the use of the new tools to desegregate schools provided by the Civil Rights Act.

In 1966, when Congress was debating the first extension of the new ESEA, controversy arose about whether accepting the new federal aid would lead to school districts being ordered to bus their students to integrate the schools. To defuse that explosive issue, Congressman James O'Hara (D-MI), a supporter of federal aid, offered an amendment to forbid federal education officials from requiring the assignment or transportation of students or teachers as a means of overcoming racial imbalance.[1] In addition to being the first "anti-busing" amendment adopted by Congress, this action was noteworthy for two other reasons, as explained to me when I started working on the education committee. First, the provision only restricted officials in the education division of the executive branch of the federal government, who were quite unlikely to order busing; it had no effect on the federal judiciary, who were far more likely to require busing. Therefore, it was an amendment with limited impact. And second, it was offered by a congressman who had voted for the civil rights laws but who represented a suburban Detroit area where white voters were expressing opposition to school busing for integration out of fear that their children might be bused to Detroit, with its large African American population. The sponsorship of this amendment gave O'Hara some "political cover" on the issue.

In 1968, the Supreme Court in *Green v. County Board of Education of Kent County, Virginia* in effect required school districts to implement their desegregation plans. Fourteen years earlier, the Court had ruled that legally segregated schools were unconstitutional and urged action to desegregate with "all deliberate speed." Leaders in the southern states ignored the Court's decision and maintained segregated schools. To them "deliberate speed" was no speed. The *Green* ruling meant that desegregation had to begin, that the delays had to end.

During the 1968 presidential campaign, Richard Nixon expressed opposition to that ruling and to any busing of school children that might be employed to carry it out. Patrick McGuinn, a professor who studies federal policy, summarized the political significance of the busing issue as follows:

> In this and subsequent elections, Republican presidential candidates would successfully use opposition to school busing and integration as a key part of their "southern strategy" to appeal to conservative Democratic voters and their assault on federal government activism more generally. Several scholars have argued that race—and particularly the debate over school integration—became the decisive issue in U.S. politics during the second half of the twentieth century and led to the unraveling of the coalition that supported the Great Society and the war on poverty, and ultimately a partisan electoral realignment.[2]

In 1970, ESEA was amended again to require that in matters of racial segregation in the schools of any state, that law as well as Title VI of the Civil Rights Act (which forbids discrimination and authorizes funding cutoffs and lawsuits as means of enforcement) had to be applied uniformly in all regions of the United States, whether the origin or cause of such segregation was *de jure* or *de facto*. The amendment included the caveat that nothing would diminish the obligation of federal officials to eliminate discrimination.

At that time, a big distinction was made between *de jure* and *de facto* segregation. The former was racial segregation created by laws, such as separate schools for white and African American children and separate public water fountains for the races. The latter was segregation that resulted from people making (or being pressured to make) choices, such as whites deciding to live in a particular neighborhood. Of course, some real estate companies' and governments' practices kept African American families from living in certain neighborhoods. Their choices of where to live were limited. But, again, at this time it was argued that there was a distinction between the two types of segregation.

The *de jure* segregation existed in the southern states where the legislatures had enacted laws calling for separation of the races. The *de facto* segregation appeared in the northern states where residential communities were segregated due to the actions of the inhabitants. In later decades, evidence emerged indicating that northern segregation often came about due to actions by governments, which meant that northern residential segregation could also be *de jure*. In the 1970s, however, the distinction was thought to mean something.

Through adoption of this amendment, southern members of Congress tried to put *de facto* and *de jure* segregation on the same plane. They hoped thereby that members of Congress from the northern states would see that they, too, were imperiled by the federal court decisions and other pressures to integrate the schools.

The southerners did not succeed with that strategy: most northerners still viewed segregation as a southern issue. But some northern liberals agreed that the burden was being placed on the southern states to eliminate segregation when segregation also existed in the north. They supported the bill to equate both types of segregation because they wanted the opposite result from what the southern members of Congress desired: these northerners wanted federal action against *de facto* as well as *de jure* segregation. Senator Abraham Ribicoff (D-CT), for example, argued that northern senators did not have the "guts to face their liberal white constituents, who have fled to the suburbs for the sole purpose of avoiding having their sons and daughters go to school with blacks."[3]

In 1970, in the midst of this congressional fighting, President Nixon awarded grants of $46 million to twenty-one southern states that had dual systems of segregated schools to help them pay for the costs of complying with federal court decrees to desegregate. Nixon was able to do this without legislation through shifting some appropriations, but he did ask Congress to make this program long-term.[4]

Here is how President Nixon explained his position:

> I am against busing as that term is commonly used in school desegregation cases. I have consistently opposed the busing of our Nation's school-children to achieve a racial balance, and I am opposed to the busing of children simply for the sake of busing. Further, while the executive branch will continue to enforce the orders of the court, including court-ordered busing, I have instructed the Attorney General and the Secretary of Health, Education, and Welfare that they are to work with individual school districts to hold busing to the minimum required by law.
>
> Finally, I have today instructed the Secretary of Health, Education, and Welfare to draft and submit today to the Congress an amendment to the proposed Emergency School Assistance Act that will expressly prohibit the expenditure of any of those funds for busing.[5]

Nixon's tactic of finding federal aid for the South, and his rhetoric about busing, showed his clear agreement with the opponents of busing for racial purposes. The president's objective was to win over for the Republicans the southern Democrats who were upset with their traditional party's support of civil rights. Since the end of the Civil War, the southern states had been reliably Democratic in their voting patterns, sending mostly Democrats to Congress and generally supporting that party's presidential candidates. There was a good reason it was called the "Solid South" for its steady support of the Democrats. President Johnson, a southerner himself, understood full well that when he signed the various civil rights acts of the 1960s, he was jeopardizing that political alignment.

Another part of Nixon's southern strategy to gain political support among white southerners was to change the makeup of the federal courts to ease the pressure on school districts to desegregate. By 1971, Nixon had appointed four new justices to the U.S. Supreme Court, and he hoped thereby to moderate the Court's decisions on busing.[6]

Despite the president's efforts, the Supreme Court in the 1971 *Swann v. Charlotte-Mecklenburg Board of Education* decision upheld as constitutional a federal court order using school busing as a remedy to eliminate *de jure* segregation. Busing of school children to do away with officially sanctioned segregation was not required by the Supreme Court's 1954 *Brown* decision, but lower federal courts in the 1960s were resorting to it as a means to desegregate racially isolated schools. *Swann* sanctioned this practice of federal judges to order the busing of school children in these cases.

Nixon was obviously not pleased with this decision, but neither were some white southern Democrats who expressed their displeasure that only the southern states were affected. Jimmy Carter, then governor of Georgia, noted: "*Swann* was clearly a one-sided decision; the Court is still talking about the South; the North is still going free."[7]

In 1971, emotions in the South were indeed aroused about court-ordered desegregation and northern support for it. That year, Congressman Pucinski and I held a meeting in Mississippi about the uses of Nixon's Emergency School Aid, which was intended to assist school districts with the extra costs of desegregation. Since Pucinski was chair of the subcommittee with jurisdiction over that issue and I was the staff director and counsel, our meeting was an oversight session to understand the needs of desegregating districts and how federal funds were being used.

When we arrived in Mississippi, we were informed by the county police chief that threats had been made against us, including the use of weapons, for coming to the state to hold that meeting. That night at the motel, I barricaded the door with a chair and slept on the floor. I was not going to take any chances. Nothing happened, and the next day the oversight meeting occurred. The witnesses from the school districts seemed resentful that we had come and were asking questions, but we did get information from them about the uses of federal funds. So, I can attest from what was said and from the attitudes I saw that at least some white southerners felt that northerners were targeting them while avoiding their own problems with segregation.

President Nixon took advantage of that resentment, and in 1972, he repeatedly spoke of his opposition to "forced busing" as he ran for reelection. Nixon took the position that he was proposing to improve neighborhood schools but that the Senate was frustrating his efforts:

> No one profits by the confusion and resentment that is generated when whole school systems are disrupted by the forced busing of schoolchildren away from their neighborhood schools. The answer to inequities in our educational system is to spend more money on learning and less money on forced busing . . . However, as you know, after passing the House of Representatives, (my) measure was filibustered to death in the Senate by pro-busing Senators.[8]

During those years—the late 1960s and the 1970s—the Democratic-controlled Congress was feeling the pressure from white constituents opposed to racial integration of the schools and from voters who were simply against busing school children to achieve that purpose. Southern Democratic congressmen, only a few of whom had voted for the Civil Rights Act, were naturally under attack due to the federal court orders against state-imposed school segregation. Now, northern and midwestern Democrats, most of whom had voted for the civil rights legislation, faced situations in which the federal courts moved against officially sanctioned racial segregation of schools in Boston, Detroit, and other cities.

Today, we may think of Democrats as advocates for civil rights and Republicans as opponents, or at least as less ardent than Democrats in their support of that cause. But until the 1970s, many Republicans supported civil rights legislation. President Abraham Lincoln, the first Republican president, had freed the slaves; and after the Civil War, Republican Congresses enacted laws to benefit the freed slaves. African Americans therefore tended to vote Republican for many decades. It was only during the Depression of the 1930s and the coming of the New Deal that African American voters began to shift loyalties toward the Democrats.

Thus, despite President Nixon's opposition to busing, many Republican members of Congress were supporters of civil rights and the elimination of segregated schools in the South. In fact, earlier in 1964, a higher percentage of Republicans than of Democrats voted for the Civil Rights Act in both the House and Senate because the Democratic caucuses included southern Democrats who almost unanimously opposed that law.[9] At the time, there were almost no Republican members of Congress from the South. Like the Democrats who felt popular displeasure with their votes for civil rights, these northern, midwestern, and western Republicans who voted the same way as the northern Democrats also became targets of constituent complaints after that vote and its consequences.

The Education Amendments of 1972, which included ESEA amendments and changes to other laws, contained the congressional response to relieve this constituent pressure. That response included new funding for desegregation and integration, and restrictions on the use of busing for desegregation.

President Nixon's proposal to make the temporary aid program for southern school districts into a permanent program authorized by law was accepted as part of that omnibus package in the form of the Emergency School Aid Act (ESAA). Congress also expanded that program to go beyond aiding school districts with the costs of carrying out desegregation decrees, and it funded districts that were voluntarily integrating. This new law also prohibited the use of federal funds to pay for busing for the purpose of desegregation unless locally requested, and forbade busing if the time or the distance endangered the health of the student or brought that student to an inferior school. Parents and guardians were authorized to sue to enforce those limitations on busing.

Nixon signed the law but expressed his displeasure that it did not contain stricter limits on busing:

> In the amendments dealing with the busing of public school children, however, this measure is most obviously deficient. Had these disappointing measures alone come to this office—detached from the higher education reforms—they would have been the subject of an immediate veto . . . Confronted with one of the burning social issues of the past decade, and an unequivocal call for action from the vast majority of the American people, the 92d Congress has apparently determined that the better part of valor is to dump the matter into the lap of the 93d. Not in the course of this Administration has there been a more manifest Congressional retreat from an urgent call for responsibility.[10]

Busing was the hot topic and grabbed all the attention. Nixon was using the issue for political purposes, and it was getting more news media coverage than other issues of the time.

Ironically, the Education Amendments of 1972 contained the greatest expansion of federal aid to postsecondary education since the mid-1960s, but one would not have known that from the political debate or the news media coverage. As my former congressional colleague Christopher T. Cross later noted, "Although the 1972 bill put in place the most significant set of higher education programs ever enacted, the White House statement that day was all about school busing, as were the press stories that followed . . . Again, issues of race—this time in the guise of busing—had eclipsed content."[11]

Nixon was reelected in 1972 and attracted some southerners to the Republican side. The Democrats retained control of the Congress but felt they had to find some additional means to further limit busing to avoid more political damage. However, they wanted to do this in a way that did not undercut civil rights or the duty of school districts to eliminate segregation.

Several Republican members of Congress were also involved in this attempt, most notably Senator Jacob Javits, a prominent leader of the moderate Republican congressional faction. Democratic senators supporting civil rights thought so highly of Javits that they often deferred to his judgment. I could understand that high regard for Javits after watching him in numerous meetings, and dealing directly with him in seeking agreement on legislation. Of all the members of Congress I met over three decades, I consider Javits as one of the best.

During several Senate-House conference committees of this period, Congressman Perkins as chief negotiator for the House and I as his chief counsel would meet with Javits and his counsel privately in the senator's Capitol office to hammer out agreements on changes to anti-busing amendments passed by the House. Javits, although a Republican and in the Senate minority, spoke often for both parties in the Senate on the issue of civil rights.

That bipartisanship on civil rights was not to last. As the Republicans succeeded in their "southern strategy," the party became less supportive of civil rights and a less hospitable place for moderate or conservative Republicans who supported their party's historic position in favor of the rights of African Americans. A casualty of this political transformation was Senator Javits, who was defeated in the Republican primary in New York State in 1980 by Alphonse D'Amato, a more conservative politician who alleged that Javits was out of line on many issues with Republicans. D'Amato went on to be elected to represent New York in the Senate.

In the 1970s, when Javits was still a leader of both Democrats and Republicans on the issue of civil rights in the Senate, it was a tricky balancing act to keep busing as a remedy to desegregate the schools while satisfying constituent opposition to busing. Congressman Richardson Pryor (D-NC) believed that it was possible to limit busing, carry out the constitutional duty to desegregate the schools, and relieve public opposition to both. Pryor had been a federal judge before he was elected to the House, and so his views received particular attention.

Pryor, a member of the judiciary committee, met with Carl Perkins, chair of the education committee, to work out an arrangement whereby both committees would jointly write legislation to defuse the controversy. Perkins agreed, and I was designated to work with Pryor and the judiciary committee as the education committee representative in crafting this leg-islation. It was an education for me in both constitutional law and politics.

The 1974 Education Amendments, which resulted from our work, contained a fuller set of restrictions on busing than had the 1972 law. These provisions were contained in a section of the law titled the Equal Educational Opportunities Act of 1974 (EEOA). The objective of the EEOA was to make busing a remedy of last resort and place parameters on its use by the courts, but not to completely bar federal courts from resorting to its use for desegregation.

The Congress walked this thin line of vociferously pointing out the problems with busing and highlighting some restrictions on its use for desegregation, but then—without saying it explicitly—permitting the use of busing to integrate the schools. For example, the EEOA said that the neighborhood was the appropriate basis for assignment to school; that desegregation plans were costing school districts large sums of money to implement; that busing was creating serious health and safety risks for children and disrupting education for others; and that excessive busing was harming children, particularly in the first six grades. The act further stated that the courts had not established a clear, rational, and uniform standard for determining when to use busing. Therefore, it was necessary for Congress to specify appropriate remedies.

The operative provisions of the EEOA further declared that assign-ment of children to neighborhood schools was not a violation of the law unless it was for purposes of segregation. If housing patterns shifted within a desegregated school district in ways that resulted in resegregation of the schools, that fact would not cause a legal action. Further, a desegregated school did not have to reflect the racial composition of the entire school district's student population. But again, these were limitations on the use of busing, not total prohibitions.

I cite this legislative language in detail because it shows the twisting and turning that legislators did to convince their constituents that they did not really favor busing, while adopting legislative language that did not completely bar busing, since that was a necessary means to achieve desegregation. Still, each set of amendments adopted during the 1960s and 1970s narrowed the options for the use of busing.

This was obviously a very difficult issue for many politicians. It was one thing for a Michigan Democrat to insist that southerners dismantle their segregated systems of education which were created by law for the purpose of separating the races. It was quite another thing for that member of Congress from suburban Detroit to support busing when many of his or her constituents had spent considerable money to buy a house in a community with good public schools and then learn that their children might be bused into Detroit to desegregate city schools that were educationally inferior. The issues of race, low-quality schools, and safety were all intertwined. How could a politician try to improve the education for African American children who were stuck in inferior schools, when the people who elected that congressional representative were more concerned about the education of their own children?

For all those reasons, these 1974 amendments limiting busing did not douse the fires. Conservative Republicans continued to attack Democrats as "elitists" in favor of busing. In 1980, for example, when Ronald Reagan ran for president, he repeated these charges, although by that time busing for racial purposes amounted to just about 3 percent of all school busing in the country.[12] Reagan's tactics were in line with Nixon's southern strategy, which ultimately proved successful in moving the southern states from the Democratic electoral column to the Republican one. Opposition to school busing was one of the means used to achieve that end.

In the 1990s the Supreme Court ruled that school districts could be released from court orders mandating busing for racial purposes. Many southern districts asked for, and were granted, that relief. Gary Orfield of the UCLA Civil Rights Project summarized the long-term impact of these laws and later judicial decisions:

> Resegregation, which took hold in the early 1990s after three Supreme Court decisions from 1991 to 1995 limiting desegregation orders, is continuing to grow in all parts of the country for both African Americans

and Latinos and is accelerating the most rapidly in the only region that had been highly desegregated—the South . . . Across the country, segregation is high for all racial groups except Asians . . . While white students are attending schools with slightly more minority students than in the past, they remain the most isolated of all racial groups: the average white student attends schools where 77 percent of the student enrollment is white. Black and Latino students attend schools where more than half of their peers are black and Latino (52% and 55% respectively), a much higher representation than one would expect given the racial composition of the nation's public schools, and substantially less than a third of their classmates are white.[13]

In sum, for decades congressional debates on education were enmeshed in this issue of school busing. These judicial and congressional decisions had a major effect on which schools students attended and, in effect, how well they were educated. Presidents, Congresses, and judges can greatly affect children's lives by their actions. These laws restricting busing had, and continue to have, an effect on who sits in the nation's various classrooms, as have the subsequent Supreme Court decisions that curtailed busing.

TITLE IX: EQUITY FOR GIRLS AND WOMEN

At the same time that the Congress and presidents were restricting a means of integrating the races in public schools, they enacted a law that proved to be monumental in bringing about greater equality of opportunity in the education of girls and women. Ultimately, this legislative mandate assisted females in making great advances in schooling, the job market, athletics, and society. So, as some doors closed on racial integration, other doors opened for greater equality for women.

These greater opportunities were created by a federal law, Title IX of the Education Amendments of 1972, which stated in part that no person in the United States shall, on the basis of sex, be excluded from participation in, be denied the benefits of, or be subjected to discrimination under any education program or activity receiving federal financial assistance.

As noted earlier, in the 1960s and 1970s, the liberation movements for African Americans, women and girls, people with disabilities, and gay men and lesbians flourished. The women's movement worked hard for passage of an Equal Rights Amendment to the U.S. Constitution that would have helped women gain better access to good jobs, earn equal pay for work comparable to that done by men, and bring about other changes. That proposed amendment became bogged down in the state legislatures, and failed to gain the approval of a sufficient number of states to be added to the Constitution.

Title IX, formally known as the Equal Opportunity in Education Act, was a more politically successful route to advancing equality for women. The antidiscrimination provisions of Title IX were sponsored by Congresswomen Edith Green (D-OR) and Patsy Mink (D-HI) and were modeled on Title VI of the Civil Rights Act of 1964.

Both House sponsors of the amendment had to overcome major hurdles themselves to become influential members of Congress. Edith Green, an educator, was only the second woman from Oregon to be elected to the U.S. House of Representatives. Once elected, she was one of only seventeen women in the 435-member chamber. Patsy Mink, a lawyer, was the first woman of color and the first Asian American to be elected to Congress. In Hawaii she had faced discrimination from whites, and while attending the University of Nebraska, she successfully campaigned against that university's policy of separate housing for students of color.[14]

When I worked in Congress, I knew both women quite well, since they were longtime members of the education committee, and I was present when they offered their amendment. From our conversations and from my observations of them in a male-dominated Congress, I understood their motivation to make it easier in the future for girls and women to succeed while avoiding some of the barriers they themselves had faced in making their own careers.

Senator Birch Bayh (D-IN), who was the sponsor of the amendment in the Senate, explained the intent of this provision:

While the impact of this amendment would be far-reaching, it is not a panacea. It is, however, an important first step in the effort to provide for the women of America something that is rightfully theirs—an equal chance to attend the schools of their choice, to develop the skills they want, and to apply those skills with the knowledge that they will have a fair chance to secure the jobs of their choice with equal pay for equal work.[15]

This legislative mandate was written in response to the discrimination that girls and young women faced in enrolling in certain courses in high school and college and that teachers faced in elementary and secondary schools in seeking certain jobs, and in recognition of the very unequal expenditures for sports for men and women at every level of education.

The law allowed for a transition period for schools and colleges to comply, and included exemptions for traditional single-sex colleges, military academies, and religious organizations. It also stated that there should be no preferential or disparate treatment of members of one sex, and excluded any effect on separate living facilities. Despite these accommodations, many people voiced loud opposition against the new law, especially about its impact on sports. Coaches contended that their teams would be decimated because dollars would have to be shifted to women's sports, which were receiving much less financial aid than men's sports.

The 1974 Education Amendments created a grant program to advance gender equality, the Women's Educational Equity Act (WEEA). This effort was meant to accelerate and ease the implementation of Title IX. During the 1970s, grants were made to develop curricula and textbooks, provide teacher training, improve guidance and counseling, and fund other activities to increase the participation of women in education. Although never funded with more than a few million dollars, that program drew great opposition from conservatives. In particular, WEEA became a lightning rod for criticism of "feminists." The program's opponents were unsuccessful in eliminating this categorical program, however; even President Reagan, at the height of his political powers in the early 1980s, could not accomplish that goal. But Reagan's opposition was a major factor in sharply curtailing funding for WEEA for a period. In recent years, conservative critics have continued to charge that WEAA funds are used to "support activist/ advocacy projects, making the program even more contentious," in the words of Chester Finn.[16]

A problem complicating the implementation of Title IX was pointed out by Christopher T. Cross:

> Because Title IX was added to the bill without either House or Senate hearings, the legislative history of congressional intent is exceedingly sparse, consisting primarily of a short section in the committee report, a statement by Congresswoman Green, and some dialogue on the House floor during debate on the overall higher education bill. That absence, though not entirely unusual, would be a key part of the controversy surrounding Title IX, and its application over the following 30 years.[17]

Usually, when a lawsuit is filed involving a statute and some ambiguity exists about the meaning of a provision of the law, a court will review the legislative history to ascertain the intent. The absence of a full record of hearings and explanatory congressional committee reports hampers that judicial work. The same problem exists for federal officials writing regulations to enforce a law when there is a sparse congressional record of the intent.

To resolve some problems that arose with Title IX, the Education Amendments of 1976 excluded certain situations from coverage of the law, such as exempting the Boy Scouts and Girl Scouts, father-son and mother-daughter activities if provided for both sexes, and beauty contest awards. But the congressional proponents were able to hold off what would have been eviscerating amendments, especially regarding sports.

The opponents of Title IX were more successful in the federal courts than they had been in Congress. In 1984, the Supreme Court in *Grove City v. Bell* placed limits on shifting funds from men's to women's sports through a narrow reading of the statute. That decision determined that Title IX's provisions affected only the part of a college or university that received federal aid, and not the remainder of the institution. Grove City College did not accept federal aid other than for student loans and grants, and so pursuant to the Court's decision, the student aid office was the only part of the college to which the antidiscrimination prohibitions applied.

The congressional supporters of Title IX were not intimidated by the Court's decision. In fact, they led a successful drive that in effect over-turned the decision by passing a law specifying that the entire institution was covered if one part received funds. The Civil Rights Restoration Act of 1987[18] was important not only for Title IX but also for other civil rights laws, since a court could use the *Grove City* ruling as a precedent for nar-rowly interpreting those other laws.

The Restoration Act passed Congress, and then was vetoed by Presi-dent Reagan. The Congress overrode that veto, which requires a two-thirds majority in both the House of Representatives and the Senate. As a result, Title IX retained its role in barring discrimination against girls and women in education.

At the time, I was the congressional counsel working on both the Title IX legislation and on the various anti-busing provisions. I couldn't help but see the irony of the Congress moving forward to forbid discrimination on the basis of sex, while the reverse was occurring in the busing controversy.

In sum, from the 1960s until today, many forces in society have helped to bring about greater equality for women. Title IX was a major factor, both symbolically and in actuality. While Title IX cannot be credited with all of the improvement that women have experienced, the results in educa-tion are impressive. Currently, girls score higher in reading at every grade level tested by NCLB, and are on par with boys in mathematics achieve-ment—reversing past math performance. Girls finish high school at higher rates than boys, and women enter and complete college at higher rates than men. Female professors have greater access to college and university posi-tions than they previously had. Women are also making greater advances in gaining professional degrees than ever before, and are becoming the ma-jority in law and medical schools.

These are all dramatic changes from the prevailing situation for women prior to 1972. Of course wage disparities still exist between men and women, and there are other obstacles to full equality. Title IX has, nonetheless, opened doors to girls and women that had been closed before. Title IX is an example of bold policy making, as its supporters sought to reverse a Supreme Court decision and challenged the power of collegiate sports. Title IX's prohibition against discrimination is a landmark that clearly brought about both social and educational improvement.

In short, the country is stronger because the talents of girls and women are being more fully used than before. The federal government, in setting a nondiscrimination policy by statute, is at least in part responsible for that achievement.

STUDENT BIBLE STUDY GROUPS AND GAY/STRAIGHT ALLIANCES

A final example of education policy making to address social issues is the Equal Access Act of 1984 (EAA). This legislation about the use of school facilities by student groups was enacted after fierce debate involving both the separation of church and state and students' rights to free speech. It proves the point that one should be careful about what one asks for—and also about what one does not want.

In the early 1980s a number of student Bible study groups asked to use the facilities at their public high schools for meetings. Some school districts gave permission, but some refused, citing the doctrine of separation between church and state. Conservative religious organizations turned to Congress to pursue a law that would permit these meetings. They found a champion in Congressman Carl Perkins, the chair of the Education and Labor Committee of the U.S. House of Representatives. Perkins's support surprised many education organizations because the committee he headed was traditionally one of the most liberal in the Congress, and he had led the fight for many elements of the nation's "safety net," which identified him as an economic liberal. What was not generally known was that Perkins had been "reborn" religiously and that this legislation was very popular in his religiously conservative congressional district. As his committee's chief counsel for education, I was aware of this personal motivation.

Perkins found an unlikely ally on this bill in Congressman Barney Frank (D-MA), one of the most liberal members of Congress and a representative from a New England district that had little in common with Perkins's rural, poorly educated, and religiously conservative area. Frank's support for the legislation was important because the proposal, as introduced, was referred to both the education committee that Perkins headed and the judiciary committee on which Frank was a senior member. According to the rules of the House, the bill would have to be approved by both committees in order to proceed to consideration by the full House of Representatives.

Frank's support was based on the general principle that if a school district allowed one student group to use its facilities, it should allow other groups the same opportunity within certain parameters, such as a condition that the group was not sponsored by any public authorities. In other words, the student organizations had to be student-led and not guided by a teacher or other public official.

The proposed legislation contained those safeguards. It made it unlawful for any public secondary high school that received federal assistance and permitted student groups to use its facilities for meetings to deny the same rights to any student group on the basis of religious, political, philosophical, or other content of the speech at such meetings.

In 1984, the bill was introduced with the prominent cosponsorship of Congressmen Perkins and Frank, both well-respected progressive Democrats in the House. Both the education and the judiciary committees to which it was referred engaged in fierce debate about the merits and constitutionality of the legislation. In the end, though, both committees approved the bill, and it went to the full House for consideration.

There another vociferous debate occurred. Liberals did not want to encourage student Bible or prayer groups to meet in public schools because they feared it would show official sanctioning of religion. Conservatives were more than happy to show their support for these groups and to insist on their right to meet in public buildings. During the debate, Frank tried to get his liberal colleagues to see the general principle involved, but with little success.

I can attest to the hostility of liberals to the legislation. As Perkins's counsel, I worked with the judiciary committee on getting the two committees to approve the bill. Then I had to assist in organizing to secure passage of the legislation through the House. During this entire process, angry Democratic members of the education committee and their staffs wanted to know why Perkins and I were involved in what they considered a "right wing" attack on separation of church and state. At the same time, I had to meet on a regular basis with the conservative religious groups led by Pat Robertson and Jerry Falwell, well-known televangelists, to line up support for the legislation. These were organizations that I ordinarily would not engage with. Due to all this stress, one Friday my back gave out and I had to be taken by ambulance to a hospital emergency room for treatment. The following Monday, I was back in the middle of the controversies.

After a heated debate, the House approved the bill and then included it in a broad piece of legislation authorizing education programs for science and mathematics and other initiatives meant to strengthen the nation's economy. The Senate leadership did not want to deal with this issue of student prayer groups, so the House strategy of including the provision in another bill would offer a chance to have it approved as part of a larger piece of legislation.

That is exactly what occurred. In the Senate-House conference committee on the math and science bill, the Senate negotiators accepted the House proposal while reaffirming the limitations that any prayer meetings could not be publicly sponsored or endorsed. Thus, the Equal Access Act appears as Title VIII of the Education for Economic Security Act.[19]

Conservative members of Congress took credit for this bill and celebrated the outcome that student Bible study and prayer groups must be allowed to meet in their high schools, if the students requested it and the school district allowed other groups to meet. Liberals were disappointed that legislation supported by Pat Robertson, a prominent conservative religious and political leader, and his allies had gotten through the Congress.

The story, though, does not end there. In the 1990s and later, as the gay liberation movement gained ground, a number of gay/straight clubs were founded in high schools to encourage acceptance of gay men and lesbian women. Several public schools denied permission for these groups to meet in high schools. Lawsuits were filed by the student clubs, and judges relied on the Equal Access Act to require the public authorities to allow those meetings if other groups had been allowed to use the facilities.

The worm had turned. Conservatives who were happy that student Bible study groups could meet in high schools now had to face the fact that the law that made this possible was being used to afford the same rights to gay/straight groups. Barney Frank was correct; he understood at the beginning the universality of the rule that student-led groups of whatever persuasion had to be allowed to meet in high schools with a policy that permitted such meetings. There could be no public endorsement of these groups, and neither could public officials pick and choose which groups they would allow to meet depending on the officials' personal beliefs or preferences.

The law has been praised for the useful way that it guides decisions on free speech, as Joshua Dunn, a political science professor whose research focuses on legal history, has pointed out:

> While the EAA was promoted by religious organizations concerned about religious discrimination in public schools, it has been a remarkably helpful tool for courts in resolving free speech controversies. In some ways, the act saved the courts from themselves. The Supreme Court's Establishment Clause doctrine is a notorious mess that has sown substantial confusion among school officials about what kinds of religious activities are allowed in public schools.[20]

The religious advocates for this legislation in the 1980s might be surprised that it has turned out to be used so even-handedly to resolve contentious disputes. Good law may come from various intents.

The Equal Access Act was another national policy that shows the interplay of the schools, other aspects of society, and politics. In dealing with student clubs that have a religious purpose and those that encourage greater toleration, the elements of evenhandedness and school neutrality are key. The opportunity for student groups of different beliefs to meet in public high school buildings is important in itself. But it is also important as a civics lesson to the teenagers who are students in those buildings. Respect for religious views and tolerance of others' views should be integral parts of American society.

9

Lessons Learned from Federal
Involvement in Schooling

THIS TALE OF FEDERAL involvement in education has taken us from the
heady days of 1965, when ESEA was created, to 2015, when NCLB is being
dismantled state by state through waivers of its main provisions. During
this half century, other federal programs and policies have been adopted to
improve education or address pressing social problems. What can all these
experiences over fifty years teach us about how to create a more useful role
for the federal government?

HIGHLIGHTING ISSUES

Throughout these fifty years, whenever the federal government has identified a problem in education and adopted a policy to address it, states and
school districts have taken note and directed their attention to that issue.
With the 1965 passage of ESEA, the education of disadvantaged children
became a focus for educators. When federal courts in the early 1970s ruled
that the education of children with disabilities had to be improved, states
and school districts began a reform that led to national legislation affecting
all states and schools. In 2011, when the Department of Education required

141

states to change their systems of teacher evaluation in order to receive a waiver from the provisions of NCLB, the states took action.

This ability of the federal government to direct attention to an issue is invaluable since there is so much noise in the educational system—criticisms, reforms, issues featured in the news media, reports from think tanks—that it is difficult to hear the main messages. Amid this cacophony, educators and citizens need to sort out what matters most. The federal government should therefore use this power prudently, since state and local governments will respond to the adoption of federal policies. Only the most important issues—only those areas where action is badly needed and where the greatest improvement can occur—should be the business of the federal government.

Bringing about greater equity in education is one such issue. Since the 1960s, equity has been a federal concern because of previous neglect by the states and local school districts. Some progress has been made in the intervening years, but there is a need for continued attention to the vital goal of providing a good education among those who are not privileged by family wealth or other means. The social culture of the United States emphasizes individualism and "standing on your own two feet" to such an extent that the needs of the less-advantaged tend to be overlooked. The federal government is a powerful voice on their behalf. Among other issues significant enough to require the attention of the federal government are civil rights, access to higher education, and the basic business of collecting reliable statistics and supporting research.

In carrying out the responsibility of identifying the most pressing issues, the federal government must comply with statutory limitations on federal involvement with the schools. The original 1965 ESEA included a prohibition against federal control of education to allay fears that this new federal role would upend the traditional control of public education by local school districts. Section 604 of the original law stated:

> Nothing contained in this Act shall be construed to authorize any department, agency, officer, or employee of the United States to exercise any direction, supervision, or control over the curriculum, program of

instruction, administration, or personnel of any educational institution or school system, or over the selection of library resources, textbooks, or other printed or published instructional materials by any educational institution or school system.[1]

How did this provision affect the ability of the federal government to identify needs in education and to adopt policies to address them? An example may help to explain the effect, since this prohibition remains in the law although in a somewhat altered form.

As described in chapter 7, the 1968 amendments to ESEA included a new program of grants to school districts that subtly encouraged bilingual education as an instructional approach for teaching English to students with limited proficiency in the language, and then in 1974 that support of bilingual education became much more direct.[2] Did that federal policy encouraging funding of one instructional practice violate the prohibition against federal control of any "program of instruction"?

Federal grant programs have their constitutional basis in the "spending clause" of the U.S. Constitution, which authorizes the federal government to use funds to improve the general welfare of the country. If states and local school districts apply for federal funds and voluntarily and knowingly accept the conditions placed on that funding, then they must abide by those requirements.[3] In those situations, the federal government is not controlling or directing local decisions. It is simply operating a grant program with known requirements, and so the prohibition against federal control has no effect.

Thus, in the 1968 Bilingual Education Act as well as in the amended 1974 law, the federal government could encourage the teaching of English through an approach that used the native language of the student, namely bilingual education. And in 2001, the Congress could change that grant program to place stiff restrictions on the use of bilingual education and instead emphasize other instructional methods such as immersion into English, which does not use the student's native language. Neither federal policy violated the prohibition against federal control because school districts agreed to those conditions when they received grants.

Therefore, the federal government can bring the nation's attention to serious problems in education. The only caution is that those acts must be grounded in constitutional provisions, particularly the spending clause, and be carried out as the U.S. Supreme Court has prescribed; for example, states must be openly aware of the conditions on receipt of federal aid.

STRONG POLICIES

When the federal government has adopted forceful policies, the effect is greater than when weaker policies have been used—this is common sense. The means of carrying out federal policies exist along a continuum of forcefulness.

Supreme Court decisions are the most powerful means of ensuring action on a policy, and lower federal court rulings are also potent. The Supreme Court's 1974 *Lau* ruling, which held that the San Francisco school district violated the constitutional rights of students who were not proficient in English because they were not afforded additional assistance to learn English, changed practices throughout the country. Lower federal court decisions, which found violations of the Fourteenth Amendment in school districts' treatment of children with disabilities, not only affected the defendant school districts but more importantly spurred congressional action in writing what has come to be known today as IDEA.

Brown v. Board of Education, although it was issued somewhat before the time frame of this book, was tremendously important not only in desegregating the schools but also in establishing the ideal that America should be a country for all peoples. In sharp contrast, the Supreme Court's *San Antonio Independent School District v. Rodriguez* closed the federal doors to efforts to bring greater fairness in the funding of public education. This 1973 case involved Texas's substantial reliance on local real estate taxes to fund the schools even though that meant that property-poor school districts had much less available for education than did property-rich school districts. The Court said that there was no remedy at the federal level, and so sent the issue back to the states.

As powerful as they are, federal court rulings can be affected by congressional action. Over a period of many years, the Congress enacted laws that sought to limit the Supreme Court's *Swann* decision, which held that the lower federal courts could order busing of school children for the purpose of desegregation. While enacting those laws, Congress tried not to go head-to-head with the courts, since they could rule those laws as unconstitutional, but eventually Congress succeeded in limiting busing, assisted by presidential appointments of judges disposed against that practice. With Title IX, Congress changed the law after the Supreme Court ruled in *Grove City* that only one part of that institution of higher education would be affected by the prohibition on discrimination against women. The Civil Rights Restoration Act, in effect, overruled the Court's decision by clarifying congressional intent that entire institutions were affected, not only by Title IX but also by other civil rights laws. Even though court rulings are a powerful federal tool to execute policy, they are not necessarily the last word.

Federal laws can also be forceful. IDEA revolutionized the education of children with disabilities by instituting new requirements for including these children in regular classrooms, developing IEPs that detailed the services each child needed, giving parents a process for seeking changes, and requiring that school districts provide the necessary services to these children regardless of the level of federal funding. These types of provisions are not found in any other federal education law. State and local compliance with IDEA's requirements costs more than the federal appropriation for the law, but states and school districts have to bear those extra costs because they accepted the IDEA grant.

As forceful as some federal laws have been, that strength has not always ended the debate on their worth. NCLB is the strongest federal education law ever enacted, affecting most school children in the United States, but keen controversy has surrounded that policy since it was first implemented in 2002. Some states resisted at first in complying with the law; others sued the federal government over the costs they were incurring; and some parents refused to let their children take the required tests.

Unlike most other federal laws, not one word of NCLB has been changed since it was passed, despite those objections. According to our interviews on Capitol Hill recounted in chapter 5, NCLB's congressional and presidential sponsors wanted it to become part and parcel of American schooling, which they believed would happen if it stayed in effect for a long period of time. But that determination not to change NCLB just directed the energy for change elsewhere, namely toward using waivers from the Department of Education to release states from various mandates of that law.

The federal government has a third set of tools for carrying out policies in the form of directives to take certain actions, and prohibitions of certain conduct, that must be followed without any funds set aside to assist with implementation. Title IX was a strong force in removing barriers in education for girls and women, and the Equal Access Act is also a potent tool for ensuring that local school administrators make school facilities available even-handedly to student clubs; but neither has dedicated funding to assist states and local school districts in complying with its provisions. As a companion to Title IX, the Women's Educational Equity Act provided very limited funding for grants to develop technical supports, but there was no large grant program to implement requirements as there is with IDEA.

Strong federal laws and directives have been proposed by members of Congress across the political spectrum—conservatives and liberals, Democrats and Republicans. Two congresswomen sponsored Title IX. Congresswoman Edith Green was a moderate-to-conservative Democrat, and Congresswoman Patsy Mink was a liberal Democrat. As mentioned in chapter 8, the Equal Access Act originated with conservative organizations which were concerned that student Bible study groups were being barred from the use of public schools; but then the legislation was sponsored by the populist Carl Perkins and the liberal Barney Frank.

Many directives have also come from conservative members of Congress who wanted to change certain practices in the public schools or establish new policies. This sponsorship is ironic, since conservatives complain more than liberals do about governmental interference in daily affairs. President Bush's NCLB alone contains numerous such directives. One directive expanded a requirement known as the Buckley amendment, which was first enacted in 1970 and named after Senator James Buckley (R-NY), the original sponsor. As first enacted, the Buckley amendment limited public access to education records and gave parents the right to review the curriculum materials used in the classrooms. NCLB expanded this policy to limit access to records of students' scores on tests taken pursuant to NCLB.[4] Further, U.S. Armed Forces recruiters were granted the right in NCLB to receive from school districts students' names, addresses, and telephone listings unless parents objected.[5] An additional directive continued by NCLB required school districts to sign a certificate that they did not have a policy preventing constitutionally protected prayer in the public schools.[6] School districts were also forbidden from banning Boy Scout troops from using school facilities, even if the district had a policy of not discriminating on the basis of sexual orientation.[7]

Earlier laws contained other directives, such as forbidding anyone from bringing guns onto school premises. Although the federal government has not provided funding to carry out these policies, state and local school districts routinely comply with all these directives that prohibit conduct or encourage particular activities.

An interesting example of a recent directive concerns high school dropouts. In 2008, President George W. Bush's administration issued a regulation under NCLB requiring all states to report high school completion and dropout data in a uniform manner. Prior to that, states used a hodge-podge of methods to collect the data that they sent to the federal government in this area. The new regulation mandated that every state collect data on the numbers of students who finished high school with a diploma within four years after they entered ninth grade.[8] This meant that for the first time, states submitted consistent data that could be used to report accurate figures for the states and the nation of the percentage of students who completed high school "on time."[9]

By contrast to these court rulings, demanding laws, and directives, federal grant programs can be strong or weak. IDEA is certainly strong with its procedural guarantees for IEPs and the requirement that services must be provided to children regardless of the amount of the federal appropriation. In its earlier form, the Title I program attracted some additional state and local funding for disadvantaged children, but it was certainly weaker than IDEA since there was no guarantee of services beyond the provision of federal dollars. In its new form, Title I as amended by NCLB is strong in motivating school districts to direct funding to raise test scores, regardless of whether the federal appropriation will pay for those services.

Some federal programs carry out specific, narrow purposes and their effects are measured by fulfilling those objectives; for example, an ESEA program provided schools with library books and audiovisual materials with no expectation of causing major reform in those buildings. Other programs, such as many of the original ESEA Title III demonstration projects, had an effect as long as the funding lasted and then the effect withered away.

In Washington, DC, some programs seem major because they receive millions of dollars in appropriations. But when that money is spread out among many school districts, it may not amount to much for any individual district. That is a major limitation on the effectiveness of federal education programs, and makes them weak in changing practices over the long term.

ADEQUATE FUNDING

As a general policy, the federal government should pay for a change in education if it has made a commitment to do so. It should also pay more if it imposes heavy new responsibilities on states and school districts. In many cases, however, neither one of these has happened. Consequently, resentment and opposition from states and local school districts has grown.

IDEA is an example of a federal program that violates the first rule. The federal government has never paid for the full 40 percent of the extra costs of educating students with disabilities that it pledged to cover when the law was passed. Since IDEA requires school districts to provide all of the necessary services to help a child with a disability, this violation of the federal government's pledge has meant that state and local governments have had to pay proportionately more for those extra costs of educating children with disabilities, which leaves less state and local funding for educating other children.

NCLB is an example of legislation that violates the second rule. Although that law does not contain any promise of funding similar to IDEA, it clearly imposed heavier duties on school districts through its requirements to ensure that students meet proficiency targets on state tests. In the first years of NCLB, states produced studies detailing those extra costs. Under pressure from Senator Ted Kennedy (D-MA) and other Democrats, President Bush agreed to an increase in Title I funding for two years: after that, the federal funding did not substantially increase.

The New America Foundation, which monitors federal appropriations, concluded that since NCLB was enacted in 2002, "federal appropriations for Title I have remained fairly flat."[10] They suggest that the increases immediately after the passage of NCLB did not amount to much. Therefore, states and school districts were left to foot the bill. Obviously, this caused resentment and helped to undermine the law.

The state of Connecticut sued the federal government for causing it to spend its own funds to implement NCLB, and the Pontiac, Michigan, school district and others also sued based on the same issue. These plaintiffs believed they would win in court since they could document additional costs and since the NCLB law explicitly stated that there was no authority to "mandate a State or any subdivision thereof to spend any funds or incur any costs not paid for under this Act"[11]—meaning that states and school districts could not be forced to spend their own funds on compliance unless that policy was specified.

In the Pontiac case, the lower federal court ruled that the plaintiffs had no cause of action because the Congress had not said that NCLB would be fully funded by the federal government. Appeals to overturn that decision failed in the Court of Appeals, and then in the Supreme Court.[12] In the Connecticut suit, the lower federal courts and the Supreme Court ruled that the state's case was premature and therefore not sustainable in court.[13] Neither case came back from these defeats.

In failing to provide sufficient funding for its mandates or onerous new requirements, the federal government is also failing to realize any possibility that it will become a true partner with states and school districts in paying for improvements. For a policy to have maximum effect, all sources of funding—federal, state, and local—ought to support it. All oars should be pulling in the same direction. It would seem wise for the federal government to increase its funding of education if it wants to bring about broad improvement, especially if it wants to influence the shape and direction of that improvement.

In 2009, Congress nearly doubled the federal contribution to elementary and secondary education when it passed the ARRA to help states and local school districts avert teacher and administrator layoffs and other ill effects of the severe economic recession. That strategy succeeded, and the worst was avoided. That large funding increase demonstrates that the federal government can contribute more to support education. The only question is whether the will exists to do so. This issue of costs will be treated in part IV when a new proposal for federal involvement in education is discussed.

STATE AND LOCAL IMPLEMENTATION

State officials, local school administrators, teachers, and other state and local personnel are responsible for carrying out federal education policies. The federal government does pay for some administrative costs of federal programs, but not enough to cover all costs, such as the accountability demands of NCLB. In effect, the federal government is piggybacking on the current structure of schools to implement its policies, and is benefitting from the willingness of educators and administrators to back up federal ideas.

The downside of that reality is that the effects of federal policies are blunted when state and local practices are inequitable. A prime example, first described in chapter 4, involves Cicero, Illinois. That school district, which educates children who mostly come from low-income families, spends $10,000 less per student than the Winnetka school district in the same state, which educates mostly children from affluent families. Title I provides a few hundred dollars per child more to Cicero, but that amount in no way makes up for the huge imbalance in state and local funding.

Also, in general, schools with concentrations of poor and minority students have less experienced teachers and teachers with fewer advanced degrees. The more affluent schools have the more experienced teachers with more advanced degrees. Again, federal policies meant to bring greater equity to schooling are frustrated by inequitable state and local practices.

Another point concerns the flexibility over federal funds that recent laws have given local administrators. In particular, Title I has changed from a targeted assistance intervention for certain disadvantaged children to a means of providing schools that enroll at least 40 percent poor children with a pot of funds they can use to improve the entire school. In other words, schools that meet this poverty criterion have a form of general aid, but the benefit of that additional flexibility is limited by local imbalances in state and local funding and the distribution of experienced teachers among schools. While the flexibility is useful, the overall scheme of education is not fair to disadvantaged students.

One lesson learned over the years is that if the regulatory burden involved in local administration of federal policies is too heavy, there will be the risk of pushback. In 1981, that occurred when educators who had worked with Congress to write laws shifted their loyalties to the Reagan administration to ease some of the burdens coming from those laws.

It is a balancing act for the federal government. Obviously, if a federal objective is set and meant to be implemented at the state and local levels, there will be some administrative burden. The challenge for the president and the Congress is to be aware of that and only require what is necessary to carry out policies that are needed to improve education.

BROAD SUPPORT

Despite limited federal funding and a substantial administrative load, IDEA has survived. That fact disputes the lesson just mentioned about not imposing a substantial administrative burden on schools receiving federal funds. Support for IDEA from all levels of society is the chief factor in that success.

Title IX is also a success despite having irritated powerful high school and college athletic departments. Again, the answer is support from a broad spectrum of society; girls and women comprise a slight majority in

American society. Their fathers and brothers and other men are another source of support.

The handling of school busing is an example of what happens when a policy lacks broad support. In the 1970s, the federal courts could order the use of busing in the South despite local opposition in those states. By the 1990s, opposition to busing had spread broadly throughout the country, and it lacked the popular support to be sustained. Bilingual education is a similar example. Early on, there was support for that approach—or at least not wide opposition. By 2000, strong opposition led to the enactment of legal restrictions on its use.

The challenge, then, is how to develop broad support for a federal policy? At a minimum, the task is to avoid widespread opposition to it.

The specific challenge is to find or build general support while concentrating on major problems that chiefly affect limited (and often relatively powerless) segments of the population One such challenge relates to policies to ameliorate the effects of poverty on schooling. In 1967, when I first started working for the Congress, debates were ongoing about the relatively new Great Society legislation and the other programs added after the initial burst of legislating in 1965. As legislative bills were being considered to amend the old programs or add new ones, the Democratic members of Congress argued among themselves about whether to create programs that affected a broad range of people or programs with narrow coverage, particularly for persons with low incomes. Proponents of the latter point of view argued that focused aid was needed to help the poor to do better and that broad coverage would dilute this assistance. Supporters of the wide-coverage position argued that political support would always be limited for such narrow programs and that the middle class had to be involved to sustain the programs and achieve sufficient appropriations. Meanwhile, Republican members of Congress usually wanted a focused approach so that the programs and funding would not grow too much.

Medicare is an example of a Great Society program that has a broad reach and has endured through dramatic changes of political control in Washington. Head Start is an example of a focused program that has survived but continues to struggle with funding and its existence as a federal activity in the face of proposals to turn it over to the states.

The lesson is that federal policies in education should have a broad reach among the population whenever that is possible. For example, federal support for higher academic standards helps all students, and should be widely supported. But it especially helps students in schools with concentrations of children from low-income families since they are often held to low expectations. The difficulty comes when a particular problem is limited to a smaller segment of the population. Although that is a challenging circumstance, advocates need to seek political support to help maintain that effort. This lesson is obviously difficult to implement, especially because the United States has such significant percentages of children who live in poverty and could benefit from special supports.

APPLYING THE LESSONS

In this chapter, I have tried to draw on my nearly five decades of experience with federal policies in education to see what could be learned about encouraging greater improvement in the future. The experiences of the past can be educative in providing guidance for the years ahead.

So far in this book, we have been through many national debates about education, through many controversies as laws were passed, and through years of implementation of national policies. From all that, we have distilled, as described above, five lessons that are important in establishing national policy for the schools:

- The federal government ought to identify only important issues for federal policy since states and school districts will direct attention to those issues.
- The federal government has a range of ways to carry out policy, with some being more forceful than others.
- The federal government ought to keep any promises it makes to pay for implementation of its policies and ought to help to pay for burdens it places on states and local districts.

- The federal government ought to carefully consider the administrative burden resulting from its policies, since it depends on state and local governments to carry them out, and also ought to consider shoring up the capacities of those other levels of government.
- The federal government ought to seek broad support for its policies, since that assists in their continuation.

The process of setting federal policy is not always clear and clean, and so not all of these lessons have affected every policy. In other words, circumstances do not always permit policy makers to act on everything they have learned, or should know.

IDEA is the prime example. Its administrative burden is substantial, so it violates that lesson. The government has not paid what it said it would, and so it violates that lesson. But IDEA has the great advantage not only of being the right thing to do, but also of affecting people at all income levels and in all social classes. Therefore, support comes from among all sectors of the population. It is quite an advantage to hold that trump card.

Thus, these lessons may apply in varying degrees, or not apply at all, depending on the issue, and may interact with or counterbalance each other in different ways. The wisest course of action is to learn from the past, but federal policy makers have not always been reflective. They have, however, generally been assertive. In some of the short accounts of policy making described earlier, political or social conservatives won the battle. In others, liberals prevailed. Neither political camp, however, was timid about challenging U.S. Supreme Court decisions and taking other bold actions to further its causes. Boldness can be an attribute in securing change, although it should be tempered by wisdom of the past.

As the examples of federal policy in this book show, Democrats and Republicans have sometimes worked together, or coalitions of liberals and conservatives from both political parties have come together for a cause. The period of the 1950s through the 1980s was a time when that could more easily occur, before the partisan divisions and acrimony grew that engulf Congress today. It is far better to have bipartisan policies, if for no other reason than they are more likely to endure.

What should motivate everyone to find the best federal policies is that once they are adopted they can have widespread and profound effects. The enactment of Title I changed the way the schools educated disadvantaged children. A similar dramatic change was that children with disabilities were made part of the regular classroom experience. More recently, states have raised their academic standards and millions of students have had to sit for tests holding their teachers and schools accountable for their academic achievement.

Federal actions have consequences, and therefore these five lessons should serve as guideposts in finding the best ways to improve American education. Now, let us see if we can follow a logical path to better policies using those guides.

Part IV

FRESH THINKING ABOUT THE FEDERAL ROLE IN EDUCATION

THE PREVIOUS CHAPTERS have reviewed fifty years of federal policy making in education as a way to inform us about what to do in the future, or at least to understand some precautions to take as the future approaches.

Part IV is about that future. If current federal policy to improve the public schools is not achieving what is needed, what are better solutions to the major problems? The chapters that follow seek to answer that question by looking at the essential elements of an education and reviewing the research on how to improve them. Based on that knowledge, I propose a new approach to federal involvement in education. This approach will differ from what the federal government has done in the past, but will be based on what has been learned from the experiences of previous decades.

Two strategies are central to this approach: a new state grant program, which I will call the United for Students Act, described in chapter 11, and new constitutional and legal approaches, set out in chapter 12. Although the state grants and legal approaches will operate differently, they have the same goal: securing a good education for every American child.

The policies recommended to attain that goal are ambitious. Some may even say that they will not be, or even cannot be, realized because of all the political and economic difficulties that would have to be overcome. But I have learned that when a high goal is set, one can achieve more than when aspirations are low. Daily life and political pressures, of course, intervene, and dreams are not always fully realized. But if one does not start from the ideal, then progress is meager because the objective was minor.

I have also learned that one must state the truth as clearly and boldly as one can. The fact is many American children do not have a good education because of the way the country has structured its schools. Inequities in financing schools, inequalities in the assignment of effective teachers among schools, low academic expectations, and lack of preparation for entry to school are major obstacles to many children getting a good education. Those impediments didn't just happen; they didn't just come out of nowhere. They were created, or at least their presence was ignored, by us as a people. If we want to secure a good education for all children, we will have to face reality and do some difficult things. If we don't, we have no right to complain about the poor quality of public education.

10

The Greatest Problems
in Schooling

AN IMPORTANT LESSON emerging from the fifty-year review of federal involvement in the schools is that federal policies should focus only on the country's most important problems. The question is, how do we identify those issues?

I recommend that we begin with the essential elements of education, weigh what research tells us about them, and look for possible ways to improve those elements. By necessity, the research review will be brief, since many books and studies are released every year on just one of the issues to be considered—teacher quality—to say nothing of the other three areas discussed in this chapter. With that important caveat in mind, let us begin this process.

To my way of thinking, the essence of education comes down to a student, a teacher, and something to be taught and learned. Everything else in education grows out of that relationship or feeds into it. A person with a desire to learn, another person with the knowledge and skills to foster that learning, and material to be learned (whether in a book, Web resources, hands-on experiences, or another format)—these are the fundamental elements of education. Naturally, as with most things in life, money must be available to make this happen, so that becomes the fourth component.

Those four elements are so basic to education that they should be the starting point for discussing the greatest problems facing our schools. In other words, using those four factors as the framework, what are the basic impediments to teaching and learning that need correcting?

If a student does not want to or is not prepared to learn, if a teacher lacks the knowledge and skills to engage students and facilitate learning, and if the learning material is inadequate, the whole enterprise is threatened. If funds are insufficient to pay the teacher, supply the learning materials, and cover the costs of the classroom or other environment, that also threatens the process of education. Even if other parts of schooling are working well, the first four essential elements must be in place for success.

If the discussion were to start at a different point, it would probably lead in another direction. For instance, if charter schools were the starting point, then the discussion becomes whether they are effective or not, or how can we improve them. That conversation's implicit assumption is that charter schools are a possible remedy for problems in schooling, so the natural topics are whether that is true and how we can make those schools better.

However, instead of discussing possible solutions at the very beginning, I prefer to start the conversation by focusing on the very essence of education—teaching and learning as viewed through those four essential elements. Then, using that framework, we can search for what makes teaching and learning better. This strategy keeps the focus on the essential relationship in education of learner and teacher. It also allows us to work our way to solutions instead of jumping to them.

This chapter therefore looks at the highlights of research on teaching and learning, these basic building blocks of education. The questions addressed are: what factors go into determining whether students are ready to learn, teachers are effective, the content to be learned is challenging, and the funding is adequate? The chapter also examines the presence of these four elements in U.S. public schools to see how close the country is to the ideal of providing a good education to every child.

STUDENTS PREPARED TO LEARN

Students are the beginning point. After all, the purpose of education is for them to learn. For that to occur, they must want to learn and be prepared to receive an education. Parents play the most important role in readying their children for school, but other factors also have an effect.

For decades, research has shown that high-quality preschool education is a solid investment in preparing young children for school. The studies are especially clear about the benefits for children from low-income families. The Perry Preschool Program in Michigan and the Abecedarian Program in North Carolina are the best known demonstrations of the long-enduring effects of a high-quality intensive preschool experience for children.[1]

A comprehensive review of the research on preschool programs reached this conclusion:

> Well-designed preschool education programs produce long-term im-
> provements in school success, including higher achievement test scores,
> lower rates of grade repetition and special education, and higher educa-
> tion attainment . . . The strongest evidence suggests that economically
> disadvantaged children reap long-term benefits from preschool. How-
> ever, children from all socioeconomic backgrounds have been found to
> benefit as well.[2]

Steven Barnett, who conducted this review, added an important caveat to this conclusion stressing that the preschool experience must be of high quality. "Current public policies for child care, Head Start, and state preK do not ensure that most American children will attend highly effective pre-school programs," he said.[3] Many programs do not have the essential elements to achieve quality, such as well-educated teachers receiving adequate pay, supervision of teachers, and use of assessments for improvement.

High-quality preschool programs are an important contributor to children's emotional and cognitive development. A key factor in the success of these programs is that they enlarge the vocabulary of children. Early verbal stimulation has been shown by research to be later linked to better test scores and academic achievement. By age three, children who come from families in which both parents went to college have heard thirty million words more, on average, than children from families in which neither parent went to college. For children who do not have the advantage of college-educated parents, this deficiency is associated with lower IQs and low language ability. Unfortunately, those children are often also from families of low socioeconomic status. A preschool experience of high quality can help these children expand their vocabularies.[4]

Where do we stand in the United States with ensuring that all children start school ready to learn?

The United States has a way to go in providing these preschool opportunities to all students. The Equity and Excellence Commission appointed by the U.S. Secretary of Education raised this question in its 2013 report:

> Would a country serious about early childhood preparation accept that only 65 percent of 4-year-olds from the lowest-income backgrounds attend preschool (with many attending low-quality programs), compared with 90 percent from the highest-income backgrounds, when the best-performing (foreign) school systems make such access universal and view it as critical to national success?[5]

The United States clearly needs to expand preschool education to children from low-income families, who generally have the greatest need for verbal stimulation and other skills necessary to prepare them for formal education. But low-income children are not the only group that could benefit from the expansion of preschool education. Surprisingly, children from middle-income or "lower middle class" families have the least access to preschool programs. As researchers W. Steven Barnett and Donald J. Yarosz noted,

> The participation pattern by income suggests that public policies raise pre-K participation rates for low-income families. However, young children in poverty still have much lower rates of preschool education enrollment than children whose families have higher-than-average incomes. Families with modest incomes may face the greatest difficulties in obtaining access to preschool programs.

In 2005, 63 percent of four-year-old children from families with incomes between $10,000 and $20,000 participated in preschool education, while children from families with incomes of $100,000 or more had an 89 percent participation rate. It is the families near the middle of the range of incomes that had the lowest participation: 55 percent of children from families with incomes of $20,000 to $30,000 were in programs, as were 58 percent of children from families with incomes of $30,000 to $40,000, according to Barnett and Yarosz.[6]

This data supports the need to expand preschool education, but Barnett's second point based on his comprehensive research review is just as noteworthy—there is a need for higher quality preschool programs than exist now. Preschool experts Sharon L. Kagan and Jeanne L. Reid have similarly emphasized both the value of expanding access to preschool education and the necessity of creating an "infrastructure" to ensure quality. By infrastructure they mean that the people who operate and teach in local preschool programs are prepared for their work, appropriately credentialed, monitored and accountable, and fairly paid; it is also important that they have opportunities to improve. This web of supports and regulations is missing or minimal in the complexity of federal, state, and local preschool programs and tax provisions.[7]

The conclusion drawn from research is that preparing students for school is important, especially for those from families with lower incomes and from parents who are not well educated. In conjunction with providing more preschool education, we need to ensure that these programs are of high quality. The data also show that the United States has work to do in making available to all four-year-olds a preschool education of high quality.

Preparation for schooling goes beyond a good preschool education. To be able to learn, a student cannot be hungry, or suffering from medical problems, or living in an unsafe environment. Students also need parents or other adults who care and encourage them to learn and take school seriously. Summer programs can help children from low-income families retain what they learn during the school year; research has shown that in the summer months, these children lose some of the academic gains made during the school year while children from higher-income families retain more of what they have learned due to a supportive environment.[8]

The Coleman report and other social science research have identified the family background of students to be the most important factor in predicting whether a child will do well in school. That is the main reason why preschool preparation is so important for children from low-income families, who are less likely to have had the verbal stimulation or to have learned the self-direction that higher-income children have experienced at home.[9] That is also the reason why other factors, such as poor access to health services, hunger, and the lack of reinforcing summer educational activities, should be included to some degree in comprehensive efforts to level the playing field for these children.

EFFECTIVE TEACHERS

The most important "within school" factor influencing a student's success is a good teacher. A study of students in Tennessee who were exposed to three years of highly effective teachers showed a 50-percentile-point difference in achievement compared with students exposed to three years of the least effective teachers. The benefits of having an effective teacher persisted for years.

Other research has reached similar conclusions, such as a Los Angeles area study which showed that students assigned to a teacher who was in the top quartile of effectiveness gained, on average, five percentile points compared to their peers with similar pre-test and demographic characteristics. Students assigned to a teacher in the bottom quartile lost five percentile points, on average.[10]

Thus, teachers matter, and the influence of effective teachers on students lasts for years. These conclusions are widely accepted; and therefore, attention has been directed for many years to preparing teachers to be effective. National commissions have been convened and have made recommendations. National organizations, such as the American Association of Colleges for Teacher Education, the National Board for Professional Teaching Standards, and the Council for the Accreditation of Educator

Preparation, have worked to improve teacher preparation and training. The Carnegie Corporation, the Joyce Foundation, and many others have funded research and demonstration programs to improve teaching.

From all these debates, experiments, and studies, let us look for ways to ensure effective teachers. First, we will consider who goes into teaching, then teacher preparation, and finally the evaluation of current teachers.

Teacher Recruitment

Who goes into teaching? The short answer is: too few of the best and brightest.

Some politicians have tried to make political hay over the issue of teacher qualifications and the need to raise standards for the profession. Former New York City Mayor Michael Bloomberg asserted in November 2011 that American teachers came "from the bottom 20 percent and not of the best schools."[11]

Critics charged that Bloomberg was overstating the numbers of teachers who scored low on tests. Michael Di Carlo of the Albert Shanker Institute looked for the sources of this assertion and found that about 30 percent of teachers who graduated from college in 1992–1993 were in the bottom quartile, and only 40.9 percent were from the top half of those taking SAT/ACT tests. Data on a different set of teachers—1999 college graduates who also took SAT/ACT tests and whose first job was teaching—showed that 47 percent came from the bottom third, 29 percent from the middle, and 23 percent from the top third of test takers.[12]

Di Carlo's rebuttal to Bloomberg was revealing: not all teachers were in the bottom 20 percent; instead, only about half of teachers scored in the bottom third of test takers! The mayor may have overstated the numbers, but even so, the point was made that too few of the best and brightest go into teaching in the United States.

The Equity and Excellence Commission in its 2013 report looked at how few high achievers enter teaching. The commission said:

> Would a country serious about teacher excellence settle for having only
> 30 percent of its educators coming from the top third of the college pool

when the best school systems in the world recruit nearly all of their school talent from the top third of the academic cohort? And how is it that we are alone among the advanced countries in assigning our least-prepared teachers to those who most need our best?[13]

Business organizations have also pointed to the qualifications of recruits for teaching. McKinsey and Company, a prominent international management consulting firm, in a 2009 report, concluded:

> In our education system research and work in more than 50 countries, we have never seen an education system achieve or sustain world-class status without top talent in its teaching profession. If the U.S. is to close its achievement gap with the world's best education systems—and ease its own socio-economic disparities—a top-third+ strategy for the teaching profession must be part of the debate.[14]

McKinsey said that the United States was not doing enough—only 23 percent of new teachers come from the top third of the academic cohort, as do just 14 percent of teachers in high-poverty schools. This contrasts with the world's top-performing school systems, such as those of Singapore, Finland, and South Korea, which recruit 100 percent of their teacher corps from the top third and then screen them for other important qualities as well.

Education researchers confirm the basic point about too few of the highest-scoring students going into teaching. In considering whether the SAT or ACT scores of college graduates going into teaching are below the average for college graduates, Richard Ingersoll concluded:

> In our own analyses of national data for NCES's Baccalaureate and Beyond Survey for the undergraduate class of 1999–2000, we found that this is especially true for those majoring in education, who tended to have the lowest average SAT scores. Moreover, with most fields and majors, we found that those who became teachers had lower SAT scores than those in the same field/major who did not go into teaching.

Ingersoll also used a six-category ranking of the selectivity of colleges and universities as a means of measuring the academic ability of those entering teaching. He reached these conclusions:

> About a tenth of newly hired teachers come from the top category of higher education institutions. About a fifth to a quarter come from the bottom two categories. About two-thirds come from middle-level institutions. This has shown little change in recent decades.[15]

Ingersoll's latest research confirms these trends, although some evidence shows a decline in male teachers coming from the top institutions and a possible increase in the academic ability of females entering the profession. Overall, though, there has been stability for decades in the major trends.[16]

Can the bar be raised? Ingersoll points to a paradox. Compared to other occupations and professions, teaching is relatively complex work, but it also is an occupation with relatively low pre-employment entry requirements. He concludes:

> Despite its complexity, from a cross-occupational perspective, teaching has long been characterized as an easy-entry occupation. Compared with other work and occupations and, in particular compared to high-status traditional professionals, such as physicians, professors, attorneys, and dentists, teaching has a relatively low entry "bar," and a relatively wide entry "gate."[17]

If that bar is raised so that higher-scoring college students become teachers, other aspects of teaching will have to change to keep these new recruits in the profession. Some indication of those changes comes from a recent poll of college students not majoring in education.

"Today's top college students tend to see teaching as a profession for 'average' individuals that simply doesn't pay enough, and one that has seen its prestige decline over the last few years," summarized reporter Stephen Sawchuk. The poll's sponsor, Researchers for Third Way, a centrist think tank, observed that "the teaching profession has a major image problem." To break this "perception of mediocrity," the college students who were polled recommended higher pay for teachers, which they associated with higher-status jobs.[18]

The message is clear. If we want high-scoring college students to go into teaching similar to what happens in other countries' high-performing systems of education, we will have to pay for that, as well as make other changes that treat teachers as true professionals. Are we ready to do that, or is all our talk about the importance of education just hot air?

How should the bar be raised? Research has established a relationship between a teacher's verbal aptitude test scores and that teacher's effectiveness in the classroom. More than two decades ago, Eric Hanushek, a researcher in this area, summed up the results at that time: "Perhaps the closest thing to a consistent conclusion across studies is a finding that teachers who perform well on verbal ability tests do better in classrooms."[19]

Later research has confirmed that teacher effectiveness is related to verbal ability. In 2002, Linda Darling-Hammond and Peter Youngs, also noted researchers in this area, reviewed studies defining highly qualified teachers and found evidence that verbal ability contributed to teacher effectiveness. They also found evidence connecting teacher effectiveness and their content knowledge and preparation.[20] In addition, other research has shown that more-effective teachers scored high in college on standardized tests and also attended institutions of higher education that were more selective in admissions.[21]

What effects will result from raising the bar? These findings argue for raising the admission requirements for teaching to give priority to candidates who demonstrate high verbal ability, attain high test scores, and come from colleges that are harder to get into since they are more competitive or selective in admissions. As with most things, positive and negative results will occur.

Harvard's Thomas J. Kane cautions that raising admission standards can be costly by eliminating from the pipeline anyone who could be discovered as effective later. He admits that there is some evidence to support higher standards, but he asserts that it is not overwhelming. Kane prefers to combine higher admission standards with better training once teachers are on the job. Citing hundreds of studies that show teachers improve their effectiveness in their first years of teaching, he concludes that "we know that clinical training matters."[22] Kane's concern about eliminating some people from teaching if entry requirements are raised may be particularly relevant for candidates from minority groups who may not score high on standardized tests.

That is a legitimate concern, but let me give you another side of the story. What about the students who have teachers who are not well qualified?

For nine years, I served on the Board of Trustees of the Educational Testing Service (ETS), which produces the Praxis exam. That test, which measures the knowledge and skills needed to teach, is administered by states to candidates for teaching to determine whether they should be certified or licensed to teach in that state.

While on the board, I asked at a session about how states used that test and was told that the different states had various cut-scores or various levels of performance that applicants had to achieve to pass the test and become certified or licensed. Some states accepted lower performance and others demanded higher performance. Since the board had been discussing how to raise the quality of the teaching profession, I asked why ETS did not specify a minimum test score that should be used to ensure the best-qualified people become certified teachers. The answer from the company's management was that that practice would discourage some states from buying the test, which obviously would not be financially good for ETS. Particular states were identified as allowing low scores for certification. Those states had some of the nation's poorest populations and had high concentrations of minority students.

Is it fair to poor and minority students to allow teachers with low test scores to become their teachers? Test scores cannot tell everything, and the results of one test should not be used alone to make major decisions about a student's or teacher's future. But a low score on Praxis does show something about the qualifications of a candidate to be certified as a teacher. At least, the question should be raised about whether that person is qualified to teach, and the candidate should be allowed to refute that conclusion by providing other evidence.

I describe this incident to show that the nation is not taking seriously the need to get the best people into the classrooms. If we were serious, we would be working harder to recruit as teachers more students who have high verbal abilities.

A caveat. Achieving high test scores showing verbal ability, or having a degree in a certain field, does not necessarily translate into that person being a good teacher. High achievement should only be the entry requirement. After that, candidates for teaching should be examined to see if they have the attributes to be a teacher.

McKinsey's chief recommendation, for instance, was that the United States establish a top-third+ policy that would recruit those in the top third cohort in college to enter teaching and then "rigorously screen students on other qualities they believe to be predictors of success, including perseverance, ability to motivate others, passion for children, and organizational and communications skills. That's the 'plus' in top third+."[23] McKinsey suggests beginning this process in high-need districts because they have the widest achievement gaps among students and the highest turnovers of teachers.

To summarize this section on teacher recruitment, the need to bring more of the best and brightest into teaching is clear; but they should also want to teach and demonstrate the characteristics of a good teacher. It is a combination of factors that count, not a sole factor. Another factor that is important is to have well-trained teachers. That is what we will discuss next.

Teacher Preparation

Obviously, it is important to train prospective teachers to be effective before they begin teaching. The irony, though, is that effective teachers can be identified by certain characteristics such as consistently producing high student test scores, but there is no research-based agreement on how they came to be effective that would help with instilling these characteristics in others.

Much work has been done to create teacher preparation programs that will help teachers to be effective. However, in a 2005 synthesis of teacher education research conducted by the American Educational Research Association, the conclusion was that no particular program structure such as four-year undergraduate, fifth-year post-baccalaureate programs, or alternative routes was superior. Only certain strategies, under the right conditions, seemed to work, such as clinical experiences, that will be discussed later.[24]

Other reviews have reached similar conclusions. In 2010, the National Research Council (NRC), after citing the lack of good data in this area, stated:

> We found no evidence that any one pathway into teaching is the best way to attract and prepare desirable candidates and guide them into the teaching force . . . In general, the evidence base supports conclusions about the characteristics it is valuable for teachers to have, but not conclusions about how teacher preparation programs can most effectively develop those characteristics.[25]

Secretary of Education Arne Duncan, when announcing an Obama administration initiative to develop ratings of teacher preparation programs, stated his frustration: "We have 1,400 schools of education and hundreds and hundreds of alternative certification paths, and nobody in this country can tell anybody which one is more effective than the other."[26] His proposal to rank preparation programs seems aimed at making public various factors involved in teacher preparation, with the expectation that eventually the factors that lead to preparing effective teachers will become evident.

Hope for deeper understanding about how to prepare effective teachers exists among researchers. According to Richard Ingersoll, research has found that teacher education, preparation, and qualifications, *of one sort or another*, are significantly and positively related to student achievement (my emphasis).[27] The task is to gain greater knowledge of these pieces, seek broad agreement that they are important, and then put the segments together to create a comprehensive approach to teacher preparation.

Consequently, we should not give up on teacher preparation or on licensure which requires a prospective teacher to demonstrate competence. It would be a mistake simply to allow anyone with a college degree to become a teacher. Other professions, such as law, dentistry, medicine, and even massage therapy, insist on preparation before practice and also on testing for licensure. Our children deserve teachers, as well as dentists, who are well trained and have to demonstrate it to be licensed.

One "piece" of teacher preparation with evidence of its effectiveness is clinical experiences for soon-to-be teachers. Thomas Kane, cited above, said that there are hundreds of studies demonstrating that clinical programs improve a prospective teacher's skills. An example is the 2008 National Bureau of Economic Research study which found that teachers who had more extensive clinical training (including a full-year internship) before they began to teach produced higher student achievement gains.[28] Unfortunately, such opportunities are not offered to all recruits.

While most education schools strive to prepare new recruits, their universities rarely fund the extensive clinical training that is typically required and supported by other professions such as engineering, architecture, and nursing, according to Barnett Berry, a teacher preparation expert. Furthermore, universities historically have funded schools of education below the average of other university departments, and generally far below most other professional preparation programs, Berry notes.[29]

Another piece of teacher preparation that has evidence of effectiveness is induction programs where novice teachers are provided with support and guidance in the early stages of their careers under the tutelage of trained mentors. Research has found that new teachers who had two years of induction with trained mentors produced notable gains in student academic achievement. These gains were similar to those attained by the students of veteran teachers. So, clearly, certain aspects of teacher preparation can bring about improvement.[30]

Evaluation of Current Teachers

The last major area of teacher quality to discuss is the evaluation of teachers already in the classroom. As with teacher preparation, there is intense disagreement on the best way to evaluate teacher effectiveness. Therefore, it is difficult to advise teachers on the best, research-based approaches to improve their classroom performance.

National Board certification is the exception in determining the effectiveness of current teachers, but unfortunately due to costs and political pushback that certification has been earned only by a small minority of teachers when it should be widely used throughout the country. One-hundred thousand teachers are board-certified out of 3.3 million public school teachers in the country.

The Obama administration has pushed hard to get the states to review and improve their teacher evaluation systems. Until recently, the process too often was superficial, and most teachers were classified as good or excellent without much evidence to support that designation. Due to federal insistence on revision of these systems—most notably, through states' applications for NCLB waivers and Race to the Top grants—forty-three states and the District of Columbia are now in the midst of making major changes.[31]

The greatest controversy with these revisions is the degree to which the evaluations of teacher effectiveness ought to be based on student scores from state accountability tests used to comply with NCLB. Research has shown that these tests are not reliable for this purpose when they are the sole component in teacher evaluation systems.[32] Although not the only component in most state systems, student test scores in some states are given great weight, which raises many of the same concerns.

The Obama administration and many states are nevertheless pushing ahead to create systems that place heavy reliance on these assessments. Debates about the validity of that approach are contentious, resulting in no consensus about a specific system to evaluate the performance of classroom teachers. In fact, it is not even clear whether these new systems will survive because lawsuits have been filed in several states that challenge the validity of using student test results to evaluate teachers' performance, especially to make such important decisions as whether to retain teachers and how much to pay them.

As with teacher preparation, the evaluation of teachers is so vital that the search for the best methods must continue. My hope, though, is that student test scores will not be used improperly. Policy makers should heed the researchers and test-preparers who stress that tests in current use were not created to be valid in assessing teacher performance for purposes of major decisions such as pay and job retention.

Special Effects on Disadvantaged Students.

Exposure to more effective teachers would generally improve education for students and would most strongly benefit the lowest achieving students. Unfortunately, children of lower socioeconomic status who attend schools with high concentrations of similar students are more likely than students with higher socioeconomic status to have less experienced teachers and teachers who are instructing out of their field of expertise.[33]

Retention of good teachers in schools with high concentrations of poor students is also a serious problem. Pay is a factor, but so are working conditions. Michael Rebell and Jessica Wolff of Teachers College at Columbia University noted that large class sizes, poor leadership, inadequate facilities, lack of instructional materials, and other factors that constitute poor working conditions are most pervasive in schools with significant concentrations of children from low-income families. As a consequence, teachers leaving high-poverty schools are more than twice as likely as teachers leaving affluent schools to cite this as their reason for quitting.[34]

Summary

A qualified teacher is essential to a student receiving a good education. In this section, we have explored the various facets of ensuring that a teacher is qualified. Needless to say, it is complex.

More of the best and brightest should be recruited as teachers, but they should possess the attributes of a good teacher and should have earned high test scores. The area of teacher preparation needs further research and experimentation, but there are certain aspects, such as clinical experiences and induction programs using trained mentors, that have proven to produce effective teachers. Evaluations of current teachers is an area both controversial and in need of more work; nonetheless, better evaluations than those used in the past are sorely needed.

A last important point needs to be made: to get more effective teachers, a combination of things needs to change, not just one or two things in
isolation. Vivien Stewart, who was involved in a series of multi-country
meetings on teacher quality, concluded:

> The top performers [among countries] take a comprehensive approach.
> Two key features of that approach include recruiting high-quality en-
> trants into the profession, and making sure the teacher preparation
> programs are rigorous by developing strong subject matter skills for all
> teachers and providing more extensive clinical experience early on. Once
> teachers are in school, every new teacher has a mentor and there are ca-
> reer paths to enable teachers to grow in their professional roles. As they
> gain experience, they can take on leadership roles in the school focused
> on curriculum, mentoring, leading professional development to address
> the school's problems, and more.[35]

It is a package deal. Get better academically prepared people into
teaching, prepare them well, give them clinical experiences and induction
assistance with trained mentors, and evaluate their job performance—but
also pay them well and give them decent conditions in which to work.[36]

CHALLENGING CURRICULUM

The third essential element of a good education is the curriculum, or what
is taught, as represented by the reference to learning material at the beginning of this chapter.

Curricular changes can have a far greater effect on student achievement, be more certain in their impact, and be less expensive than many
other reforms, such as encouraging more charter schools, asserts Grover
Whitehurst of the Brookings Institution. For those reasons, Whitehurst
took the Obama administration to task for placing too much emphasis on
other changes and "leaving curriculum reform off the table or giving it a
very small place [that] makes no sense." [37]

Those comments are particularly ironic because the Tea Party is criticizing Obama for endorsing and advocating for the Common Core State Standards in reading and mathematics. The state officials who developed the Common Core repeatedly urged the administration to keep its distance from those standards so they would not be perceived as federal standards. All of this criticism and defensiveness is rooted in America's tradition of local control of education.

Regardless, research has shown the value of teaching students a more demanding curriculum. Such a rigorous curriculum was envisioned by those who developed the Common Core State Standards; that was the whole point of the exercise.

American high school students who are taught more rigorous academic content have higher academic achievement, according to one such study.[38] Lower achieving children can attain state standards and world-class standards if they are removed from classroom groups that use less demanding curriculum and, instead, are exposed to better teachers, curriculum, and instruction. Making these beneficial changes for low achieving children does not adversely affect high achieving students, according to another study.[39] Placing low achieving students in more demanding classes and having them do better is counterintuitive, but this research certainly raises the issue of whether too little is being asked of students. Are some students not doing well because they are not being challenged by their teachers and the subject matter?

If a rigorous curriculum is important, how rigorous is the curriculum that is currently being taught in America's classrooms?

ACT, the organization that administers the country's most widely used college entrance examination, has expressed concern about high school students' lack of academic preparation for college. ACT therefore argues for greater rigor in the courses required for high school graduation:

> If we do not raise the rigor of core courses, U.S. students are in danger of entering the workforce unprepared for the challenges of competing in a technology-based global economy . . . It is crucial that we strengthen the high school core curriculum to improve the readiness of all students.[40]

Children from low-income families are particularly harmed by a low-expectations attitude about the content taught. The Department of Education recently documented stark racial and ethnic disparities in course offerings. Eighty-one percent of Asian American high school students and 71 percent of white high school students attend high schools that offer the full range of math and science courses (algebra I, geometry, algebra II, calculus, biology, chemistry, physics). However, fewer than half of American Indian and Native Alaskan high school students are in high schools with the full range of math and science courses. Black students (57 percent), Latino students (67 percent), students with disabilities (63 percent), and English language learners (65 percent) also have diminished access to the full range of courses.[41]

Until recently, the content of instruction in American elementary and middle schools was generally a local decision made by the teacher, school, or school district. At the high school level, teachers had to pay attention to any course requirements set by the state for awarding a diploma, but states usually did not specify the content to be taught.

As a result, U.S. schools lacked a center of gravity because teachers did not know what they were expected to teach or what students were expected to learn. Therefore, a school district could choose any textbooks or tests because there was no common curriculum. Professional development could focus on whatever seemed relevant. In the name of local control of curriculum, schooling had no clear curricular objective, which meant that some students learned a lot and others not so much.

The academic standards movement that began in the late 1980s was intended to change that situation. In the following decade, states developed academic standards for English language arts, mathematics, and in some cases for other subjects. After fifteen years of experience with widely varying state standards, governors and chief state school officers decided that they needed national standards for English and mathematics—which became the Common Core State Standards. Those academic standards were developed by these state officials without federal involvement or direct federal funding. As of July 2014, those standards have been adopted by forty-two states and the District of Columbia.

Today, the Common Core standards are under attack by the Tea Party and increasingly by Republican conservatives. Opposition has also come from some liberals, but to a lesser extent than from the right end of the political spectrum. On the other hand, a strong majority of local school administrators firmly supports the standards. As noted in chapter 6, a June 2014 poll by the American Association of School Administrators found that 93 percent of responding administrators believe the Common Core standards are more rigorous than what is being taught now in the schools and will ensure that students graduating from high school will be prepared for college or a job. Most also believe that the political debates about these standards are misinformed and getting in the way of implementation.[42]

Those educators have it right, and the opponents have it wrong. It would be a serious mistake to step backwards and abandon this effort to bring greater rigor to American education. Precedent shows that on their own, many of the nation's 14,000 school districts will not pursue a more demanding education for all their students. Even if they wanted to, they may not know how to accomplish this or may lack the financial means to develop their own curriculum and teaching materials. Our country has already been through those experiences.

In addition, the United States is a mobile society in which families move from one state to another. It is common to hear parents say that the schools are less or more demanding in their new state than in their former state. Their children should face the same expectations for academic achievement in any state.

The Common Core State Standards anchor education. Decisions about textbooks, professional development, and assessments can now be made in a coherent way. That is how other advanced nations operate their school systems, and it is the logical way.

The Next Generation Science Standards, a set of national standards in science, have been adopted by twelve states and the District of Columbia as of October 2014. But the controversy about the Common Core, as well as potential disputes about evolution and global climate change, may give some state decision makers cold feet about adopting the science standards. That, too, would be a step backward. Instead, the country should move forward with state adoption of the new science standards and the development of national standards for social science, arts, and other areas.

The abandonment of the Common Core would be a particular disadvantage for children from low-income families, who are currently being offered an inferior education, as the data presented earlier indicate. The Common Core may be their best prospect for receiving a more demanding curriculum.

SUFFICIENT FUNDING

Ideally, every child should have an equal chance to obtain a good education. In the United States, inequities in state and local funding of public schools stand in the way of that ideal being realized.

When confronted by these inequities, those who oppose changing current systems of finance or providing additional funds to even out the playing field often assert that there is no evidence that the amount of money spent on education results in higher student learning. That argument has gained currency with some American politicians because the United States is one of the world's top spenders in education and because student test scores have not risen as fast as spending has. These critics, however, ignore two important facts about education spending.

First, per-pupil expenditures in the United States are not equal for all students; instead, the pattern is the opposite of what it should be. Students from families of higher socioeconomic status often have more resources spent on their education than do children from low-income families.[43] Ironically, the higher-income students would probably do well in most schools, while the lower-income students desperately need extra assistance to overcome such early disadvantages as a more limited vocabulary.

Andreas Schleicher of the OECD, which monitors trends in the world's economically advanced countries, summarized the funding situation in this way: "The bottom line is that the vast majority of OECD countries either invest equally into every student or disproportionately more into disadvantaged students. The U.S. is one of the few countries doing the opposite."[44] Only Luxembourg spends more per student than the United

States. It is not just the volume of resources that matter, however, according to the OECD. It is also important to see how countries invest their resources and how well they succeed in directing the money to the areas where it can make the most difference. An OECD report concluded:

> The United States is one of only three OECD countries in which, for example, socio-economically disadvantaged schools have to cope with less favourable student-teacher ratios than socio-economically advantaged schools, which implies that students from disadvantaged backgrounds may end up with considerably lower spending per student.[45]

Second, most of the increased spending over the last several decades has gone toward the extra costs of services for children with disabilities and to school lunch programs and other indirect expenses. Only a fraction of the increases has gone toward improving regular instruction for the majority of children. The legal requirements of the IDEA have resulted in greater spending on children with disabilities, and increases in the number of poor children mean higher costs for school lunches.

Juan Diego Alonso and Richard Rothstein of the Economic Policy Institute made a similar point:

> Conventional views of the rise of education spending are exaggerated because inflation in educational services is more rapid than inflation in the economy overall. When an appropriate education price deflator is applied, elementary and secondary education school spending increases since 1967 have been substantial, but not as much as commonly believed . . . Most of the real increase in school spending has not been on increasing the resources of schools' regular academic programs. Rather, larger increases were devoted to special education, a program that consumed very few dollars in 1967. The conventional argument—that there has been a productivity collapse in elementary and secondary education because funds have increased without a corresponding improvement in academic outcomes—we concluded is flawed. It is unreasonable to

expect additional funds to produce higher academic achievement for regular students if the additional funds have been directed to students with special needs.[46]

In their studies leading to those conclusions, Alonso and Rothstein found that for a representative sample of school districts, spending in 1967 for regular education was 79.6 percent of total per-pupil spending; by 2005, it was only 55 percent. Special education increased from 3.7 percent of this total in 1967 to 21 percent in 2005. Spending on the education of English language learners went from 0.3 percent to 2.1 percent. Other increases included those for food services, alternative education, and security.[47]

Opponents of increasing school aid often point to two studies that suggest "money doesn't matter." The Coleman report of the 1960s and a paper by Eric Hanushek in the 1970s have repeatedly been cited as a research basis for opposing increases in spending on education. Both of those studies have been recently reanalyzed using more sophisticated scientific methods than were available in the past. These re-analyses have concluded that neither study contains evidence for the position that money does not matter, according to Bruce Baker of Rutgers University. Baker and other scholars contend that the earlier conclusions were based on faulty data and analysis, and that experts can now demonstrate that funding levels in general have an effect on educational achievement and that particular ways of spending funds can have a marked effect.[48]

Michael Rebell, a leader of the movement to secure fairer state funding systems, noted:

Although state defendants in many of these litigations argued that "money doesn't matter" to school quality and student achievement, 29 out of 30 state courts that have considered that proposition have rejected it, as have most of the economists and policy analysts who have considered the issue . . . Indeed, even Eric Hanushek, the economist whose work is most often cited to support the "money doesn't matter" proposition and who has testified for the state defendants in more than a dozen of the adequacy litigations, has himself agreed with the commonsense logic that "money spent wisely, logically and with accountability would be very useful indeed" (*Montoy v. State* 2003).[49]

A recently released study of the effects of the additional spending on education resulting from successful state school finance lawsuits found remarkable improvements in educational outcomes for children from low-income families. The study took a long-term perspective by reviewing the effects of lawsuits since 1971. In districts that substantially increased their spending as the result of these court actions, "low-income children were significantly more likely to graduate from high school, earn livable wages, and avoid poverty in adulthood."[50] The study found positive effects in these areas for students who had a full twelve-year education in those districts with substantially increased spending.[51]

A study by the Boston Consulting Group, based on its work in numerous school districts and states, showed a connection between higher spending and higher test scores. In analyzing state expenditures for education and a state's NAEP scores in grade four reading and grade eight mathematics, the study found a significant correlation between increased spending per pupil and student scores in grade four reading, both for low-income students and their non-low-income peers. Further, the greater the proportion of total public spending that came from state sources rather than from local property taxes, the better those students' outcomes on NAEP. The study also recommended that children in high-poverty areas needed more resources to secure an equal opportunity.[52]

Together, these findings from various studies indicate that the United States needs a fairer system of school finance, but that equal spending per student needs to be buttressed by sufficient funding to support all schools.

California's experience from several decades ago shows the danger of seeking equity in spending across districts without also ensuring that the total level of funding available for schools is adequate. In the 1970s, California equalized its spending per pupil for education after the state supreme court declared in the *Serrano* decision that the prevailing system was unconstitutional. Then, Proposition 13 was adopted in 1978 by popular referendum, thereby limiting the amount of local and state revenues that could be raised. As a result, spending was equalized—but at a low level of expenditure.[53]

To prevent that outcome, states need to ensure that an adequate amount of tax revenue is available for the schools. Recognized school finance experts could conduct "adequacy" studies in a state to determine how much is needed in the aggregate to provide a good education. These experts could also estimate a basic per-pupil expenditure for all students and supplemental payments for special needs students. Those special needs payments could be for children with disabilities, English language learners, and students in schools with concentrations of low-income families.

How revenues are raised is another important aspect of school finance. In particular, people with low incomes could be paying taxes at higher rates than more affluent persons, and still be raising less money to educate their children than wealthier citizens do. Two residents of the same state who live in different school districts can have the same tax rate, but their taxes will produce greatly varying revenues for their school districts. This is because property wealth varies greatly among districts; the same tax rate produces different amounts of revenue when real estate has different values in different districts. Fairness for taxpayers should mean that the same tax rate provides the same amount of revenue regardless of local property wealth.

The Equity Center in Austin, Texas, explained this injustice for taxpayers in a recent report:

> A wealthy district can raise far more money with a tax rate of $1.04 than a property-poor district with a tax rate of $1.17. In fact, the 80 percent of districts in the first four quintiles [in Texas] cannot raise as much money taxing their property-owners at $1.17 as the top quintile can at a $1.04 tax rate. These disparities constitute taxpayer inequity.[54]

While greater equity in spending per student should be the objective of school finance reform, it is also important to ensure that adequate funds are available for all students and that taxpayers in school districts with low real estate wealth are treated fairly.

CONCLUSION

To summarize, the essence of education is a student who is prepared to learn, a teacher who is effective at instruction, challenging academic content, and sufficient funds to pay for these other components. All four areas need improvement, based on research and analysis, if the United States is to do better in education. The next two chapters will offer recommendations for how the country can do this enormous job.

11

Federal Aid to Improve Teaching and Learning

THE LAST CHAPTER described the most important problems facing American education from the point of view of the teacher-student relationship or, to state it differently, from the perspective of improving teaching and learning in the classroom. Drawing from the research and data presented in the last chapter, this chapter and the next lay out proposals for the federal government to assist in bringing about better teaching and learning.

A RECAP

A summary of what has been learned so far will help in understanding where to go from here. This summary includes both substantive and procedural conclusions about federal involvement in education and has been drawn from the material presented up to this point.

Examination of fifty years of federal efforts to improve elementary and secondary education has shown the benefits derived from that aid, but has also shown that the academic results for students were not as great as were anticipated by the creators of those stratagems. The first reform was to use targeted assistance programs, principally Title I, to increase the academic achievement of disadvantaged children; overall that produced modest gains in academic achievement. The second reform was the use of academic standards/tests/accountability, but that did not result in a general, broad increase in student achievement.

The main reason these results were not better was summed up well by Cohen and Moffitt in their book on federal aid: Title I "sought to improve instruction without using the instruments that actually bear on instruction: teaching, teacher education, and curricula." As to standards/testing/accountability, this was an attempt at creating a system without correcting for fragmentation resulting from state and local governmental weakness. Essential factors were not addressed, such as common curricula, oversight of teacher education, and inconsistency among these elements of teaching and learning. Cohen and Moffitt's explanation for these weaknesses is rooted in the view of the federal role: "All of these and other matters related to classrooms were, of course, thought to be off limits to the central government."[1]

In other words, the substantive conclusion is that the results in academic achievement were not as much as hoped, and the reason is procedural: the approaches federal policy used were too indirect, too extenuated to have the desired effect.

The lesson is that the issues of curriculum and teacher quality are so essential to better teaching and learning that they should no longer be considered out of bounds. As explained earlier, the Department of Education is not violating the statutory provision barring federal control of education if it uses a grant program to bring about improvement in teaching and learning.

An example may help to explain this point. Chapter 7's short history of bilingual education showed that the federal government has been involved for decades in encouraging the use of one approach to learn English or another. First, from the 1960s through the 1980s, preference was given to bilingual instruction; and later, from 2001 to today, federal legislation makes it difficult for school districts to use bilingual education. These federal policies on methods of instruction were advocated at various times by political liberals and conservatives, by Democrats and Republicans. Those legislative provisions did not violate the prohibition against federal control of instruction because they were structured as conditions on the receipt of federal aid.

The obvious conclusion for anyone seeking to broadly influence the quality of education in America is to recognize that an effective way to do so is to embed policies to improve teaching and learning in a federal grant program. States would be eligible for aid if they knowingly and willingly accepted the grant with those improvements as conditions for receiving the funds.

The features of the United for Students Act (USA)—the federal grant program I propose—are influenced by the lessons presented in chapter 9 which are drawn from fifty years of federal involvement in schooling. In brief, those lessons are to concentrate on the most important issues, use strong measures to achieve the greatest success, recognize that states and localities will be carrying out the program, pay for changes, and seek broad support. As was noted in that chapter, these lessons cannot always be fully incorporated in a grant program; but they should be used as principles to guide the formation of new federal policy.

The name for this program, the United for Students Act, is meant to signify that we have learned these lessons. Improving the education of all students is an extremely important issue, and one that will entail some costs involving additional federal dollars. The federal government, the states and local school districts should work together on that task, and not be at cross-purposes. The objective is to help all students and so broad support from the public should be sought. We should take on this campaign with enthusiasm since it is so important for our children as well as for the entire country.

OVERVIEW OF THE GRANT PROGRAM

The proposed United for Students Act can be described in a nutshell. States agree to tackle many of the most serious problems in education in exchange for increased federal funding in the form of general aid for the schools. The federal government would also, over time, free up current categorical funds as states show progress in resolving these problems.

The objective is to have all three levels of government work in tandem by implementing the same policies to secure a good education for every American student. Although the situation has improved in recent years, too often in the past local school districts, states, and the federal government pursued different policies. If states agree to the policies set out here, then funds to implement these policies would come not just from the federal government but also from state and local sources. Obviously, if the three levels of government are in accord, the policies are more likely to be achieved.

Necessary Improvements

The policies I suggest for inclusion in the United for Students Act are based on the issues discussed in the last chapter. Those policies were identified by concentrating on the essence of education: a student, a teacher, material to be learned, and adequate funding. That chapter reviewed the research on those basic elements of education and identified ways to improve each element to provide American children with a greater opportunity to receive a good education.

Drawing from that review of the research and data, this new program would provide grants to states if they implement policies in these five areas:

- *Preparation for schooling.* Children should be better prepared for school by providing four-year-olds, especially those from low-income and lower-middle-income families, with a high-quality preschool education. In addition, social, health, and mentoring supports should be available to children from low-income families.
- *Improvement of teacher quality.* A comprehensive approach is necessary, including (a) recruitment of candidates for teaching who demonstrate solid academic achievement in college through such evidence as high grade point averages and who score in the

top third of those taking the ACT, SAT, or the Graduate Record Exam (tests for admission to college and graduate school) *and* who also show the attributes needed for teaching; (b) preparation in an accredited program; (c) at least a year of clinical teaching and at least a year of induction and mentoring; (d) state licensure; (e) evaluations that fairly measure teaching effectiveness; (f) salaries commensurate with teachers' responsibilities and sufficient to retain them; and (g) working conditions respectful of teachers as professionals.

- *Extra resources for difficult schools.* School districts should recruit the most effective teachers to work in schools with concentrations of students from low-income families, usually the schools with the greatest academic problems. Bonuses in pay and good working conditions will be needed to attract and retain such teachers in those schools.
- *Challenging content.* The Common Core State Standards for reading/English language arts and mathematics and the Next Generation Science Standards should be the basis for what is taught since they establish rigorous learning outcomes. Curricula and other learning materials can be derived from those standards.
- *Adequate and fair funding.* An adequate level of funding for public education, as documented by objective experts, should be provided in a state. Further, every student's education should be supported by the same per-pupil expenditure throughout the state, except for variations among different areas in the cost of living. In addition to that amount, supplements for students with special needs should be provided to school districts. In raising funds for education, a state should treat taxpayers fairly so that the same local tax effort produces the same level of revenue in every district regardless of any disparities in real estate values.

Needless to say, these policies are comprehensive and deal with very difficult issues, such as teacher assignments and tax rates. Therefore, these policies will be difficult to implement because of costs and political problems.

But it is important to start with a view of what is necessary to provide a good education to every child in America. Anything less will shortchange children and youth.

The agenda of the United for Students Act is comprehensive because teaching and learning is complex. Making education more effective will require more than one reform; it necessitates multiple improvements.

Will these demanding policies prove possible to implement?

PROGRESS TO DATE

Despite the lofty aims of each policy listed above, states and local school districts have already made progress in implementing many of these improvements. We are not standing with building plans in hand and a dream house in our mind's eye; rather, we are walking in as the carpenters are raising the walls.

Preschool Education

Considerable progress has been made in providing preschool education for four-year-olds. For years now, Republican and Democratic state governors have adopted the expansion of preschool education as a signature issue, and state programs and funding have followed. In addition, President Obama has proposed new grants to increase services and improve quality.

The recent severe economic recession caused a small drop in enrollment in state-funded prekindergarten (a major category of preschool education), but state revenues and fiscal conditions in 2014 showed renewed growth. Even better, over time the quality of these programs has improved.[2]

Some progress has also been made with increasing health services, nutrition, and summer programs to help students retain gains. The Affordable Care Act, for example, should improve the health of children from low-income families through expanded medical care. The National School Lunch and Breakfast programs are also expanding. President Obama has created a grant program, modeled on a project in Harlem, New York City, which provides comprehensive education and social services in high-poverty areas. Much more needs to be done, but the groundwork has been laid.

Teacher Quality

For years, many efforts have been made to improve teacher quality. Preparation programs for teachers, including alternative routes to gain state teaching certification, have long been hot topics. In more recent times, the evaluations of current classroom teachers have also received great attention due to the Obama initiatives. Since so much time, effort, and funding have been and are being directed at those issues, we will presumably learn much more within a few years about how to improve the effectiveness both of new teachers through better preparation programs and of current teachers through more sophisticated evaluations.

A key recommendation in this new proposal is that candidates for teaching should show evidence of high academic achievement but also demonstrate that they have the attributes needed to teach. In some people's minds that would simply mean an expansion of Teach for America (TFA), an alternative means of recruiting new teachers popular on the campuses of selective colleges and universities.

TFA has been very successful in recruiting top ranking college graduates to teach in some of the most challenging schools in America. Debates about the program center on whether the brief training that TFA recruits receive is adequate preparation to be a good teacher, whether these teachers leave the profession at a faster rate than conventionally prepared teachers, and whether it is fair to poor children that their schools be the ones where these new teachers learn how to teach.

Teach for America is answering the criticism that its recruits do not receive adequate training by expanding its preparation programs. But deliberations about recruiting more academically advanced candidates for teaching need to go beyond the merits of TFA. While the TFA approach may be one way to do it, states ought to work with local school districts to make it standard procedure to recruit from the top tier of college graduates. It does not benefit American students to have so many teachers who scored low on standardized tests and came from lower-quality colleges and universities.

Several major education organizations are working to improve the numbers of candidates for teaching who have better academic backgrounds. The Council for the Accreditation of Educator Preparation (CAEP) has revised its standards for accrediting colleges of education so that by 2016–2017 "the average grade point average of its accepted cohort of candidates meets or exceeds the CAEP minimum of 3.0, and the group average performance on nationally normed ability/achievement assessments such as ACT, SAT, or GRE is . . . 50%."[3] In subsequent years, the testing requirement increases so that by 2020, the average performance is in the top third. Presumably, this means that eventually teacher candidates on average will come from top students based on grades and standardized tests.

The USA proposal requires the accreditation of teacher preparation institutions for several reasons. One is to ensure a review of the worthiness of the preparation program. Another is that CAEP's new requirements would help to ensure an improvement in the academic skills of recruits for teaching. But the bar for entry into the profession ought to be set higher than that so that it is not an average performance of course grades and test results that is considered, but an individual requirement.

With regard to entering the profession, the Educational Testing Service (ETS) has developed "New Praxis Core Academic Skills for Educators Tests," which states could use to determine whether a candidate for teaching possesses the academic skills to be licensed in the state. According to ETS, these tests "are more rigorous and measure critical thinking and academic skills in reading, writing and mathematics."[4] Hopefully, states will not be able to set low cut-off scores on these new tests, which would undercut the intent to raise the academic skills standard for newly licensed teachers.

Another option is from the American Association of Colleges for Teacher Education and Stanford University which together have developed an exam to measure the teaching readiness of candidates for the classroom. This assessment includes performance-based measures of teaching skills, which can complement written tests of subject knowledge. It has the great strength of having been constructed by teachers and teacher educators.[5]

The suggested new policy also recommends clinical training of new or prospective teachers. Barnett Berry has noted that only a limited number of universities offer this type of training, especially if it entails extra costs to the institutions.[6] With regard to induction programs, the New Teacher Center and other organizations have made some progress with their efforts to raise awareness of the value of induction and mentoring programs for new teachers.[7] But there is a long way to go.

Raising the bar for entrance into teaching and better preparing teachers will not be sufficient to produce lasting improvement in teaching and learning. The job of a teacher itself must become better respected and more professional. The recommendations so far would help, but teachers must be better paid so that they will stay in teaching. They also need better working conditions.[8]

Over 41 percent of new teachers leave the profession within the first five years of entry.[9] To staunch that outflow of talent, states must have comprehensive approaches to recruitment, preparation, evaluation, compensation, and professional conditions for work.

In sum, progress has been made in finding ways to improve the quality of the teaching force, as with higher standards for accreditation of colleges of education, improved tests for state licensure, evidence of the effectiveness of clinical experiences, and induction programs. But continued and greater efforts are essential, including states adopting and implementing comprehensive teacher quality plans.

Difficult Schools

In the most challenging elementary and secondary schools, improving the quality of teaching has been a topic of conversation for decades, and the debate has intensified with the attention NCLB has brought to the lowest performing schools. Unfortunately, no long-term solutions have emerged, mostly because school districts traditionally do not assign the most effective teachers to those schools. Teacher union contracts have been an impediment to such assignments, but even if this obstacle is worked out, teachers always have the option of leaving one school district and going to another if they do not like their school assignment in the first district. Or they can vote with their feet and leave the profession entirely, as so many do in the first five years of their teaching career.

Bonuses to attract teachers to challenging schools have not always worked, perhaps because they have not been large enough to make a difference. A recent experiment in Tennessee, however, has shown success with a $5,000 bonus to retain effective teachers. Peabody College researchers found "some preliminary evidence of a causal link between the bonus offer and retention of high quality teachers." Interestingly, the more disadvantaged schools showed greater success than others.[10]

Curriculum

As for the content to be taught, many states are well on their way to using the Common Core State Standards as the basis for developing curricula in reading/English language arts and mathematics. Several states have also adopted the Next Generation Science Standards. Implementation of the Common Core is proving challenging and will take longer than first anticipated, but that policy is far advanced. The serious problem is the opposition of the political right and how it has spurred many Republican politicians to wilt in their support of the standards.

Funding of Schools

Progress has also been made in school finance. Since the U.S. Supreme Court in 1973 turned over this responsibility exclusively to the states, most states have been sued, and the plaintiffs have usually prevailed. At first, the lawsuits were based on inequities in funding among students as condoned by states; later, the basis for the suits shifted to allegations about inadequate educational opportunities being provided to students despite state constitutional guarantees. Regardless of the legal grounds, once victory was gained, the implementation of those decisions proved difficult to secure. In New Jersey, the plaintiffs had to repeatedly return to the state supreme court because the state legislature refused to fully carry out the court's decree. In New York, after a resounding victory in the state's highest court, funding was increased for the first two years; but then progress was stymied by the economic recession.

Within the last decade, Ontario, which has the largest student enroll-ment of any Canadian province, comprehensively reformed its schools. A key element was removing from local school boards the ability to levy lo-cal property taxes. As in the United States, this reliance on property tax had led to great inequities in funding—with per-pupil spending varying from $4,723 to $9,148—because some districts had greater property wealth than others.[11] Under conservative political leadership at the time, Ontario moved to provincial-level funding, meaning that there is no longer a rela-tionship between spending per student and local property wealth per stu-dent. If Ontario can do it, why can't Illinois?

Illinois was cited earlier for the sharp difference in availability of re-sources in poor Cicero and wealthy Winnetka. In July 2014, the Illinois senate approved a school finance bill that would bring greater equity to funding the state's schools. So there is some progress in Illinois.[12]

That state is modeling its school finance reforms on what California has done—changed its system to a uniform payment for every child de-pending on grade, additional payments for children with high needs, and higher payments to districts with heavy concentrations of such children.[13] That approach is akin to the recommendations in this proposal.

Summary

Policies to promote improvements in teaching and learning are being im-plemented in states and school districts, or are at least being recognized as necessary. Some policies are further along in implementation than others. Preschool education has seen real progress, and the implementation of rig-orous new standards for reading, mathematics, and science is well under way in American classrooms—despite some political opposition. Favorable court decisions have led to advancements in school finance. Less progress has been made in recruiting high-scoring college students into teaching and getting the most effective teachers into the most challenging schools.

The news is therefore both good and bad. None of these polices for improvement is foreign to states and local districts. The five policy areas need a further push, and some states need that encouragement more than others. Assistance from the federal government would move things along.

THE DETAILS

If the basic concept of encouraging states to undertake difficult but crucial reforms in exchange for more and unrestricted federal aid is accepted by national policy makers, the United for Students program could be constructed in many different ways. The following discussion suggests one way to do it.

First, should a state have a choice about whether to participate? Since the policies will be difficult to implement, a state should be able to choose to apply for the United for Students grant or not. If a state opts out of participating, its current situation would be frozen. In other words, the state would receive only the amount of categorical aid that it does now and would administer Title I and other programs as is done now. The state would also be bound by NCLB requirements, whether modified by a waiver it has received from the Department of Education or without such a waiver.

Second, what would a state promise to do if it applied for a United for Students grant? If a state chose to participate, then it would agree in writing to fully implement within ten years the policies laid out above. The state would submit a description of its current status in each of those five areas, as well as a plan for each area describing the degree to which each policy would be implemented each year for the next ten years. This progress should be continuous, and not expected in a burst near the end of the decade; that was one lesson learned through experiences with adequate yearly progress under NCLB. The state would also agree to provide information to the Department of Education to enable the secretary to monitor its progress each year.

Third, what responsibility would the Secretary of Education have? The secretary would review the state's application for approval, but he or she would not have the right to require any state to adopt a particular way of implementing the five policies. The secretary would, however, be authorized to define terms, such as a "high-quality" preschool education, and to approve a list of experts whom a state would use to determine adequate funding.

With the aid of an expert organization such as the Government Accountability Office, the National Research Council, or the National Academy of Education, the secretary would develop for each state means of measuring its annual progress in implementing the policies, and would seek agreement with the state on these measures. For instance, an annual teacher survey could be administered to determine whether working conditions have improved. Using these indices or measures, the secretary would monitor each state's annual progress.

Fourth, how much federal funding would a state receive? The state would receive a substantial payment of new, unrestricted funds to undertake these challenging reforms, and then it would receive large general aid payments as it showed progress. Both the initial and the later payments would be continuing federal general aid supports for the schools.

To be precise, once a state's application was approved, the federal government would give that state a grant equal to 20 percent of the federal aid for elementary and secondary education within the state. The current federal categorical aid programs would continue in that state until the fifth year. In that year, if the Secretary of Education determines that the state has fulfilled its responsibilities and is halfway to achieving the five policies, then half of the funds in the categorical programs would be given to the state as general aid. In other words, the federal categorical programs would shrink by half. In addition, the secretary could also eliminate some of the NCLB requirements that bind the state. The state would also be given an unrestricted grant equal to 40 percent of its federal funds, as an ongoing annual grant. On the other hand, if a state has only shown some progress, then the secretary could prorate the amount of categorical aid that is converted into general aid, and the state would not receive any new unrestricted funding.

At the end of the decade, the secretary would determine whether the state has fully implemented these policies. If so, then the state would receive as general aid the remaining amount in the federal categorical programs, and those programs would no longer operate in that state. At that point, no NCLB provisions would apply to the state. From that point forward, the state would also receive an additional unrestricted United for Students grant equal to 40 percent of its federal funds.

This process is intended to achieve these policies while respecting the role of the states. States have a choice whether or not to participate in the United for Students program. Those that do participate would receive extra federal funds in an unrestricted way. States implementing the policies would be relieved from NCLB requirements and from categorical programs. The federal government would provide substantial aid. The state's entire education system would be improved so that all parents would see a better education for their children.

If most states participate, then the federal government achieves reform goals that have a real impact on improving teaching and learning. It would cost the federal government more money, but that is only fair if the states undertake really hard work to create fairer systems of school finance and assign the most effective teachers to challenging schools. Also, the federal categorical programs and NCLB would be phased out gradually to hedge bets that states will succeed in implementing these policies.

The lessons learned over fifty years of federal involvement have obviously affected the formation of this proposal. Only the most important goals have been identified, strong action by the states is expected to address those issues, deference is given to states to choose the methods while federal-state agreement is sought on the means to measure progress, substantial federal funds are committed to deal with these important issues, and the entire process is open to the public to secure support for the enterprise.

COSTS

The federal government's special commitment in this arrangement is to provide additional funds to the states to solve these difficult problems. To illustrate the amounts of money involved, I will use the current appropriations for the elementary and secondary education programs in the Department of Education.

The initial federal costs of the United for Students program would be the first year's payment of an additional 20 percent of a state's federal elementary and secondary education funding. In fiscal year 2014, Title I, IDEA, and other categorical grants totaled about $35 billion for all states. If all states chose to participate—an unlikely situation—the extra funding would be about $7 billion.

If another 40 percent were awarded to all states in the fifth year, the cost would be another $14 billion. At the end of the decade, the final 40 percent payment to all states would amount to an additional $14 billion.

Therefore, the total costs if all states participated and fully carried out the policies would be an additional $35 billion, in current dollars, over the present level of support, with all of the aid after the ten-year mark being in the form of general rather than categorical aid. The federal contribution to public elementary and secondary education would thus be doubled, from $35 billion to $70 billion, representing an increase from 10 percent of the total costs to 20 percent.

Where would the federal government find the extra federal funds for the new $35 billion? One possibility would be a faster wind-down of the war in Afghanistan. That war and the Iraqi war have cost the United States $6 trillion, according to a study done by the Kennedy School at Harvard University. The interest alone on the debt assumed to pay for those costs is $260 billion as of early 2014.[14] If the Afghan war were to finish earlier, less money would be spent on war and more could be spent on education.

Another possibility is to look for the funds in other parts of the Department of Defense budget. For instance, the initial payment of $7 billion to all the states to participate in implementing all these reforms could be found by eliminating just one war plane. Each F-35 Joint Strike Fighter costs $7 billion, according to the National Priorities Organization.[15] In subsequent years, the fifth year payment of $14 billion could come from axing two planes. For the tenth year payment, two more would go on the chopping block.

Since these payments to the states are meant to be annual, ongoing support for state reforms, the remainder of the funding could come from eliminating waste and fraud in the Department of Defense, the Department of Homeland Security, and the National Security Agency. Those agencies have had huge increases in their budgets since 9/11. In those vast sums of money, there are bound to be items that are wasteful, and perhaps there is even some fraud in contracting.

Another possible source of funding is a federal tax on new supplies of energy produced by improved methods of obtaining sources for fuel. A tax on fracking, a means of extracting increased amounts of oil and gas from rock formations, could produce the needed revenue. Since March 2008, oil production has increased 58 percent in the United States, and natural gas output has risen 21 percent, according to federal and international agency statistics cited in the *Wall Street Journal*. These developments have made the United States the world's largest producer of both fuels.[16] Why can't we have two national goals: to be energy independent, and to have better-educated children? We would be investing for the future if we educated our children better while we enjoyed this increase in supplies of energy.

In 2009, the Congress passed the ARRA during the economic recession, which doubled the funding for the major categorical programs, provided the states with nearly another $100 billion of general aid to schools, and gave the Secretary of Education more than another $5 billion for Race to the Top and other programs. While that legislation provided those funds over two to three years, it does demonstrate that increased funding is possible, if the political will is there.

In sum, squeezing out waste and abuse, eliminating some weapons, and/or raising some taxes on new supplies of energy would provide the funds to bring about comprehensive reform in America's public schools. The only question is whether the nation's political leaders share the determination to do this. They certainly remind us repeatedly about how important education is; now the issue is, will they do something about it?

SCHOOL FINANCE

If the proposed United for Students Act were passed, it would lead to the implementation of a multiplicity of reforms that will improve teaching and learning, but it will also have benefits for how public schooling is funded in the United States. If adopted by the president and Congress, this new federal role in education would diversify the funding base for public education in the country.

The federal government now provides about 10 percent of the country's total costs of elementary and secondary education. This proposal would increase that amount to 20 percent. The federal government has the fiscal capacity to make this increased contribution because it has broad taxing powers and a national taxing base.

Local school districts and state governments currently provide the remaining 90 percent of funding. School districts rely on local property taxes for almost all of their contributions, and state governments receive their revenues from income taxes, sales taxes, and other sources. The states vary in how much they rely on each of those sources. For example, Florida is dependent on sales tax revenue since it does not have a state income tax.

In an economic recession, state sales tax and income tax receipts fall, leading to lower state revenue. Since states must balance their budgets every year regardless of any such decline in revenues, funding for public education is at risk whenever there is an economic downturn. In 2009–2010, states had plans to cut back sharply on funding for education and other areas because of the major recession of those years. The ARRA saved many jobs and buffered the schools from a severe jolt.

The revenue that local school districts receive from real property taxation is more stable than state revenues. But in an economic downturn, school districts also run the risk that property tax revenue will shrink if property values decline or if property is abandoned. That threat to school funding was also softened by the $100 billion paid to the states for support of education by the ARRA.

If the federal government were to provide a larger share of the costs of education, this would bring permanent, greater stability to school funding to protect teachers' jobs and other essential elements of education. That was what the ARRA did for a few years.

In the United for Students Act, some provision would be included to ensure that states maintained their own tax efforts in support of education so that the increased federal funds would in fact be additional to, and not in lieu of, current state and local funding. In ESEA and other federal laws now in effect, "maintenance of effort" provisions assure this result while providing some flexibility for unusual circumstances.

IDEA and Categorical Aid

What would happen to IDEA under the United for Students Act? That law would remain in effect with its IEPs, due process procedures, and similar provisions. The funding for IDEA, however, would be affected by this new proposal. If a state has achieved half of its goals after five years, then half of the state grant available under IDEA would be folded into the general aid grant to that state. At the end of a decade, if the state has fully achieved its goals, then the full amount of the state grant would be converted into general aid for the state. The state funding formula adopted as part of the United for Students Act would require supplemental payments to school districts for students with special needs, such as children with disabilities. Therefore, there would be no decrease in funding for the education of children with disabilities.

Nearly all other categorical elementary and secondary education programs in the Department of Education would be repealed, but IDEA is unique. While a grant program, many consider it a necessary civil rights statute for students with disabilities, and as such it would remain.

With regard to the larger issue of whether it is wise to repeal most categorical programs, proponents of targeted aid for categories of students may argue that this approach could produce higher student achievement if given the additional sums promised to states by the United for Students Act. The weakness of that argument is that categorical aid, including Title I schoolwide programs, would still be encumbered by inequities in state funding of schools and in local practices that assign more inexperienced and out-of-field teachers to schools with concentrations of children from low-income families.

Let's say that the law was amended so that states had to correct those inequities to receive the categorical aid. This would mean that states would have to make demanding reforms, but the additional federal funds they receive would be tied to providing services in those categorical programs and unavailable to help pay for undertaking those reforms. Therefore, it is unlikely that this approach would work.

CONCLUSION

The proposed United for Students Act would take from the original creators of federal aid the concept of federal funds as general assistance for the support of the public schools. It would take from the creators of the accountability reform the idea that something besides money is needed to increase student academic achievement. This new program also takes guidance from research about the areas that should be the focus of federal policy.

This chapter calls for politicians to undertake uncomfortable tasks, such as shifting or raising revenues. It also calls on candidates for teaching to become better educated. It calls on current teachers to consider working in schools where it is difficult to teach.

Two truths about American education must be faced. Students need to increase their academic achievement, and students from low-income families often attend schools that do not offer them an equal educational opportunity. These problems exist because we have created our educational system that way. We can provide every child with a good education only if we have the courage to undo inequities and raise standards for all students. There is no easy way.

12

Constitutional and Legal Guarantees
of a Good Education

THE LAST CHAPTER proposed to provide grants to the states from the federal government to improve teaching and learning every school day in every classroom of the country's elementary and secondary schools. This chapter proposes to improve education through constitutional and legal means. If American schools are to become better, both funding and legal strategies are needed.

WHY CONSTITUTIONAL AND LEGAL STRATEGIES?

When the federal government takes action on behalf of all citizens, these actions should focus on the most important issues facing the country. The need to improve the public schools has become such an issue.

In 2002, during his weekly radio address following passage of the No Child Left Behind Act, President George W. Bush declared that "education is the great civil rights issue of our time."[1]

At the National Action Network gala in April 2011, President Barack Obama echoed that sentiment: "The best possible education is the single most important factor in determining whether [our children] succeed. But it's also what will determine whether we succeed. It's the key to opportunity. It is the civil rights issue of our time."[2]

Buttressing that view about the opportunity to secure a good education for all were the comments of Secretary of Education Arne Duncan at Howard University on July 15, 2014, commemorating the fiftieth anniversary of the Civil Rights Act. "Education, I'm convinced, is the civil rights issue of our generation," said the Secretary. "If you can ride at the front of the bus, if you can drink from the same water fountain, but you cannot read, you're not truly free."[3]

These presidential and secretarial assertions emphasize how crucial it is today for children to receive a good education. These statements are also a reminder that the battles of the 1950s, 1960s, and 1970s to secure basic civil rights for African Americans and other racial and ethnic minority groups involved the use of multiple strategies, including seeking U.S. Supreme Court decisions, congressional approval of civil rights legislation, and creation of federal grant programs.

If attaining a good education is as important as Bush, Obama, and Duncan have said, then that objective cannot be left solely to the state grant program described in the last chapter. Other ways ought to be used to broadly achieve this policy, similar to the means used to secure civil rights for all Americans in the last century.

THE BENEFITS OF A SUPREME COURT DECISION

In chapter 9, Supreme Court and other federal court decisions were identified as among the most forceful means the federal government has available to set policy in education. Obviously, issues involving education can be brought to the federal courts because the Supreme Court and lower federal courts have ruled in education cases. Previous chapters discussed several of those decisions.

The Supreme Court cases mentioned earlier in this book—*Brown v. Board of Education, Lau v. Nichols, San Antonio Independent School District v. Rodriguez,* and *Grove City v. Bell*—show that access to the federal courts has long been available to citizens seeking redress on education issues. That access is limited, however. Citizens can file lawsuits if they assert claims grounded in such constitutional provisions as the Fourteenth Amendment dealing with civil rights, or the "spending clause" allowing conditions to be placed on state and local receipt of federal aid.

The Tenth Amendment is pertinent to this discussion because some people believe this part of the Constitution is an absolute barrier to federal involvement in education. However, that amendment, which reserves respectively to the states and the people all power not delegated to the federal government by the Constitution nor prohibited by it to the states, has *not* been interpreted by the federal courts as being an obstacle to the federal government's involvement in education. Other provisions of the Constitution, such as the spending clause and the Fourteenth Amendment, have been cited by judges as the basis for federal action in education.

Although the Tenth Amendment is not a barrier to federal activity, the current constitutional grounds are limited. Education should have a firmer constitutional basis than it has at present. To secure that objective, we need to establish the constitutional right to a good education. I will explain how to do this shortly, but first let us discuss the reasons for taking this action.

To begin with, a constitutional right would enable parents and students to sue in federal court to enforce that right. In other words, the doors of the federal courts would be more open to lawsuits to remove impediments to a good education.

As noted earlier, court decisions are among the most forceful ways of implementing a federal policy. The Supreme Court decision in *Lau v. Nichols* provided additional educational services to children with limited English language proficiency. Several lower federal court decisions preceded congressional approval of IDEA, which revolutionized the education of children with disabilities.

Why shouldn't the students in Cicero, Illinois, have the right to sue in federal court because the state of Illinois has created a system in which their overwhelmingly poor district has $10,000 less per student spent on their education than in Winnetka, a district with almost no poverty?

Second, if education were a right under the Constitution it would be easier to address issues across state boundaries. For instance, the difference in spending per child can be as substantial between states as it is among school districts within states. A national effort to have fair funding of education throughout the country would benefit millions of students attending school in states with limited ability to finance education. Remember, as noted in chapter 1, that was a reason that Senator Taft gave for changing his mind on federal aid, and that led him to support its passage. Another example is that teachers who move from one state to another usually cannot transfer their retirement savings from the first state to the second, or combine their payments from both states to create one account. A state usually only pays for a teacher's time spent in the classrooms of that state. An interstate retirement system would give greater mobility to teachers.

Third, the battle to secure the right to a good education would occasion a full and open national debate about the importance of education and the obstacles standing in the way of securing a good education for all children.

Finally, the symbolic value of recognizing education as meriting constitutional protection would be worthwhile in itself. The federal, state, and local governments would have to direct more attention to providing a good education for all children, if for no other reason than they might eventually be sued in federal court for not doing so. Education would be taken more seriously than it is now.

IMPEDIMENTS TO A SUPREME COURT DECISION

How would this reversal be achieved? A lawsuit must be filed to overturn the 1973 Supreme Court decision in *San Antonio Independent School District v. Rodriguez,* which held that education was not a protected interest under the Constitution.[4] This decision is an obstacle that can and should be removed.

Of course, it is serious business to ask the Supreme Court to reverse itself, but that is what happened on the issue of busing for desegregation, as described in chapter 8. Similarly, with Title IX, Congress in effect overturned the Court's *Grove City v. Bell* ruling by passing a law with a clearer intent than the Court had read in the original act.

In *Rodriguez*, the plaintiffs were poor families in a school district with a low real estate tax base. They sued the state of Texas, claiming that the state's reliance on local property taxation favored more affluent students attending school districts with greater property wealth, to the disadvantage of poorer families in districts with lower property values.

The equal protection clause of the Fourteenth Amendment, which forbids a state from invidiously discriminating against its citizens, was the legal basis for the suit. To invoke that clause, the interest involved must be a fundamental right protected under the Constitution, or the group must be a "suspect" class, which has been defined as a group that has historically been subject to discrimination. If either of those conditions is met, then strict scrutiny is given to the state's action. Strict scrutiny is a high standard for a state to meet. It requires the state to demonstrate that the legislature passed the law to further a "compelling governmental interest," and that the law is "narrowly tailored" to achieve that interest. If no fundamental right or suspect class is involved, then the standard is merely that the state's action must either be rational or subject to a somewhat more demanding standard of "intermediate scrutiny."

In *Rodriguez*, the Supreme Court found that education is not a fundamental right, and that there was no suspect class. Proceeding then to apply the rational standard, the Court determined that Texas's decision to rely partially on local property taxation was constitutional.

Education was not found to be a fundamental right because the U.S. Constitution does not mention education, according to the Court. There was no suspect class because poor people lived in many school districts and were not concentrated only in property-poor districts. Furthermore, the Court said, the plaintiffs were not completely without schooling because Texas provided an adequate education.

Rodriguez was a very discouraging court decision. At the time of the decision, I was working with members of the House to prepare for a conference committee with the Senate to iron out the differences between the House- and Senate-approved versions of major amendments to the

Elementary and Secondary Education Act. Senator Ralph Yarborough (D-TX) had moved through the Senate a major aid bill to give the states assistance to equalize funding among their school districts.

The Yarborough Senate bill found "a federal responsibility to assist states in equalizing educational opportunity so that a child may be able to obtain an appropriate education regardless of his place of residence within the state."[5] Under the proposed bill, a state could receive a grant if the quality of education among school districts within that state was not the result of the wealth of the school districts. In other words, federal funds would be available if a state supplemented with additional state revenue the lesser sums raised in property-poor school districts so that their children would have comparable sums spent on their education as the children who lived in property-rich school districts. Thus, the federal grants would reward a state for having equalized spending for education among its school districts. But, states would also be expected to go beyond simple equal spending and to provide greater amounts for students with greater educational needs and in school districts with greater costs. This legislation had obviously been inspired by the *Rodriguez* litigation that originated in Yarborough's state.

Momentum was building behind the Yarborough bill as the conference was organizing. Congressman Perkins, the House committee chair and the key voice in the conference for the House side, had declared his enthusiastic support for the proposal. But in *Rodriguez* the Court went against the plaintiffs and upheld the state's system of finance. That action took the wind out of the sails of the bill's supporters, thereby sinking the legislation. If the case had gone in the other direction, the United States today would have a fairer system of funding of public education. Unfortunately, the problem is still with us.

Analysis of *Rodriguez*

For purposes of this discussion, the interesting parts of the decision are those that laid out the specific reasons for ruling against the plaintiffs. These reasons may no longer be relevant, which gives hope that a return to the Supreme Court might result in a different ruling.

In asserting that education was a protected interest, the plaintiffs had said that education was necessary for the exercise of rights guaranteed by the Constitution. In deciding against an implicit inclusion of education in the Constitution, the Court said that it had "no indication that the present levels of educational expenditures in Texas provide an education that falls short" of enabling people to exercise the constitutional rights of free speech and voting.[6] The Court, moreover, expressed doubt about ruling against the state because the Court lacked "specialized knowledge and experience" in matters of education or taxation that states possessed.[7]

Rodriguez forced plaintiffs seeking to sue states for inequitable school financing to go to state courts and to rely on provisions of state constitutions. That recourse to state courts is precisely what occurred. Within the last thirty-five years, forty-five states have been sued, and the plaintiffs have won in 60 percent of the cases. Since the late 1980s when the plaintiffs' arguments shifted from unequal funding to inadequate financing, 70 percent of the plaintiffs have prevailed.[8] It has been a struggle, however, to get the state legislatures and the governors to comply fully with these court decisions. In many states, the changes in funding have been much less ambitious than the advocates had anticipated with the court decisions.

A reversal of *Rodriguez* would help in the area of school finance, and it would also help to address broader problems in education, such as the need to improve teacher quality. It would give advocates for improvement a powerful tool.

Michael Rebell of Columbia University's Teachers College, who has been a leader in this state litigation movement, sees an opportunity for a reconsideration of *Rodriguez*. His hopes center on the Court's comments in the decision about two points—first, that the plaintiffs did not prove that an inadequate education resulted from financial inequities, and second, that the adequacy of education was a complex subject requiring specialized knowledge that the Court lacked but the state possessed. Rebell believes there are answers today to those concerns that may not have existed in 1973. So the door may be open for education to be considered a fundamental right and therefore to have the protection of the Fourteenth Amendment if the earlier ruling's concerns can be addressed.

With regard to the first point— that the plaintiffs did not present evidence to the Court showing that students were not receiving a good education as a result of the unequal funding system—Rebell draws on his work in leading the successful challenge to New York State's system of school finance. That lawsuit relied heavily on evidence that citizens were not being educated adequately to be informed voters or good jurors in the courtroom. Those facts, which were so persuasive in New York, would counter the Supreme Court's assertion in *Rodriguez* that Texas was supporting an adequate educational system and therefore education did not have to be recognized implicitly as a fundamental constitutional right in order to equip citizens to exercise their rights of voting and free speech.

With regard to the second point—that the Court did not believe it had the specialized knowledge to deal with the issue of the adequacy of education—Rebell's answer is that four decades of state court decisions on school finance systems have provided the material that the Supreme Court needs to make an informed decision about whether a program of education equips students with the necessary skills to be informed citizens. He summarizes the decisions from the state courts in this way: "The courts have tended to insist that states provide students an education that will equip them to obtain a decent job in our increasingly complex society and to carry out effectively their responsibilities as citizens in a modern democratic polity."[9]

Several additional points made by the dissenters in *Rodriguez* should be considered by plaintiffs preparing to ask the Court to reconsider the decision. As noted above, when there is no fundamental right or suspect class, the Court still applies a legal standard called "rational basis" to determine if the state's actions are constitutional. At a minimum, a statutory classification must be rationally related to a legitimate state interest. Texas asserted that the purpose of its system of school funding was to encourage "local initiative and local choice."[10]

While the majority of Supreme Court justices found that the taxing scheme was related to Texas's stated interest, the dissenting justices disagreed. The dissent pointed out that because of the low property tax value of the plaintiffs' school district, even if the district taxed at a much higher rate than the wealthier school districts, it could not attain a similar per-pupil funding. Texas's statutory scheme was not rational in producing such results.

This inequity in taxation in Texas has been laid bare in other states by cases challenging school financing systems on state constitutional grounds, as mentioned above. Over the last forty years, numerous state court cases have demonstrated that state funding schemes are not related to the state interest of an adequate education. Consequently, even if education is not deemed a fundamental right, states have no rational basis, given the history of state funding cases, for establishing these inequitable funding schemes.

Ten years after the *Rodriguez* decision, the Supreme Court heard another school case out of Texas. In *Plyler v. Doe*,[11] the Court struck down a Texas statute that withheld state funds for the education of undocumented children. While many argue that being subject to either the rational basis or the intermediate scrutiny standard, instead of the higher strict scrutiny standard, provides such deference to the state that it is often the death of a lawsuit, that reasoning did not hold in *Plyler*. There, the Court found that there was no basis for the law to create a difference, a classification, between documented and undocumented students. The Court stated that the Texas law "imposes its discriminatory burden on the basis of a legal characteristic over which children can have little control."[12] Similarly today, children have no control over where they live—however, this "birth lottery" perpetuates inequities in the education many children receive and leads to limiting their opportunities in life.[13]

Considering the Court's reasoning in *Rodriguez* and the decision in *Plyler*, it would be wise to prepare a case to bring to the Supreme Court involving the issue of whether education is a fundamental right under the Constitution. The door is open, and plaintiffs whose education has been lessened due to state action ought to sue. Advocates for a better education for all should show the same boldness as those in the past who were supporters of other causes and fought Supreme Court decisions that stood in their way.

A New Case

Rebell argues for revisiting *Rodriguez* on behalf of children from low-income families. The remedy he would seek would be to intensify school improvement for these children but also to provide these children with comprehensive services to overcome the disadvantages of low socioeconomic status. He makes a persuasive case that this is how the country must improve the condition of poor children, who make up 22 percent of the young population.

Another approach could be to file a case on behalf of children from lower-middle-income families who do not have the benefits of a high-quality preschool education. The poor have subsidized preschool, and the rich pay for their own preschool for their children. But parents in the middle-income range are losing out.

As the experiences with IDEA and Title IX illustrate, broad support from different sectors of society can enable a policy to withstand criticisms, such as burdensome administrative practices and inadequate funding with IDEA, and the opposition of some college athletic departments with Title IX. Any effort to reverse the Supreme Court's ruling that education is not a protected right under the Constitution should seek the benefits of this right for many children, if such a case can be made in a particular set of circumstances.

These facts support a strategy of returning to the Supreme Court for a decision that would recognize education as a fundamental right under the Constitution. I realize that critics will say it is unrealistic at this time to expect the Supreme Court to reverse itself on that issue. Critics might point out that the majority of justices on the Court are politically conservative and may oppose expanding individual rights to a good education. The justices may also have concerns about expanding federal involvement in education at a time when the current federal role in education is under attack for NCLB, any connection to the Common Core Standards, and Obama's Race to the Top program.

If the campaign to overturn *Rodriguez* fails, then, action should be taken on the next item, seeking a constitutional amendment.

PURSUING A CONSTITUTIONAL AMENDMENT

If the Supreme Court refuses to recognize education as a fundamental right, then an amendment ought to be prepared which states that the opportunity for a good education is every person's right under the Constitution. This amendment should draw on the wording of the state constitutions that have similar provisions for public schooling. Another source of expertise for properly phrasing this right are the plaintiffs and their attorneys who have sued the states to improve systems of school finance.

This proposed amendment to the Constitution could acknowledge that school districts and charter school authorities have daily responsibility for the public schools and that the states have general authority to maintain public schools. The federal government, though, should assist in securing a good education for every child. It could also emphasize that the importance of having a good education has grown over time. Therefore, recognizing the right to a good education for every child would ensure that students are prepared for further learning and training, employment, citizenship, and responsible membership in society.

A draft amendment should be submitted to the Congress for consideration and circulated among organizations for discussion and endorsement. A national debate about the merits of education and ways to improve it would be a healthy beginning of a movement to advocate for a change to the Constitution.

The congressional debate should center on the most serious problems in education—namely, expanding high-quality preschool, improving teacher quality, teaching a rigorous curriculum, and providing adequate funding. Those issues should also form the basis for a national campaign to gain popular support for the amendment.

The congressional sponsors should round up cosponsors and try to move legislation to create this amendment through the Congress. Then it must be submitted to the states for approval. It is a long route, and many past proposed amendments have not been approved.

I know that some will consider this attempt to amend the Constitution quixotic. But change does not happen unless people take risks and stimulate discussion. Change may not come directly from the adoption of this amendment but rather may come from the associated debate and controversies because they will help to raise popular awareness of the problems.

PUSHING FOR LEGISLATION

In the 1960s and 1970s, the organizations working for the rights of women tried to get the Equal Rights Amendment to the Constitution approved. They succeeded in gaining congressional approval, but fell short of getting three-fourths of the states to vote for that amendment. So they switched their strategy. Title IX was part of the new strategy to gain equality for girls and women. It only affected institutions or activities that received federal education grants and aid, but it had a broad impact. The same strategic flexibility may be needed to ensure that children and young people are provided with a good education.

If the Supreme Court does not rule the right way, and if a constitutional amendment is not approved, then a new law could be the third action item, the fallback position. Members of Congress could introduce legislation that would authorize the U.S. Attorney General to bring suit against states or school districts that show a pattern of not providing a good education. This would allow the federal government to go to court to protect the rights of students who are receiving an inadequate education. As history has shown, it often takes government intervention to vindicate the rights of the oppressed, and such a statute would provide that basis. This law would be modeled on Title VI of the Civil Rights Act, which bars discrimination on the basis of race in any program or activity receiving federal financial assistance.

This statute would apply to any state or school district receiving federal aid. It would state that every child should have the opportunity to be prepared for education, have an effective teacher, learn from a rigorous curriculum, and attend a school with sufficient funding to pay for this. The Attorney General would be authorized to bring suit against states and school districts that demonstrate a pattern of inadequate education. In other words, if a state or local school district did not provide those four elements, it could be sued for violating the statute. Such a bill would not authorize lawsuits by individuals to enforce this right, but citizens could submit petitions to the Attorney General asking for legal action.

The advocates for these constitutional and legal protections should consider seeking this statute at the same time they pursue a constitutional amendment. If the statute were to be enacted, with or without a constitutional amendment, it would give the federal government a useful tool to seek improvement in education. The success of the Civil Rights Act of 1964 is an example of what can be done with such authority from a law.

A COORDINATED CAMPAIGN

Both a constitutional or legal right to a good education and a revision of current federal aid to education (described in the last chapter) should be pursued at the same time. If a law revising federal aid is enacted and the debate is still continuing over the lengthier process of seeking a Supreme Court decision or constitutional amendment, the looming possibility of a court decision or amendment may encourage the states to move faster on the changes incorporated in a revised federal aid law. Progress may be made one way or another.

CONCLUSION

A national campaign to improve public education in the United States should employ a variety of strategies to achieve that objective, including grant programs, constitutional guarantees, statutory protections, and other means.

African Americans used those tools in their fight for equality, and they have made great progress, but their battle is not completely won. It would no doubt be the same with securing a constitutional right to a good education. It would still be a battle to achieve gains, but using all means available to the federal government would certainly help.

Conclusion

FROM THE HAPPY DAYS OF 1965, when ESEA held the promise of greatly improving American education, to the present contentious times, when both the political right and left are challenging the Common Core State Standards, this book has taken us on a long journey. At times, the reader must have felt that because of all the fighting and controversy we would never arrive at the destination of knowing how the federal government can work to produce better schools.

We have now reached the point where we can recommend some ways to accomplish that goal, although I am fully aware that these ideas will not be accepted by all. In fact, these recommendations for a different and broadened federal role in education go against the political temper of the times. Because of attacks from the Tea Party, Republican state governors are running away from the national academic standards that they helped write. Liberals are attacking the federal government's emphasis on tests and raising doubts about the left's traditional support for federal aid to education.

Despite the political tenor of the times, one must state the truth as one sees it. Fifty years of federal involvement in education demonstrate, to my mind, that a strong federal role is essential to attaining the best schools for most students. There will be missteps, such as there were with NCLB, and there may be overregulation as in the late 1970s. But overall, only the federal government can bring the national spotlight, the financial resources, and the leadership needed to help states and local districts to improve public schools.

The United States has a strong tradition of local control and state authority over the public schools. History has shown, however, that 14,000 school districts on their own cannot raise the quality of all schools because they vary so much in fiscal capacity and focus so intently on the daily operations of the schools. The states have potential to play a big role, but governors and legislatures weaken state governments through keeping wages for employees unappealing and setting strict limits on the number of state jobs.

The federal government must be involved. A revised federal role should have two aspects: a constitutional or legal right to a good education, and a state-federal program to improve classroom teaching and learning. Both are needed to move the nation.

Many might say that these ideas are too idealistic, that the plan I have outlined cannot be carried out. That could be true today—but not necessarily tomorrow.

My purpose has been to propose a fresh start in thinking about the federal government's role in education. First, though, it was necessary to trace the origins and evolution of the federal role in education. Then, it was important to document the results of federal programs. The next stage was to put aside for a moment issues about the current federal role and understand the major problems in American education. Once those problems were identified, thought could finally be given to how the federal role should be revised to deal directly with them.

It has been a long journey, but I hope that an understanding now exists that real change should occur in the federal role in education. What I hope does *not* happen is that Congress makes a few minor changes in the current federal laws and thinks that it has done its job. That won't do.

If this book has identified the right issues for a common federal-state campaign of school improvement, then organizations and groups should push to implement these solutions. It may take several years or longer. Remember Senator Taft was involved in debating federal aid to education in the mid-1940s, and it did not come about until the mid-1960s.

An example of long-term thinking comes from school choice advocates. In the 1950s, Milton Friedman argued for tuition vouchers for private schools, but it was not until 1990 that the first program was put in place in Milwaukee. Although there still are only a limited number of voucher programs, they are becoming more commonplace. Voucher advocates have followed a strategy of refining their arguments, persisting in making them, and waiting for the right political moment to pass laws permitting them. A recent example of that strategy's success can be found in Indiana, which has adopted a new statewide voucher program involving the middle class.

Advocates for better public schools should take a lesson from the voucher advocates. Public school supporters often know what they are against, but not what they are for. They should work to get agreement on goals such as the ones set forth in this book, refine the arguments, be persistent, and then move when the politics turns favorable.

Not all of the goals outlined in this book may be realized soon, but if they are the right ones, people ought to adopt them and work to put in place as many as possible. Based on nearly three decades of working in Congress helping to make policy and writing legislation, I know there are hundreds of permutations of each element of this new approach. So, it is better to put aside the details, and seek agreement on the big concepts.

The major objective is to have people think differently, to get out of the box of tinkering with the current set of federal laws and programs. The solution to making American schools better is not to amend NCLB; instead it is to deal directly with improving teaching and learning in the classroom.

The biggest lesson I have learned over half a century of involvement in education politics and policy is that if you are not working to implement your own agenda, then you are working off someone else's agenda. It is time public school advocates established their own ambitious agenda and set out to achieve it.

Appendix

Chronology of Major Events, 1948–2013

1948	President Harry Truman supports general aid for public schools.
	Senator Robert Taft secures Senate approval of general aid bill that dies in the House.
	Harry Truman is elected president.
1952	*Dwight D. Eisenhower is elected president.*
1954	The U.S. Supreme Court rules in *Brown v. Board of Education* that legally segregated schools are unconstitutional.
1956	*President Eisenhower is reelected.*
1958	The National Defense Education Act becomes law.
1960	*John F. Kennedy is elected president.*
1963	Kennedy is assassinated, and Lyndon Johnson assumes presidency.
1964	The Civil Rights Act becomes law.
	Lyndon B. Johnson is elected president.
1965	The Elementary and Secondary Education Act becomes law.
1966	The first anti-busing amendment is approved by Congress.
1968	The Bilingual Education Act becomes law.
	The Supreme Court rules in *Green v. County Board of Education of Kent County, Virginia* that desegregation plans must be implemented.
	Richard M. Nixon is elected president.

1969	Nixon proposes elimination of some new education programs and funding cutbacks.
	Congressman Carl Perkins begins a campaign to oppose Nixon's proposal, and wins.
1970	An anti-busing amendment is adopted that equates *de jure* and *de facto* segregation.
1971	The Supreme Court rules in *Swann v. Charlotte-Mecklenburg Board of Education* that busing can be used for desegregation.
1972	Title I is increasing administered as targeted assistance, not general aid.
	Anti-busing amendments are adopted in the Education Amendments.
	Title IX affecting girls and women is adopted in the same law.
	President Nixon is reelected.
1973	Section 504 of the Rehabilitation Act is adopted affecting persons with disabilities.
	The Supreme Court rules in *San Antonio Independent School District v. Rodriguez* that education is not a fundamental interest under the Constitution, and thus challenges to state systems of school finance must be filed in state, not federal, courts.
1974	Some amendments are adopted making Title I a targeted assistance program.
	More anti-busing amendments are adopted.
	The Supreme Court rules in *Lau v. Nichols* that children must be given assistance to learn English.
	The Bilingual Education Act is broadened to provide more services, and the Equal Education Opportunity Act to remove language as a barrier to receiving an education is passed.
1975	The Individuals with Disabilities Education Act becomes law (under a different title).
	The *Lau* Remedies regulations are issued by the U.S. Office of Education.
1976	*Jimmy Carter is elected president.*
1978	Education Amendments are adopted with strong bipartisan support.

1980	The U.S. Department of Education replaces the U.S. Office of Education. *Ronald Reagan is elected president.*
1981	Reagan succeeds in cutting back on federal programs and funding. The Bilingual Education Act allows some funding for English-only programs.
1982	The *Sustaining Effects Study* finds modest academic improvement through Title I.
1983	*A Nation at Risk* is released.
1984	The Equal Access Act affecting student clubs becomes law. The Supreme Court in *Grove City v. Bell* limits the effects of Title IX. *President Reagan is reelected.*
1987	The Civil Rights Restoration Act restores the broad effects of Title IX.
1988	Title I is amended by Congressman Augustus Hawkins to emphasize the need to increase students' academic achievement. Congress increases funds available for English-only programs under the Bilingual Education Act. *George H. W. Bush is elected president.*
1989	Bush convenes the nation's governors at a Charlottesville summit on education.
1990	Bush signs the Americans with Disabilities Act.
1992	Bush's legislation related to national goals and state-wide reform is stymied in Senate. *Bill Clinton is elected president.* The first charter school legislation is passed in Minnesota.
1993	The *Prospects* study finds modest effects for Title I.
1994	Goals 2000 and the ESEA amendments create a national standards-based program. Bilingual Education Act is amended to permit more English-only programs.
1995	The Senate votes against the first President Bush's national history standards.
1996	*President Clinton is reelected.*

2000	*George W. Bush is elected president.*
2002	The No Child Left Behind Act becomes law.
	The Bilingual Education Act becomes the English Acquisition Act.
2004	*President Bush is reelected.*
2008	*Barack Obama is elected president.*
2009	The American Recovery and Reinvestment Act becomes law.
2010	The Common Core State Standards are released by the governors and school chiefs.
2011	The NCLB waiver program begins.
2012	*President Obama is reelected.*
2013	The Next Generation Science Standards are released.

Notes

Introduction

1. Chester E. Finn Jr., "Agenda-Setters and Duds: A Bully Pulpit, Indeed," in *Carrots, Sticks, and the Bully Pulpit: Lessons from a Half-Century of Federal Efforts to Improve America's Schools*, eds. Frederick M. Hess and Andrew P. Kelly (Cambridge, MA: Harvard Education Press, 2011), 228.
2. Christopher B. Swanson and Janelle Barlage, *Influence: A Study of the Factors Shaping Education Policy* (Bethesda, MD: Editorial Projects in Education Research Center, 2006), 59.
3. Emily Richmond et al., "High School Graduation Rate Hits 40-Year Peak in the U.S.," *The Atlantic*, June 6, 2014, http://www.theatlantic.com/national/archive/2013/06/high-school-graduation-rate-hits-40-year-peak-in-the-us/276604/; Andrew Mytelka et al., "College-Going Rates for All Racial Groups Have Jumped Since 1980," *Chronicle of Higher Education*, July 10, 2014, http://chronicle.com/blogs/ticker/college-going-rates-for-all-racial-groups-have-jumped-since-1980/25533; Child Trends DataBank, "Appendix 1—Dropout Rates of 16 to- 24-Year-Olds, by Gender and Race/Hispanic Origin: Selected Years, 1970–2012," Sept. 2013, http://www.childtrends.org/wp-content/uploads/2012/10/01_appendix1.pdf.
4. OECD, *Education at a Glance 2012: OECD Indicators* (OECD Publishing, 2012), http://dx.doi.org/10.1787/eag-2012-en.
5. OECD, *PISA 2012 Results in Focus: What 15-year-olds know and what they can do with what they know* (OECD Publishing, 2012), http://www.oecd.org/pisa/keyfindings/pisa-2012-results-overview.pdf.
6. PISA, "About PISA," http://www.oecd.org/pisa/aboutpisa/;PISA, "PISA Overview," National Center for Education Statistics, http://nces.ed.gov/surveys/pisa/.
7. Arne Duncan, "Speech to the National Assessment Governing Board" Jan. 13, 2014, http://www.ed.gov/news/speeches/remarks-us-secretaty-education-arne-duncan-national-assessment-governing-board-education.
8. Marshall S. Smith, "Rethinking ESEA", in *Carrots, Sticks, and the Bully Pulpit: Lessons from a Half-Century of Federal Efforts to Improve America's Schools*, eds. Frederick M. Hess and Andrew P. Kelly (Cambridge, MA: Harvard Education Press, 2011), 233.
9. U.S. Department of Education, *For Each and Every Child—A Strategy for Education Equity and Excellence* (USDE: Washington, DC, 2013), 15, http://www2.ed.gov/about/bdscomm/list/eec/equity-excellence-commission-report.pdf.

Chapter 1

1. U.S. Department of Education, National Center for Education Statistics, *Digest of Education Statistics*. *Table 91, Total Number of Public School Districts and Public and Private Elementary and Secondary Schools: Selected Years 1869–70 through 2009–10* (Washington, DC: NCES, 2011). See note 7 in the table regarding the comparability of numbers.
2. Thomas D. Snyder, ed., *120 Years of American Education: A Statistical Portrait* (Washington, DC: National Center for Education Statistics, 1993), 31.
3. New America Foundation, "Federal, State, and Local K–12 School Finance Overview, Table: Share of Public Elementary and Secondary School Revenue," http://febp.newamerica.net/ background-analysis/school-finance/print, in Stephen Cornman, Patrick Keaton, and Mark Glander, "Revenues and Expenditures for Public Elementary and Secondary School, Districts: School Year 2010–11 (Fiscal Year 2011) (NCES 2013 344)" (Washington, DC: National Center for Education Statistics, 2013).
4. Eugene Eidenberg and Roy D. Morey, *An Act of Congress: The Legislative Process and the Making of Education Policy* (New York: W.W. Norton, 1969), 13.
5. Robert Taft, "Statement" (1948), quoted in Christopher T. Cross, *Political Education: National Policy Comes of Age*, updated ed. (New York: Teachers College Press, 2010), 6.
6. Maurice McCann, "The Truman Administration and Federal Aid to Education" (paper presented at the annual meeting of the American Educational Research Association, New York, NY, April 4–8, 1977), 9, 22.
7. Michael Harrington, *The Other America; Poverty in the United States* (New York: Macmillan, 1962).
8. Eidenberg and Morey, *An Act of Congress*, 102.
9. Senator Wayne Morse, "Remarks on Consideration of the Elementary and Secondary Education Act of 1965," *Congressional Record* (Washington, DC: U.S. Government, April 7, 1965).
10. *Congressional and Administrative News*, U.S. Code, Vol. 1, 89th Congress 1st Session (Washington, DC: U.S. Government, 1965), 1450.
11. Congressman Carl Perkins, "Remarks on Consideration of the Elementary and Secondary Education Act of 1965," *Congressional Record* (Washington, DC: U.S. Government, March 24, 1965).
12. Lyndon B. Johnson, "Remarks in Johnson City, Tex., Upon Signing the Elementary and Secondary Education Bill," *The American Presidency Project* (April 11, 1965), http://www .presidency.ucsb.edu/ws/?pid=26887.

Chapter 2

1. Samuel Halperin, "ESEA—Twenty Years Later: A Political Retrospective," quoted in *A Compilation of Papers on the Twentieth Anniversary of the Elementary and Secondary Education Act of 1965* (Washington, DC: Committee on Education and Labor, U.S. House of Representatives, 1985) 10–11.
2. *Elementary and Secondary Education Act* of 1965, Public Law 89-10, *United States Statutes at Large* 79 (1965), 27.
3. Ruby Martin and Phyllis McClure, *Title I of ESEA: Is It Helping Poor Children?* (Washington, DC: Washington Research Project of the Southern Center for Studies in Public Policy and the NAACP Legal Defense and Education Fund, 1969).
4. John F. Hughes, *Implementing Title I of ESEA—Major Themes*, quoted in *A Compilation of Papers on the Twentieth Anniversary of the Elementary and Secondary Education Act of 1965*

(Washington, D.C.: Committee on Education and Labor, U.S. House of Representatives, 1985), 50, 54.

5. Floyd Eugene Stoner, *Implementation of Ambiguous Legislative Language: Title I of the Elementary and Secondary Education Act*, (PhD diss., University of Wisconsin, 1976) 12, 18, 22, 132.

6. John F. Jennings, *Why National Standards and Tests? Politics and the Quest for Better Schools* (Thousand Oaks, CA: Sage Publications, 1998), 127–128.

7. U.S. Congress, *Elementary and Secondary Education Amendments of 1974*, House Report 93-805, 9.

8. Jennings, *Why National Standards,* 127–128.

Chapter 3

1. *Elementary and Secondary Education Act*, Public Law 95-561, Section 125 (November 1, 1978).

2. *Elementary and Secondary Education Act*, Public Law 95-561, Section 126 (November 1, 1978).

3. David K. Cohen and Susan L. Moffitt, *The Ordeal of Equality: Did Federal Regulation Fix the Schools?* (Cambridge, MA: Harvard University Press, 2009), 88-90.

4. Cohen and Moffitt, *Ordeal,* 97–98.

5. Mary Jean LeTendre, "Effective Title I Programs," in *A Compilation of Papers on the Twentieth Anniversary of the Elementary and Secondary Education Act of 1965* (Washington, DC: Committee on Education and Labor, U.S. House of Representatives, 1985), 76.

6. Charles Radcliffe, "How and Why A Reagan Republican Saved Title I by Changing It to Chapter One," in *A Compilation of Papers on the Twentieth Anniversary of the Elementary and Secondary Education Act of 1965*, (Washington, DC: Committee on Education and Labor, U.S. House of Representatives, 1985), 64.

7. Christopher T. Cross, *Political Education: National Policy Comes of Age*, updated ed. (New York, NY: Teachers College Press, 2010), 86.

8. Wayne Riddle, e-mail message to author, July 24, 2014.

9. John F. Jennings, *Why National Standards and Tests?* (Thousand Oaks, CA: Sage Publications, 1998), 127-8

10. *Improving America's Schools Act*, Public Law 103-382, 108 (1994): 3518.

11. Diane Stark Rentner, Alexandra Usher, and Nancy Kober, *What Impact Did Education Stimulus Funds Have on States and School Districts?* (Washington, DC: Center on Education Policy, July, 2012).

12. U.S. Department of Education, "Setting the Pace: Expanding Opportunity for America's Students Under Race to the Top," *Executive Office of the President* (jointly with the USDE, March, 2014), http://www.whitehouse.gov/sites/default/files/docs/settingthepacerttreport_3-2414_b.pdf.

Chapter 4

1. David K. Cohen and Susan L. Moffitt, *The Ordeal of Equality: Did Federal Regulation Fix the Schools?* (Cambridge, MA: Harvard University Press, 2009), 81–82.

2. Ibid.

3. National Institute of Education, *The Compensatory Education Study: Executive Summary* (Washington, DC: NIE, July 1978).

4. Ming-mei Wang, Moraye B. Bear, Jonathan E. Conklin, Ralph Hoepfner, *Compensatory Services and Educational Development in the School Year,* Technical Report 10 from the Study of the Sustaining Effects of Compensatory Education on Basic Skills (Santa Monica, CA: System Development Corporation, May 1981) xxxi-xxxv, 24–25, 27–28; System Development Corporation, *Does Compensatory Education Narrow the Achievement Gap?,* Technical Report 12 from the Study of the Sustaining Effects of Compensatory Education on Basic Skills, prepared for the Office of Program Evaluation, U.S. Department of Education (Santa Monica, CA: System Development Corporation, Dec. 1981); Wayne Riddle, *Title I, Education for the Disadvantaged: Perspectives on Studies of Its Achievement Effects* (Washington, DC: Congressional Research Service, Library of Congress, 1996), 14.

5. System Development Corporation, *Does Compensatory Education*; Riddle, *Title I,* 14.

6. RAND Corporation, *Federal Policy Options for Improving the Education of Low-income Students,* vol. I, 1993; Riddle, *Title I,* 12–13.

7. Commission on Chapter 1, *Making Schools Work for Children in Poverty* (Washington, DC: Dec. 1992), 101; Riddle, *Title I,* 12.

8. Cohen and Moffitt, *Ordeal,* 99.

9. Michael J. Puma, Colvin C. Jones, Donald Rock, Roberto Fernandez, *Prospects: The Congressionally Mandated Study of Educational Growth and Opportunity,* Interim Report (Washington, DC: U.S. Department of Education, July 1993), 163–181; Riddle, *Title I,* 11.

10. Michael Puma, "The Prospects Study of Educational Growth and Opportunity: Implications for Policy and Practice" (paper presented at the annual meeting of the American Educational Research Association, Montreal, Quebec, Canada, Apr. 19–23, 1999), 10.

11. Jesse H. Rhodes, *An Education in Politics* (Ithaca, NY: Cornell Press, 2012), 33.

12. Cohen and Moffitt, *Ordeal,* 89.

13. *Elementary and Secondary Education Act,* Public Law 95-561, Section 123 (Nov. 1, 1978).

14. Cohen and Moffitt, *Ordeal,* 88–92.

15. Illinois state report cards 2013, "Winnetka District 36" and "Cicero District 99," http://webprod.isbe.net/ereportcard/publicsite/getSearchCriteria.aspx.

16. Puma, "Prospects Study," 8.

17. Wayne Riddle, *Appropriations for ESEA Title I, Part A, in Current and Constant (FY2014) Dollars, FY 1966–2014,* a table prepared on March 5, 2014, and sent by e-mail to the author.

18. Ibid.

19. Cohen and Moffitt, *Ordeal,* 100.

Part II

1. Bill Bushaw and Shane J. Lopez, "The 45th Annual PDK/Gallup Poll of the Public's Attitudes the Public Schools," *Kappan* (Sept. 2013), tables 31 and 32, p. 20.

Chapter 5

1. "A Nation at Risk" (Archived Information: April 1983), www2.ed.gov/pubs/NatAtRisk/risk.html.

2. James Harvey, e-mail message to author, July 2014.

3. Patrick J. McGuinn, *No Child Left Behind and the Transformation of Federal Education Policy, 1965–2005* (Lawrence, KS: University Press of Kansas, 2006), 49.

4. John F. Jennings, *Why National Standards and Tests? Politics and the Quest for Better Schools* (Thousand Oaks, CA: Sage Publications, 1998), 179.

5. Jennings, *Why National Standards,* 6, 7, 18.

6. M. S. Smith and J. O'Day, *Putting the pieces together: Systemic school reform,* CPRE Policy Brief, RB-06-4/91 (New Brunswick, NJ: Consortium for Policy Research in Education, 1991).

7. Marshall Smith and Jennifer O'Day, "Systemic School Reform," *Journal of Education Policy, Special Issue: The Politics of Curriculum and Testing* 5 (1990), 233–267.

8. Lynne Cheney, "The End of History," *Wall Street Journal,* Oct. 20, 1994.

9. Christopher T. Cross, *Political Education: National Policy Comes of Age,* updated ed. (New York, NY: Teachers College Press, 2010), 113.

10. Jennings, *Why National Standards,* 44–75.

11. Dan Balz, "Stands on education cost GOP among women, governors told," *Washington Post,* Nov. 27, 1996, A6.

12. McGuinn, *No Child Left Behind,* 193–194.

13. Paul Manna, *School's In* (Washington, DC: Georgetown University Press, 2006), 157.

14. Mitch McConnell, "Interview with Major Garrett," *National Journal* (Washington, DC: Oct. 23, 2010).

15. Jennifer McMurrer, "ESEA/NCLB Waiver Watch," (Washington, DC: Center on Education Policy, May 3, 2014), www.cep-dc/index.cfm?DocumentSubTopicID=48.

16. Jennifer McMurrer and Nanami Yoshioka, "States' Perspectives on Waivers: Relief from NCLB, Concern about Long-tern Solutions" (Washington, DC: Center on Education Policy, March 4, 2013).

Chapter 6

1. Jack Jennings and Diane Stark Rentner, "Ten Big Effects of the No Child Left Behind Act on Public Schools," *The Phi Delta Kappan* (Bloomington, IN. Oct. 2006), 110–113.

2. Alexandra Usher, *AYP Results for 2010–11, November 2012 Update* (Washington, DC: Center on Education Policy, Nov. 1, 2012).

3. U.S. Department of Education, "NAEP Overview," National Center for Education Statistics, from http://nces.ed.gov/nationsreportcard/about/; "What Are the Differences Between Long-term Trend NAEP and Main NAEP," Institute for Education Statistics, http://nces.ed .gov/nationsreportcard/about/ltt_main_diff.aspx.

4. Naomi Chudowsky, Victor Chudowsky, and Nancy Kober, *Rising Scores on State Tests and NAEP,* (Washington, DC: Center on Education Policy, Sept. 2010).

5. Nancy Kober, Naomi Chudowsky, and Victor Chudowsky, *State Test Score Trends Through 2008–9, Part 2: Slow and Uneven Progress in Narrowing Gaps* (Washington, DC: Center on Education Policy, Dec. 14, 2010).

6. "NAEP-Mathematics and Reading 2013," The Nation's Report Card, http://nationsreportcard .gov/reading_math_2013/#/achievement-gaps.

7. U.S. Department of Education, "The Nation's Report Card: Mathematics and Reading, 2013," Institute of Education Sciences, http://nces.ed.gov/nationsreportcard/pubs/main2013/ 2014451.aspx.

8. David Grissmer, Sheila Nataraj Kirby, Mark Berends, and Stephanie Williamson, *Student Achievement and the Changing American Family* (Santa Monica, CA: Rand, 1994).

9. Erik Robelen, "District Leaders Mostly Back Common Core, But Troubled by Implementation, Curriculum Matters Blog," *Education Week,* www.blogs.edweek.org/edweek/curriculum/ 2014/06/superintendents_mostly_support_co.html?intc=es.

10. Liana Heitin, "Common Core Will Improve Education, Most District Chiefs Say," *Education Week* (July 1, 2014), http://www.edweek.org/ew/articles/2014/07/01/36gallup.h33.html?k.

11. Javier C. Hernandez, "Charters, Public Schools and a Chasm Between," *New York Times*, May 12, 2014, A1, A13.

12. NCES, *Charter Schools, Fast Facts* (Washington DC: National Center for Educational Statistics, 2014).

13. Zach Miners, "Charter Schools Might Not Be Better," *U.S. News and World Report*, Education, June 17, 2009.

14. CREDO, *National Charter School Study 2013* (Palo Alto, CA: Center for Research on Education Outcomes, 2013), 23.

Part III

1. New America Foundation, *Federal, State, and Local K–12 School Finance Overview*, Table: Share of Public Elementary and Secondary School Revenue, Source: National Center for Education Statistics (June 30, 2013), http://febp.newamerica.net/background-analysis/school-finance/print.

Chapter 7

1. U.S. Department of Education, *History: Twenty-five Years of Progress in Educating Children with Disabilities Through IDEA* (Washington, DC: 2000), www2.ed/gov/policy/speced/leg/idea/history.html.

2. Ibid.

3. Charles Radcliffe, "How and Why a Reagan Republican Saved Title I by Changing It to Chapter One," in *A Compilation of Papers on the Twentieth Anniversary of the Elementary and Secondary Education Act of 1965* (Washington, DC: Committee on Education and Labor, U.S. House of Representatives, 1985), 62

4. Ibid., 65.

5. Gloria Stewner-Mansanares, "The Bilingual Education Act: Twenty Years Later," *The National Clearinghouse for Bilingual Education* 6 (Fall 1988): 1, 2.

6. *Lau v. Nichols*, 414 US 563 (1974).

7. Bilingual Education Act, Sec. 703 (a) (4) (A)(i), P.L. 93-380, 88 Stat. 503, (1968).

8. Stewner-Manzanares, "Bilingual Education Act," 4.

9. Chester E. Finn Jr., "Agenda-Setters and Duds: A Bully Pulpit, Indeed," in *Carrots, Sticks, and the Bully Pulpit: Lessons from a Half-Century of Federal Efforts to Improve America's Schools*, eds. Frederick M. Hess and Andrew P. Kelly (Cambridge, MA: Harvard Education Press, 2011), 221.

10. Kenji Hakuta, *Mirror of Language: The Debate on Bilingualism* (New York, NY: Basic Books, 1986), 233.

11. Ronald Reagan, "Remarks to the National Governors' Association—Department of Education Conference in Columbia, Missouri, March 26, 1981," www.presidency.ucsb.edu/ronald_reagan.php.

12. U.S. General Accounting Office, "A New Look at Research Evidence," *GAO/PEMD-87-12BR* (Washington, DC, 1987).

13. Jay P. Greene, *A Meta-analysis of the Effectiveness of Bilingual Education*, sponsored by the Tomás Rivera Policy Institute (March 2, 1998), 1, http://www.languagepolicy.net/archives/greene.htm.

14. Lesli A. Maxwell, "Proposal to Restore Bilingual Education in California Advances," *Education Week*, Blog: Learning the Language, http://blogs.edweek.org/edweek/learning-the -language/2014/05/proposal_to_restore_bilingual_.html.

Chapter 8

1. Eugene Eidenberg and Roy D. Morey, *An Act of Congress: The Legislative Process and the Making of Education Policy* (New York, NY: W.W. Norton, 1969), 194.
2. Patrick J. McGuinn, *No Child Left Behind and the Transformation of Federal Education Policy, 1965–2005* (Lawrence, KS: University Press of Kansas, 2006), 36.
3. U.S. Congress, *Remarks of Senator Abraham Ribicoff, Congressional Record 116* (Feb. 9, 1970), 1461-64, in James T. Patterson, *Brown v. Board of Education* (Oxford, UK: Oxford University Press, 2001), 157.
4. Christopher T. Cross, *Political Education: National Policy Comes of Age*, updated ed. (New York, NY: Teachers College Press, 2010), 44–45.
5. Richard Nixon, "Statement About the Busing of Schoolchildren, August 3, 1971," in Gerhard Peters and John T. Woolley, *The American Presidency Project*, http://www.presidency .ucsb.edu/us/?pid=3098.
6. Eric A. Posner, "Casual with the Court," *New Republic* (Oct. 24, 2011), www.newrepublic .com/book/review/nixon's-court-kevin-mcmahon.
7. James T. Patterson, *Brown v. Board of Education: A Civil Rights Milestone and Its Troubled Legacy* (Oxford, UK: Oxford University Press, 2001).
8. Richard Nixon, "Radio Address on the Federal Responsibility to Education, Oct. 25, 1972," in Gerhard Peters and John T. Woolley, *The American Presidency Project*, http://www .presidency.ucsb.edu/us/?pid3655.
9. Desmond King, *Separate and Unequal: Black Americans and the U.S. Federal Government* (New York: Oxford University Press, 1995), 311.
10. Richard Nixon, Statement on Signing the Education Amendments of 1972, June 23, 1972, www.presidency.ucsb.edu/ws/?pid=3473.
11. Cross, *Political Education*, 50.
12. Drew S. Days III, *Turning Back the Clock: The Reagan Administration and Civil Rights* (New Haven, CT: Faculty Scholarship Series, Yale Law School Legal Scholarship Depository, 1984), 321.
13. Gary Orfield and Chungmei Lee, *Historic Reversals, Accelerating Resegregation, and the Need for New Integration Strategies* (Civil Rights Project: 2007), http://civilrightsproject .ucla.edu/research/k-12-education/integration-and-diversity/historic-reversals-accelerating -resegregation-and-the-need-for-new-integration-strategies-1/orfield-historic-reversals -accelerating.pdf
14. Ann T. Keane, "Patsy Mink", *American National Biography Online* (October 2008), www .anb.org/articles/07/07-00812.html.
15. 118 Cong. Record 5808 (1972).
16. Chester E. Finn Jr., "Agenda-Setters and Duds: A Bully Pulpit, Indeed," in *Carrots, Sticks, and the Bully Pulpit: Lessons from a Half-Century of Federal Efforts to Improve America's Schools*, eds. Frederick M. Hess and Andrew P. Kelly (Cambridge, MA: Harvard Education Press, 2011),224.
17. Cross, *Political Education*, 48.
18. Civil Rights Restoration Act of 1987, Public Law 100-259, 102 STAT 28, section 1687.

19. Equal Access Act, H.R. 5345, 98th Cong. (1984), http://www.govtrack.us/congress/bills/98/hr5345 (accessed on April 23, 2014).

20. Joshua Dunn, "Courting Education: Mitigating the Seven Somewhat Deadly Sins of Education Litigation," in *Carrots, Sticks, and the Bully Pulpit: Lessons From a Half Century of Federal Efforts to Improve America's Schools*, eds. Frederick M. Hess and Andrew P. Kelly (Cambridge, MA: Harvard Education Press, 2011), 102.

Chapter 9

1. *An Act to Strengthen and Improve Educational Quality and Educational Opportunities in the Nation's Elementary and Secondary Schools*, Public Law 89-10, 604, (1965): 79.

2. *An Act to Strengthen, Improve, and Extend Programs of Assistance for Elementary and Secondary Education, and for Other Purposes*, Public Law 90-247, (1968).

3. Gary Robinson, "United States: Lawsuit Challenging No Child Left Behind Act Allowed to Proceed" (Law Library of Congress, Global Legal Monitor, Jan. 2, 2008).

4. *An Act to Close the Achievement Gap with Accountability, Flexibility, and Choice so that No Child is Left Behind*, Public Law 107-110, 9523 (2002).

5. *An Act to Close the Achievement Gap with Accountability, Flexibility, and Choice so that No Child is Left Behind*, Public Law 107-110, 9528 (2002).

6. *An Act to Close the Achievement Gap with Accountability, Flexibility, and Choice so that No Child is Left Behind*, Public Law 107-110, 9524 (2002).

7. *An Act to Close the Achievement Gap with Accountability, Flexibility, and Choice so that No Child is Left Behind*, Public Law 107-110, 9525 (2002).

8. "Other Academic Indicators," Code of Federal Regulations, 34 CFR Section 200.19.

9. Marie C. Stetson and Robert Stillwell, *Public High School Four-Year On-Time Graduation Rates and Event Dropout Rates: School Year 2010–11 and 2011–12, First Look* (U.S. Department of Education, National Center for Education Statistics, April 2014), http://nces.ed.gov/pubsearch.

10. Federal Education Budget Project, *No Child Left Behind Funding* (New America Foundation, April 24, 2014), febp.newamerica.net/background-analysis/no-child-left-behind-funding.

11. *An Act to Close the Achievement Gap with Accountability, Flexibility, and Choice so that No Child is Left Behind*, Public Law 107-110, 7907 (a) (2002).

12. "Supreme Court declines to hear No Child Left Behind challenge," *Jurist* (May 7, 2010), http://jurist.org/paperchase/2010/06/supreme-court-declines-to-hear-no-child-left-behind-challenge.php.

13. Stephanie Reitz, "Connecticut loses "No Child Left Behind" legal challenge," *NBC News*, www.nbcnews.com/id/41723439/ns/us_news-crime_and_courts/t/connecticut-loses-no-child-left-behind-challenge-/#.u54TvCil/.

Chapter 10

1. Extensive research exists documenting the effects of both programs. See, for example: Frances A. Campbell, Elizabeth P. Pungello, Margaret Burchinal, Kirsten Kainz, Yi Pan, Barbara H. Wasik, Oscar A. Barbarin, Joseph J. Sparling, and Craig T. Ramey, "Adult outcomes as a function of an early childhood educational program: An Abecedarian Project follow-up," *Developmental Psychology* 48, no. 4 (July 2012): 1033–1043; Peter Muennig, Dylan Robertson, Gretchen Johnson, Frances Campbell, Elizabeth P. Pungello, and Matthew Neidel,

"The Effect of an Early Education Program on Adult Health: The Carolina Abecedarian Project Randomized Controlled Trial," *American Journal of Public Health* 101, no. 3 (March 2011): 512–516; Heckman, Moon, Pinto, Savelyev, and Yavitz, "The Rate of Return to the HighScope Perry Preschool Program, *Journal of Public Economics* 94, no. 1–2 (Feb. 2010): 114–128; Peter Muennig, Lawrence Schweinhart, Jeanne Montie, and Matthew Neidell, "Effects of a Prekindergarten Educational Intervention on Adult Health: 37-Year Follow-Up Results of a Randomized Controlled Trial," *American Journal of Public Health* 99, no. 8 (Aug. 2009): 1431–1437.

2. W. Steven Barnett, *Preschool Education and Its Lasting Effects* (Boulder and Tempe: Education and the Public Interest Center and Educational Policy Research Unit, 2008), 1, 2, http://nepc.colorado.edu/files/PB-Barnett-EARLY-ED_FINAL.pdf.

3. Ibid., 1, 2.

4. Betty Hart and Todd Risley, *Meaningful Differences in the Everyday Experiences of Young American Children* (Baltimore: Paul H. Brookes Publishing, 1995).

5. Equity and Excellence Commission, *For Each and Every Child: A Strategy for Education Equity and Excellence,* (Washington, D.C.: U.S. Department of Education, 2013), 15.

6. W. Steven Barnett and Donald J. Yarosz, "Who Goes to Preschool and Why Does It Matter?," *National Institute for Early Education Research* (2007), http://nieer.org/resources/policybriefs/15.pdf.

7. Sharon L. Kagan and Jeanne L. Reid, *Advancing ECE² Policy* (Washington, DC: Center on Education Policy, 2008), 50.

8. J. S. McCombs et al., *Making Summer Count* (Santa Monica, CA: Rand, 2011), http://www.rand.org/content/dam/pubs/monographs/2011/RAND_MG1120.pdf.

9. Greg J. Duncan and Richard Murnane, eds., *Whither Opportunity: Rising Inequality, Schools, and Children's Life Chances* (New York: Russell Sage Foundation, 2011).

10. R. Gordon, T. Kane, and D. Staiger, *Identifying Effective Teachers Using Performance on the Job* (Washington, DC: Brookings Institute and the Hamilton Project, 2006).

11. Jill Colvin, "Bloomberg Says He Has 'Own Army" in NYPD, Slams Teachers," *DNAinfo New York* (Nov. 30, 2011), http://www.dnainfo.com/new-york/20111130/manhattan/bloomberg-says-he-has-own-army-nypd-slams-teachers.

12. Matthew Di Carlo, "Do teachers really come from the 'bottom third' of college graduates?," *Washington Post,* Dec. 8, 2011, http://www.washingtonpost.com/blogs/answer-sheet/post/do-teachers-really-come-from-the-bottom-third-of-colleges-graduates/2011/12.

13. U.S. Department of Education, *For Each and Every Child: A Strategy for Education Equity and Excellence.*(Washington, D.C.: USDE, 2013), 15.

14. Byron Auguste, Paul Kihn, and Matt Miller, *Closing the talent gap: Attracting and retaining top-third graduates to careers in teaching* (McKinsey and Co., 2010), 8, Mckinseyonsociety.com/closing-the-talent-gap/.

15. Richard Ingersoll, Lisa Merrill, and Daniel Stuckey, *Seven trends: The transformation of the teaching force* (Philadelphia: Consortium for Policy Research in Education Report #RR-80, University of Pennsylvania, 2014): 19–20.

16. Ibid., 21–22.

17. Richard M. Ingersoll et al., *A Comparative Study of Teacher Preparation and Qualifications in Six Nations* (Philadelphia: Consortium for Policy Research in Education, University of Pennsylvania), 98, http://www.cpre.org/images/stories/cpre_pdfs/sixnations_final.pdf; R. Ingersoll, "Four Myths About America's Teacher Quality Problem," in *103rd*

Yearbook of the National Society for the Study of Education, ed. M. Smylie and D. Miretzky (Chicago: University of Chicago Press, 2004), 1–33, http://www.gse.upenn.edu/pdf/rmi/FourMyths.pdf.

18. Stephen Sawchuk, "Poll: Top College Students See Teaching as 'Average' Profession With Low Pay," *Education Week* (Apr. 29, 2014), http://blogs.edweek.org/edweek/teacherbeat/2014/04/poll_college_students_dont_fin.html?cmp=ENL-EU-NEWS2.

19. Dan Goldhaber, "The Mystery of Good Teaching," *Education Next* 1 (Spring 2002).

20. Linda Darling-Hammond and Peter Youngs, "Defining 'Highly Qualified Teachers': What Does 'Scientifically-Based Research' Actually Tell Us?," *American Educational Research Association, Educational Researcher* 9 (Dec. 2002): 13–25.

21. R. G. Ehrenberg and D. J. Brewer, "Did teachers' race and verbal abilities matter in the 1960's? Coleman revisited," *Economics of Education Review* 14, no. 1 (1995): 1–21; R. G. Ehrenberg and D. J. Brewer, "Do school and teachers' characteristics matter? Evidence from high school and beyond," *Economics of Education Review* 13, no. 1 (1994): 1–17; R. Greenwald, L. Hedges, and R. D. Laine, "The effect of school resources on student achievement," *Review of Educational Research* 66, no. 3 (1996): 361–396.

22. Thomas J. Kane, "A Flexner Report on Teacher Preparation," *Education Next,* http://educationnext.org/flexner-report-teacher-preparation/.

23. Auguste, Kihn, and Miller, *Closing the talent gap,* 5–9, 44.

24. M. Cochran-Smith, K. Zeichner, *Studying teacher education: The report of the AERA panel on research and teacher education* (Washington, DC: American Educational Research Association, 2005).

25. National Research Council, Committee on the Study of Teacher Preparation Programs in the United States, *Preparing Teachers: Building Evidence for Sound Policy* (Washington, DC: National Academy Press, 2010), http://www.nap.edu/12882.html.

26. Motoko Rich, "Obama Administration Plans New Rules to Grade Teacher Training Programs," *Washington Post,* April 26, 2014, A12.

27. Richard Ingersoll, e-mail sent to the author, Aug. 13, 2014.

28. Donald Boyd et al., *Teacher preparation and student achievement* (National Bureau of Economic Research, NBER Working Paper Number W14314, Sept. 2008), http://ssrn.com/abstract=1264576.

29. Barnett Berry, *Teacher Education for Tomorrow,* National Council for the Accreditation of Teacher Education, October 7, 2010, 6-8, files.eric.ed.gov/fulltext/ED519712.pd.

30. Michael Strong, Stephen Fletcher, Anthony Villar, *An Investigation of the Effects of Teacher Experience and Teacher Preparedness on the Performance of Latino students in California* (Santa Cruz, CA: New Teacher Center, 2004).

31. Rich, "Obama Administration Plans New Rules," A12.

32. Daniel Koretz, "Limitations in the Use of Achievement Tests as Measures of Educators' Productivity," *Journal of Human Resources* (2002): 752–777.

33. Heather G. Peske and Kati Haycock, "Teaching Inequality: How Poor and Minority Students are Shortchanged on Teacher Quality—A Report and Recommendations by the Education Trust," *Education Trust* (Washington, DC: 2006).

34. Michael Rebell, *Moving Every Child Ahead* (New York: Teachers College Press, 2008), 94; R. Ingersoll, "Teacher Turnover and Teacher Shortages: An Organizational Analysis," *American Educational Research Journal* 38, no. 3 (Fall 2001): 499–534.

35. Marc Tucker, *Tucker's Lens: Report from the 2014 International Summit on the Teaching Profession* (Center on International Education Benchmarking, Apr. 17, 2014).

36. R. Ingersoll, "Short on Power, Long on Responsibility," *Educational Leadership* 65, no. 1 (Sept. 2007):20–25.

37. Grover J. "Russ" Whitehurst, *Don't Forget Curriculum* (Washington, DC: Brookings Institution, Brown Center Letters on Education, 2009).

38. V. E. Lee and A. S. Byrk, "Curriculum Tracking As Mediating the Social Distribution of High School Achievement," *Sociology of Education* 61, no. 2: 78–94; V. E. Lee, "Educational Choice: The Stratifying Effects of Selecting Schools and Courses," *Educational Policy* 7, no. 2 (1993): 125–148.

39. Wiley Burris and Murphy Widman, *Accountability, Rigor, and Detracking* (New York: Teachers College Record, 2008).

40. ACT, *Rigor at Risk* (Iowa City, IA: ACT, 2007): 1, 3.

41. U.S. Department of Education, Office of Civil Rights, Civil Rights Data Collection, Issue Brief No. 3, Data Snapshot: College and Career Readiness, March 2014 ocrdata.ed.gov/Downloads/CRDC-college-and-career-readiness-Snapshot.pdf .

42. Leslie A. Finnan, *Common Core and Other State Standards: Superintendents Feel Optimism, Concern and Lack of Support* (American Association of School Administrators, June 2014): 3, 6.

43. Duncan and Murnane, eds., "Whither Opportunity"; Organisation for Economic Cooperation and Development, *Strong Performers and Successful Reformers in Education: Lessons from PISA for the United States* (Paris, FR: OECD, 2011).

44. Eduardo Porter, "In Public Education, Edge Still Goes to Rich," *New York Times*, Nov. 6, 2013, First Business Page.

45. OECD, "Strong Performers and Successful Reformers In Education," 2011, 28.

46. Juan Diego Alonso and Richard Rothstein, *Where Has the Money Been Going?* (Washington, DC: Economic Policy Institute, 2010), 1.

47. Ibid., 5.

48. Bruce Baker, *Revisiting That Age-old Question: Does Money Matter in Education?* (Washington, DC: Albert Shanker Institute, 2012), 3–9.

49. Rebell, *Moving Every Child Ahead*, 98.

50. Holly Yettick, "School Spending Increases Linked to Better Outcomes for Poor Students," *Education Week*, http://www.edweek.org/ew/articles/2014/05/29/33finance.h33.html.

51. C. Kirabo Jackson, Rucker Johnson, and Claudia Persico, "The Effect of School Finance Reforms on the Distribution of Spending, Academic Achievement, and Adult Outcomes" (National Bureau of Economic Research, Working Paper No. 20118, May, 2014), http://www.nber.org/papers/w20118.

52. Marin Gjaja, J. Puckett, and Matt Ryder, "Equity Is the Key to Better School Funding," *Education Week* (Feb. 19, 2014), http://www.edweek.org/ew/articles/2014/02/19/21puckett.h33.html?tk.

53. Jon Sonstelie, Eric Brunner, and Kenneth Ardon, *For Better or for Worse? School Finance Reform in California* (San Francisco: Public Policy Institute of California, 2000); William A. Fischel, *The Homevoter Hypothesis* (Cambridge, MA: Harvard University Press, 2001).

54. Equity Center, *Money Does Matter!* (Austin, TX: Equity Center, 2010), 44; Robert Greenwald, Larry Hedges, R. D. Laine, "The effect of school resources on student achievement," *Review of Educational Research* 66, no. 3 (1996): 361–396.

Chapter 11

1. David K. Cohen and Susan L. Moffitt, *The Ordeal of Equality: Did Federal Regulation Fix the Schools?* (Cambridge, MA: Harvard University Press, 2009), 122, 188.
2. W. S. Barnett et al., *The state of preschool 2013* (New Brunswick, NJ: State Preschool Yearbook, 2013); Clare McCann, *States Have Improved Pre-K Quality Over the Past Decade* (Washington, DC: New America Foundation, May 14, 2014).
3. Council for the Accreditation of Educator Preparation, "Standard 3: Candidate Quality, Recruitment, and Selectivity," http://caepnet.org/accreditation/standards/.
4. "New Praxis Core Academic Skills for Educators Tests," *ETS The Praxis Series* (May 2013), www.ets.org/praxis/news/praxis_core_academic.
5. American Association of Colleges for Teacher Education, *New Assessment for Teacher Candidates Rolls Out After Two Years of Field Testing,* press release, Nov. 8, 2013.
6. Barnett Berry, *Teacher Education for Tomorrow,* prepared for the National Council for the Accreditation of Colleges of Teacher Education, Oct. 2010, files.eric.ed.gov/fulltext/ED519712.pdf.
7. James Aquino, *Ten reasons to have a high-quality teacher induction program* (New Teacher Center, June 3, 2014), http://www.newteachercenter.org/blog/ten-reasons-have-high -quality-teacher-induction-program.induction-program.
8. Richard Ingersoll, "Four Myths About America's Teacher Quality Problem," in *103rd Yearbook of the National Society for the Study of Education,* ed. M. Smylie and D. Miretzky (Chicago: University of Chicago Press, 2004), http://www.gse.upenn.edu/pdf/rmi/FourMyths .pdf; Richard Ingersoll and Lisa Merrill, "The Status of Teaching as a Profession," in *Schools and Society: A Sociological Approach to Education,* 5th ed., eds. Jeanne Ballantine and Joan Spade (Los Angeles: Sage, 2014).
9. Richard Ingersoll, Lisa Merrill, and Daniel Stuckey, *Seven trends: The transformation of the teaching force* (Philadelphia: Consortium for Policy Research in Education Report #RR-80, University of Pennsylvania, 2014); Richard Ingersoll and David Perda, *How high is teacher turnover and is it a problem?* (Philadelphia: Consortium for Policy Research in Education, University of Pennsylvania).
10. Matthew G. Springer, Luis A. Rodriguez, and Walker A. Swain, *Effective Teacher Retention Bonuses: Evidence from Tennessee* (Nashville, TN: Peabody College, Vanderbilt University, June 12, 2014), 24.
11. Juliana Herman, *Canada's Approach to School Funding: The Adoption of Provincial Control of Education Funding in Three Provinces* (Center for American Progress, May 2013), http://cdn.americanprogress.org/wp-content/uploads/2013/05/HermanCanadaReport .pdf, 21–27.
12. Andrew Ujifusa, "Illinois Moves Towards Significant Shift in How Schools are Funded," *Education Week blog,* http://blogs.edweek.org/edweek/state_edwatch/2014/07/illinois_moves _towards_significant_.html.
13. William Diepenbrock, "Amid Bumps, New School Funding System Rolls Out in California," *Education Week,* http://www.edweek.org/ew/articles/2014/08/08/01thr_californiafunding .h34.html.
14. Sabir Shah, "U.S. Wars in Afghanistan, Iraq to Cost $6 trillion," *Global Research News* (Feb. 12, 2014), http://www.globalresearch.ca/us-wars-in-afghanistan-iraq-to-cost-6-trillion.

15. "Fighting for a U.S. federal budget that works for all Americans," *Cost of National Security: How Much the U.S. Spends Per Hour,* https://www.nationalpriorities.org/analysis/.

16. Amy Harder, "Democrats Warming to the Energy Industry," *Wall Street Journal,* Aug. 12, 2014, A4.

Chapter 12

1. George W. Bush, "Weekly Radio Address," in *Public Papers of the Presidents of the United States 2002* (Washington, DC: Government Printing Office), http://www.presidency.ucsb.edu/index_docs.php.

2. Barack Obama, "Remarks at the National Action Network Annual Gala," *The White House, Office of the Press Secretary* (New York, NY, April 6, 2011).

3. Madeline Will, "Inequalities Linger 50 Years After Civil Rights Act, Speakers Declare," *Education Week* (July 15, 2014), http://blogs.edweek.org/edweek/campaign-k-12/2014/07/civil_rights_act_anniversary.html.

4. *San Antonio Independent School District v. Rodriguez,* 411 U.S. 1 (1973).

5. *Education Amendments of 1974* (Conference Report, July 23, 1974) 207–208.

6. *Rodriguez,* 411 U.S. 1 (1973), 37.

7. Ibid., 43.

8. Michael Rebell, "The Right to Comprehensive Educational Opportunity," *Harvard Civil Rights-Civil Liberties Law Review* 47 (2012): 22, http://harvardcrcl.org/wp-content/uploads/2012/03/Rebell.pdf.

9. Ibid., 82

10. Ibid., 68.

11. *Plyler v. Doe,* 457 U.S. 202 (1982).

12. Ibid., 220.

13. Michael Rebell, e-mail message to author, July 21, 2014; clarified that the *Plyler* decision relied on the intermediate scrutiny test, not the rational basis test, although the Court did not explicitly say so.

Acknowledgments

THIS BOOK WOULD NOT have come about without the inspired assistance I received from Caroline Chauncey, my editor at the Harvard Education Press. In addition, Nancy Kober did her usual good work editing the manuscript, and Alexandra Usher was a thorough researcher. Wayne Riddle, Jay Kober, and Amy Berman strengthened the manuscript. The reviewers of the draft provided good ideas, and made necessary corrections: Bill Bushaw, Donna Christian, Mary Cowell, James Harvey, Richard Ingersoll, Jim Popham, Michael Rebell, Diane Stark Rentncr, and Tom Wolanin. Maggie Appel-Schumacher was very helpful in arranging the lectures at The George Washington University that preceded this writing. Special thanks to Michael Feuer, the dean of the Graduate School of Education and Human Development at George Washington, for sponsoring those lectures, and to Michael McPherson, president of the Spencer Foundation, for providing a grant that assisted with the lectures and the researching, editing, and writing of this book. Lastly, thanks to Steve Molinari, my husband, for putting up with my distractions with this writing.

About the Author

JOHN F. "JACK" JENNINGS founded the Center on Education Policy in January 1995 and was its CEO and president until he retired in 2012. According to a poll of national leaders conducted by *Education Week*, that Center was one of the ten most influential organizations affecting school policy in the United States.

From 1967 to 1994, Mr. Jennings served as subcommittee staff director and then as a general counsel for the U.S. House of Representatives' Committee on Education and Labor. In these positions, he was involved in nearly every major education debate held at the national level, including the reauthorizations of such important legislation as the Elementary and Secondary Education Act, the Vocational Education Act, the Individuals with Disabilities Education Act, the Higher Education Act, and the National School Lunch Act.

Mr. Jennings served on the board of trustees of the Educational Testing Service, the Title I Independent Review Panel, the Pew Forum on Standards-Based Reform, the Maryland Academic Intervention Steering Committee, and the Maryland Visionary Panel. Mr. Jennings is currently a member of the National Academy of Education, and serves on the board of governors of the Phi Delta Kappa Foundation. He also served as chair of the PDK Foundation board.

Over the years, he has received awards from dozens of organizations, and recently was the recipient of awards for distinguished public service from the American Educational Research Association and from Phi Delta Kappa. Most recently, he has been honored with the Education Visionary Award by the Learning First Alliance (a coalition of the country's major national public education organizations), the Outstanding Friend of Public Education Award from the Horace Mann League, and the Meritorious Service Award from the National Association of Federal Education Program Administrators.

Mr. Jennings's book *Why National Standards and Tests? Politics and the Quest for Better Schools* was published by Sage Publications in 1998. He has also edited four volumes on National Issues in Education which were published by Phi Delta Kappa: *The Past is Prologue* (May 1993), *Community Service and Student Loans* (June 1994), *Goals 2000 and School-to-Work* (January 1995), and *Elementary and Secondary Education Act* (July 1995).

Mr. Jennings writes a blog for the *Huffington Post*. He has also written numerous articles, including twelve for the *Kappan*, more than any other single contributor for that prestigious magazine. He is one of the authorities on education most cited in the news media. For example, he was quoted in *Education Week* more than 500 times from 1995 to 2011.

He holds an AB from Loyola University and a JD from Northwestern University School of Law, and has been a member of several legal bars, including the U.S. Supreme Court.

His website is jackjenningsdc.com.

Index